Applications of the Myers-Briggs Type Indicator in Higher Education

Edited by

JUDITH A. PROVOST
Rollins College

SCOTT ANCHORS
University of Maine

CONSULTING PSYCHOLOGISTS PRESS
3803 E. Bayshore Road
Palo Alto, CA 94303

COPYEDITOR: Doreen Finkelstein
PRODUCTION MANAGER: Laura Ackerman-Shaw
DESIGNER: MaryEllen Podgorski
LAYOUT: Mary Gendron
MANUFACTURING: Gloria Forbes

MBTI® and Myers-Briggs Type Indicator® are trademarks of Consulting Psychologists Press, Inc.

ISBN: 0-89106-032-4

Third printing, 1991.

Library of Congress Catalog Card Number: 87-70975

044926

Table of Contents

CHAPTER 1

Introduction

JUDITH A. PROVOST and SCOTT ANCHORS

ALTHOUGH ARTICLES ABOUT MBTI use in higher education have appeared in professional journals, no comprehensive book exists to pull together the range of higher education activities that involve the MBTI ®. *Applications of the Myers-Briggs Type Indicator in Higher Education* has been written for student personnel practitioners, faculty, administrators, and counselors/psychologists interested in using the MBTI in their colleges and universities. Readers may find the book useful in either expanding current uses of the MBTI or in initiating new programs. The book presents both theory and application. The theories give a foundation and rationale for the programs described. These programs serve as models to apply in various higher education settings.

Readers are expected to be already familiar with the MBTI and know "the basics." The basics are thoroughly presented in the *Manual* (Myers & McCaulley, 1985), *Gifts Differing* (Myers, 1980), *People Types and Tiger Stripes* (Lawrence, 1982), and in other sources referenced in this book. There is no need to duplicate these excellent sources. The basics essential to finding this book helpful are knowledge of the preferences and Jungian theory of psychological type. If readers are new to psychological type, and especially if they are unclear about Jung's concept of the dominant and auxiliary, they should read Chapter 2 carefully to acquire important background knowledge. In addition, if readers desire to administer and interpret the MBTI, they need to acquire the knowledge and skill to do so from the training workshops offered by the Center for Applications of Psychological Type (CAPT) and the Association for Psychological Type (APT).

1

Much thought was given to the topics a book on MBTI uses in higher education should cover. The topics are organized by chapter. These chapters reflect a range of use from the more traditional ones of personal and career counseling to research on college attrition and other aspects of college life. Some applications focus on individual student development, others on the consultation process, some on patterns of behavior among a large group of students, and yet others on environmental issues. These topics are supplemented by an appendix of type tables reflecting distributions of types in various subgroupings within higher education. These data were provided by the chapter authors and other MBTI users around the country.

The editors set out to select contributors innovative in applying the MBTI in a variety of ways and in a variety of institutions. The contributors represent diversity in professional functions, work settings, and disciplines. Their brief biographies begin each chapter to show some of the background which shapes their thinking and practice with the MBTI. The editors also wished to have many of the psychological types represented so that readers could have the benefit of several different writing styles and methods of presentation. Thus there has been no attempt to make the writing style uniform throughout the book.

Each contributor could easily expand his/her chapter into an entire book. The editors challenged them to provide an overview of their topic, the rationale for their particular MBTI application, and a detailed description of specific programs in which the contributor has been involved. These latter descriptions include the "what, how, and why." The result of these 11 contributions is a handbook of applications and models for using the MBTI within higher education.

As most readers probably know, Isabel Myers and her mother, Katharine Briggs, began developing the Indicator in the 1940s through a desire to implement Carl Jung's theory of type. In 1962 Educational Testing Service (ETS) published Form F of the MBTI to be used for research purposes only. In the 1960s while the MBTI was still a research instrument, several higher education practitioners researched university students' behavior (Grant, 1965; Williams, 1980). Auburn and Michigan State Universities were two early sites of such research. In 1969, Myers began working with Mary McCaulley at the University of Florida to establish a Typology Laboratory for research on type, especially longitudinal studies of students. By 1979, this laboratory became the Center for Applications of Psychological Type (CAPT) and completed its transition to an independent nonprofit public corporation.

In 1975, Consulting Psychologists Press (CPP) became the publisher and made the Indicator available to qualified professionals. The Indicator's validity and reliability established it as a stable and effective tool for application, not just for research. The university research in the '60s and '70s, the availability of the MBTI through CPP, and the leadership of CAPT stimulated a rapid expansion of use within higher education. According to CPP, no other psychological instrument has had such a dramatic increase in use.

A recent informal survey of American College Personnel Association (ACPA) members by Anchors, Robinson, and Wood (1984) demonstrates the broad and varied application of the MBTI in higher education. Approximately 100 ACPA members responded to a request in *ACPA Developments* for MBTI users to complete an informal survey of use. The survey findings demonstrate that the MBTI is one of the few instruments used in higher education which crosses over functional areas. The MBTI was reported to be used in career development, academic advising, leadership training, counseling, roommate matching, paraprofessional training, understanding learning and teaching styles, conflict resolution, and development of retention strategies. The survey results indicate that the MBTI is used in all types of post-secondary institutions. Respondents were from traditional public and private institutions, two-year vocational colleges, and junior and community colleges. Respondents agreed that a major strength of the instrument was its conceptualization of the whole person and its theoretical base from which implications for practice can be derived.

Chapter 2 provides a foundation in theories of student development and type development. It is important to read this chapter before proceeding to sample other chapters. Its discussion of type development has practical implications for practitioners working in all the areas explored by later chapters.

References

Anchors, S., Robinson, P., & Wood, C. (1984). *A survey of Myers-Briggs Type Indicator users in the American College Personnel Association.* Orono, ME: University of Maine.

Grant, W. H. (1963). *Behavior of MBTI types* (research report). Auburn, AL: Student Counseling Service, Auburn University.

Lawrence, G. (1982). *People types and tiger stripes: A practical guide to learning styles.* Gainesville, FL: Center for Applications of Psychological Type.

Myers, I. B. (1980). *Gifts differing.* Palo Alto, CA: Consulting Psychologists Press.

Myers, I. B., & McCaulley, M. H. (1985). *Manual: A guide to the development and use of the Myers-Briggs Type Indicator.* Palo Alto, CA: Consulting Psychologists Press.

Williams, C. (1980). [Historical background of the MBTI]. *MBTI News, 2,* p. 8.

ANN Q. LYNCH, Ed.D., is an Associate Professor in the Counseling and Personnel Services department and in the Center for the Study of Higher Education at Memphis State University. She is a licensed counseling psychologist in Tennessee and has served as Executive Director of the Higher Education for Adult Mental Health Project. In 1970 at the University of Florida, she was introduced to the MBTI by Isabel Briggs Myers when Myers came to work with Dr. Mary McCaulley in establishing the Typology Laboratory. Ann Lynch has served as President of APT-Southeast and on the APT and CAPT faculty and editorial board of CAPT. She has used the MBTI extensively in counseling college students and couples and in working with administrators, faculty, and student services professionals. She is an ENFP.

CHAPTER 2

Type Development
and Student Development

ANN Q. LYNCH

INDIVIDUAL DIFFERENCES HAVE long been recognized in the American tradition and are the cornerstone of individuality and autonomy. Higher education is based on the premise that individuals with different motivations can be served by different institutions to reach their different goals. Perhaps more so than other parts of our society, higher education is dedicated to ensuring the fulfillment of the human potential through the recognition of individual differences.

This chapter will address individual differences from a psychological type perspective, as applied through the *Myers-Briggs Type Indicator* ®. We are assuming that most readers have a basic knowledge of psychological type. The reader unacquainted with type concepts is encouraged to refer to *Introduction to Type* (Myers, 1980a), *Gifts Differing* (Myers, 1980b) and the *Manual: A Guide to the Development and Use of the Myers-Briggs Type Indicator* (Myers & McCaulley, 1985). Two other books will also be helpful to the reader: *People Types and Tiger Stripes* (Lawrence, 1982) and *A Casebook: Applications of the Myers-Briggs Type Indicator in Counseling* (Provost, 1984).

Psychological type theory provides a way of examining some important personality differences. Theories of student development also shed light on how professionals can respond to individual differences. A sound theoretical base is important for us as practitioners to implement our work in higher education. As professionals we need a blend of theory and practice to serve students effectively. In this chapter, we first examine type development theory and its applications in higher educa-

5

tion. Then we explore student development theory and its implications for psychological type. Finally, we present recommendations for the intentional use of type to contribute to student development.

Diversity and College Students

Visible diversity among college students in terms of age, gender, and ethnicity has increased dramatically in the past few decades in most institutions. Traditional students, ages 18 to 22, with common characteristics of being recent high school graduates, having satisfactory admissions scores, being supported mainly by parents, and living on or near campus, still comprise the major focus of most colleges and universities. However, adult learners, who are defined more by their roles and responsibilities than by age, have increased substantially over the past two decades. With the increase in adult learners has come a change in the ratio of men and women. In 1979, for the first time in this country, women outnumbered men in higher education. Both of these trends are predicted to continue, accompanying the shift in U.S. age demographics. The greatest change in ethnic composition is evident in predominantly white institutions with the increase of minority students.

These "new" students bring with them diversity in academic preparation, socioeconomic status, motivations, goals, and values. Academic preparation ranges from high school noncompleters and GED graduates to advanced placement graduates and adults experienced in the work world. Entrance test scores, such as the SAT and ACT, attest to the range of entering academic backgrounds across institutions, even though there are valid questions about the predictive value of these instruments as entrance criteria. Certainly, different motivations propel students into college—fulfilling parental expectations or following the crowd, improving job capabilities, upgrading skills, earning a credential, learning for the pleasure of learning, gaining a secure future, looking for relationships, or improving self.

Type and Type Development Theory

Besides these visible and invisible differences among college students, there are cognitive and affective differences that influence learning and development. Why do some individuals from apparently similar backgrounds succumb or barely survive while others from apparently very disparate backgrounds excel? Knowing about psychological type and type development theory will help the practitioner understand students and give a rationale for predicting some, but certianly not all, important behaviors. As Myers (1980b) has explained, "Within limits, type development can substitute for *intelligence*, because average intelligence fully utilized through fine type development will give results above expectation" (p. 186). Type theory begins with recognizing the basis for what appears to be random behavior. Jung (1923) wrote that much seemingly chance variation in human behavior is not due to chance but is the logical result of a few observable differences in mental functioning.

Psychological type is dynamic, not static. The theory of type development states that everyone has the capability of using all four of the functions: two perception functions and two judgment functions. However, people differ in which functions they naturally prefer to use; that is, they will naturally choose one of the perception functions, either Sensing (S) or Intuition (N), and one of the judgment functions, either Thinking (T) or Feeling (F). Many MBTI experts explain preference by using the metaphor of handedness. Although everyone can use both hands to catch a beach ball, each of us has a natural preference for using either the right or the left hand in signing our names.

Development of the Dominant and Auxiliary

As young children, we begin to exercise a preference between two ways of perceiving or judging. As soon as that preference is established, a basic difference in development begins. The child begins to use the favored process more often and to neglect the process less favored. Just as in the handedness metaphor, we develop a natural tendency to use one hand over the other. It becomes easier for us to use that hand; therefore we use it more and become more expert with its use. The favorite function is called *dominant* and will be either a perception process, Sensing (S) or Intuition (N), or a judgment process, Thinking (T) or Feeling (F). The dominant function is the unifying process in one's life.

If a person is to become fully effective, the dominant must have clear sovereignty, with the opportunity to reach its maximum potential. Since it is natural to use one hand for signing your name, you become adept at it with use. According to Von Franz and Hillman's explanation of Jung's theory (Von Franz & Hillman, 1979), the dominant is usually reflected in behavior by kindergarten age. Sometimes for different environmental reasons the dominant process may not become developed. In such situations, the person often appears confused because there is little or no direction or intensity.

Having a well-developed dominant function is not enough; the remaining function becomes the auxiliary or supplemental process. If the person chooses a perception (S or N) function for the dominant, the judgment (T or F) function becomes the auxiliary or vice versa. To be well balanced, the individual needs an adequate (but not equal) development of the auxiliary or second process. If the right hand is preferred, the left hand is used for support or balance, or vice versa. If Intuition (N) is the dominant perception function, then Thinking (T) or Feeling (F) will be the auxiliary judgment function, or if Feeling (F) is the dominant judgment function, then Sensing (S) or Intuition (N) will be the auxiliary perception function. The development of the auxiliary usually begins in the young adult, though there is no specific timetable for this. Its development is important to effective functioning.

An extreme perceptive type, for example, with an underdeveloped auxiliary judgment process would gather information and not be able to use it to make a decision. In college students, such underdevelopment of a judgment auxiliary is often illustrated in the aimless wanderings in search of a major over a period of years. It is also evident in students who gather information for a paper but cannot decide on a topic or cannot begin the writing because they do not have "enough" material. An extreme judging type, on the other hand, without a well-developed perception auxiliary, tends to make decisions without information. This lack of development is often seen in freshman or sophomore students who choose majors and lifelong careers without the slightest bit of knowledge of the educational requirements, working conditions, or job possibilities. In writing term papers, students who have not developed a perception auxiliary will decide on the topic and write the paper with little, if any, supporting evidence.

We have only discussed two of the four MBTI personality variables, which have to do with the basic functions of Perception (S or N) and Judgment (T or F). The other two variables are called *attitudes*, or sometimes *orientations*, but are not *functions*. The attitudes indicate a person's dominant and auxiliary and where these functions are used. One variable is the attitude toward life, Extraversion (E) or Introversion (I). This variable represents the world in which the person becomes energized; that is, the direction of the flow of attention—either outward for Extraverts or inward for Introverts. The other variable, Judgment (J) or Perception (P), indicates whether a judgment or a perceptive function is used in the outer world. This orientation to the outer world also indicates how people structure or organize their lives and the degree of closure they prefer, and is sometimes referred to as "lifestyle."

The dominant function is used in the world, either external (E) or internal (I), that interests the person the most, where the person becomes energized and where the person's best work is done. For example, the Extraverted Intuitive (EN) student will show creativity for all the world to see through innovation. This student uses the dominant Intuition (N) in the extraverted mode (E). Conversely, the Introverted Intuitive (IN) student will be just as creative, but in a more private way because the dominant intuitive (N) process remains unseen in the inner world (I). Extraverted Sensing (ES) students will show themselves as action-oriented realists using the dominant Sensing (S) in the outer world (E), while Introverted Sensing (IS) types will apply their realistic and fact-oriented perception within their inner world.

The auxiliary then takes care of the less important matters in the world which holds less importance for the student. The auxiliary handles the extraverted process for the Introvert and introverted process for the Extravert. For example, the Extraverted Intuitive with Feeling as auxiliary uses the dominant Intuition in the external world and the auxiliary Feeling in the internal world; the imagination (N) is shown to the world while the subjective values (F) are kept inside.

To summarize, well-balanced type development occurs under the following conditions:

1. A dominant process (either a perception process, S or N, or judgment process, T or F) is clearly preferred and used.

2. An auxiliary process (the remaining perception or judgment process) is used to supplement the dominant.

3. The dominant is used in the preferred attitude or world (E or I) while the auxiliary is used in the opposite attitude or world (I or E).

As Myers (1980b) so eloquently put it:

Balance does not refer to equality of two processes or attitudes; instead, it means superior skill in one, supplemented by a helpful but not competitive skill in the other. The need for such supplementing is obvious. Perception without judgment is spineless; judgment with no perception is blind. Introversion lacking any extraversion is impractical; extraversion with no introversion is superficial. (p. 182)

Balance or Complementarity

Quenk (1984) described the balance between preferences and attitudes as "complementarity." She further explained that when such complementarity does not occur, one or more of the following conditions may prevail:

1. *Failure to develop one of each pair of opposites more than the other.*

If a pair of opposites is developed relatively equally, a situation of potential conflict exists, such as a competition between Sensing (S) and Intuition (N) or a competition between Thinking (T) and Feeling (F). As Myers (1980b) wrote, "Expert perception and judgment result from specialization, from using one of a pair of opposites rather than the other. One of the opposites must be 'tuned out' in order to have a chance to develop either of them" (p. 182).

If Mary (ENFP) were well developed, she would have extraverted Intuition as dominant with introverted Feeling as auxiliary. She does not seem to be able to make a choice between her objective and subjective reasons in choosing a major or in deciding whether to be in college or not. She is returning to college because her five-year-old daughter is entering kindergarten. Mary has difficulty deciding on courses, her major, and whether she can hold a job while going to school. She thinks she wants to do something with people, but she also likes reading and thinking about ideas. Her husband wants her to take a Nursing program so that she will have a definite job when she graduates. Mary recognizes they need the income, and she has been working part-time as a secretary but finds the work unchallenging. She seems to have some confusion in the Judgment function—bouncing between logical, objective Thinking (T) and value-oriented, subjective Feeling (F).

2. *Lack of clear development of the dominant function.*

In this case, the preferred perceiving (S or N) and judging (T or F) functions compete for energy and attention. Neither is clearly dominant and neither is clearly auxiliary. Such individuals may appear inconsistent and unpredictable.

Charlie (ESFP), if well developed, would have extraverted Sensing as dominant with introverted Feeling as auxiliary. He changed majors many times from Business to Health Sciences and then to Physical Education. His father wanted him to take accounting courses to get ahead. Even though he had difficulty in biology, Charlie had an interest in health from a high school summer job he had in a medical lab. He enjoyed playing team sports but would often be late for practice. Toward the end of his sophomore year, his lack of responsibility on the baseball team made the coach remove him from the team. Charlie shrugged off his desire for a sports career, dropped out of college, and got married. Now he is selling appliances in a local department store, much to his parents' and his own disappointment. Charlie did not have a clear preference between a dominant Sensing (S) and an auxiliary Feeling (F). He did not have well-developed complementarity. He vacillated when gathering practical information and allowed his decisions to be heavily influenced by others' feelings.

3. *Failure to use the auxiliary in the attitude opposite to that associated with the dominant.*

Some students may be seen as "shy," "socially inept," or "antisocial," and they may be "extreme introverts." They avoid all social situations and appear unable to express themselves interpersonally. They often become anxious and embarrassed when required to deal with people or the external world. Students who appear to be extreme Introverts may use both the perceiving and judging functions in an introverted mode. They may not have developed a comfortable way of dealing with the outside world. College students who are extreme Introverts may often be isolates, having no successful way of dealing with people or things in the outside world. They may be particularly disadvantaged since many college activities require interacting with others, working in groups, and making oral presentations.

Roger (INTP), if well developed, would have introverted Thinking as dominant and extraverted Intuition as auxiliary. He is seen by the other students as reclusive and stand-offish. At times they refer to him as the "ghost." He is hardly ever visible, preferring to remain in his room reading and studying. When he does venture forth, he seldom has a conversation with another person; yet he takes tests well and maintains a respectable grade point average. He is the kind of student whom the sensitive advisor or resident assistant may try to involve in activities without much success. Roger seems to be introverting both his dominant Thinking (T) and his auxiliary Intuition (N).

Individuals who extravert their dominant and auxiliary have fewer apparent difficulties than Introverts who introvert both functions, especially if this occurs early in life. When extreme Extraverts use both their dominant and auxiliary in an extraverted fashion, this results in a lack of trust in the inner life.

Joan (ESFJ), if well developed, would have extraverted Feeling as dominant with introverted Sensing as auxiliary. She has become overinvolved in student activities, to such an extent that she seldom goes to class. She rationalizes her activities as being practical when applied to her Public Relations major. She appears to enjoy the attention and expends much energy on being with others. At night she roams the residence hall looking for someone—anyone—with whom she can talk in detail about her day's activities. It is almost as if she is afraid to be alone. Joan seems to be extraverting both her dominant Feeling and her auxiliary Sensing.

When extreme Extraverts reach middle age and have not developed their auxiliary in the introverted mode, they may experience feelings of emptiness and meaninglessness and be perceived by friends and family as shallow. They are seen as lacking conviction and flitting from absorption to total disinterest in projects. They are often described by others as "too extraverted," "inappropriately friendly," "gushing," or "overwhelming." Quenk (1985b) poignantly delineates the lack of empathy of extreme Extraverts: "They seek out other's advice and sympathy but are unavailable to reciprocate for a friend in need" (p. 29).

George (ESTP) is an Extravert. If well developed, he would have extraverted Sensing as dominant balanced with introverted Thinking as auxiliary. However, George seems shallow and undisciplined, flitting among many different interests and people. He entered college at 29 after his second divorce, intending to make up for all that he missed. He went to every football game and appeared to delve into his studies, but by mid-term he had lost interest. He talked to the other older students about his divorce, but when a friend needed help moving, he was unavailable. He had no real friends because he was hypercritical of their behavior. George dropped out of college for the third time. He appears to be extraverting both his dominant Sensing and his auxiliary Thinking.

Effective Type Development and the Inferior Function

For effective type development it is essential first to develop trust in the preferred direction of the dominant process, with the auxiliary focused in the opposite direction. That then frees us later in life to explore less-preferred patterns. Quenk (1984) explains, "A person who is clear about the dominant versus the auxiliary, has specialized in one of each pair of opposites and uses the auxiliary in the less-preferred attitude may be seen as well developed in terms of type" (p. 17).

Quenk (1985a) reports that clinically the most frequent evidence for inadequate type development occurs in the judging function, Thinking (T) versus Feeling (F), with much reported distress in decision making. If the Thinking/Feeling function is poorly differentiated and the dominant process, the conflict is particularly disruptive. There appears to be a shifting back and forth between Thinking and Feeling. The final decision emerges in fatigue and confusion and later proves to be poor, based on reports by that person as well as by significant others.

Sharon (INFP), if well developed, would have introverted Feeling as dominant with extraverted Intuition as auxiliary. She seems to be confused in making decisions, not knowing whether to attend to objective or subjective values. Last semester, Sharon found that one of her best friends cheated on the midterm exam. Her sense of justice said that she should report the situation to her teacher, but her sense of loyalty to her friend put her in a quandary. To make matters worse, Sharon was put on the awards committee and found that her friend was eligible for honors, and that anyone found cheating would be disbarred automatically. Sharon felt caught between her two loyalties. After many hours of worry, she resigned from the committee, did not report the cheating incident, withdrew from other activities, and avoided her friend. By default, she let her subjective values prevail but continued to feel that she had betrayed her objective values. She has some confusion between Feeling and Thinking judgment as her dominant process.

A poor perception differentiation between Sensing (S) and Intuition (N) is more difficult to identify. The individual sometimes uses Sensing to gather information and sometimes Intuition, but trusts neither function. The result is a lack of self-confidence and erratic performance.

Bill (ISTP), if well developed, would have introverted Thinking as dominant with extraverted Sensing as auxiliary. He sometimes takes specific information and uses his imagination to jump to erroneous conclusions. As a Biology major, he once conducted an experiment on a frog. He extracted tissue that had a dark appearance and immediately speculated that the frog had cancer. The lab instructor told him that it was an area of tissue that was generally light in color, but these frogs came from a different locale causing that tissue to be dark. Bill felt embarrassed in reaching such a conclusion without much evidence. He does not use his Sensing well and often drifts into his less-preferred Intuition function.

Stages of Type Development

Jung (1923) wrote that the goal of the first half of life is to make one's place in the world and establish an identity through the successful achievement of a career and personal relationships. The second half of life is for balancing and completing individuation. He explained that the growth of a healthy personality goes through two important stages. In the first stage of life, we specialize; we develop clear preferences and use them freely. In the second stage of life, we strive to become more complete and less specialized. At this stage some adults become more interested in developing their third and fourth functions. They are ready for a change! Perhaps this is one motivation propelling so many adult learners to return to college. Later in life some individuals do learn to use their third and fourth functions more freely, though never as expertly as their first and second functions.

People also differ in the order in which they develop their functions and the degree of use of the four functions. The natural order to type development is: the dominant (No. 1), to the auxiliary (No. 2), to No. 3 (the function opposite No. 2); and finally to No. 4 (the function opposite the dominant, No. 1). For example, if Intuition (N) is dominant and Feeling (F) is auxiliary, then Thinking (T) becomes No. 3 and Sensing (S) becomes No. 4.

The fourth function is the least developed, the least preferred, and the most difficult to access. It is sometimes referred to as the inferior or the shadow, but the latter term causes confusion with Jung's meaning of the personal unconscious and undesirable aspects which the self represses. In MBTI circles the fourth function is simply referred to as the least preferred without any negative connotation. As Provost (1984) described, "If and when [No. 4] and [No. 3] can be utilized in mature adulthood, the outcome is often positive, even exhilarating" (p. 4).

The fourth or inferior function is the process which causes the person the most difficulty. It is slow and loaded with emotionality. The inferior function lies opposite to the dominant function. Von Franz and Hillman (1979) described the problems that the inferior function presents to individuals who are often unaware of its magnitude. They especially emphasized the slowness of the inferior function when compared with the dominant and recognized that "in this realm, one has to waste time which gives the unconscious a chance to come in" (p. 8). Jung (1923) called the inferior function infantile and tyrannical. In developing the inferior function, the person should give it a lot of time and let it develop in the attitude which is opposite the preferred attitude. For example, the dominant Extraverted Intuitive would explore Sensing through the Introverted attitude. However, it should be remembered that the inferior function cannot be relied upon to act according to needs or dictates. A person cannot cross directly to the opposite function; the functions S or N and T or F exclude each other; they are dichotomous and incompatible. Therefore, it is a serious mistake to try to help someone to "work directly on his or her inferior function" with the expectation that the fourth function will reach the capacity of the first.

Environmental Effects on Type Development

We assume first that people have a natural bent or grain and will become happier and more effective if they follow their natural pathways. The second assumption is that following a natural pathway leads to lifelong development. However, environment affects development and expression of type. Students can be affirmed for who they are in their families, or they can have their true type discouraged. Falsification of type occurs because it is not safe to be the "person one truly is," as explained by Carl Rogers (1961). Crises and stress can also contribute to inconsistencies in the expression of type. Stress may push individuals into their inferior function rather than toward type development.

According to McCaulley (1985), "true type" is shorthand for the concept that "Jung's theory appears to assume that each person has a constitutional predisposition to develop certain preferences over others, if this development is not falsified by the environment" (p. 30). She also posited some of the reasons why we cannot expect the MBTI or any other instrument to report "true types" 100 percent of the time.

Effective type development cannot be determined by scores (Mc-Caulley, 1981). It is important for practitioners to keep this in mind when giving feedback to students. Neither low nor high scores on the MBTI should be taken as absolutes regarding type development. In light of these limitations, it is truly amazing how often students report that the MBTI descriptions fit their "true type." Perhaps it would be better to expect the MBTI to be wrong and to be pleasantly surprised when the student reports that the description is accurate. McCaulley (1985) proposes that a better term than "true type" which indicates more certainty than is possible would be "currently best-fit type," to allow for growth and development.

Provost (1984) explained different developmental issues that arise in counseling, which seem generally applicable for college students as well. She proposed the following questions which can serve as a guide for those of us who are concerned with type development in students:

1. How well does the student use the functions? Which are preferred? In which does the student have confidence? Which are avoided? Are the consequences problematic?

2. What has been the pattern of function development? What are the implications for the student?

3. Has the normal developmental order of the functions been inter-fered with? By what environmental or circumstantial factors? With what consequences?

4. What can facilitate development of all four functions, but particu-larly of the natural functions? What can be done to develop a "balanced" personality, the ability to use the function appropriate to the situation and to not overuse or rely solely on one function? (p. 3)

Student Development Theory and Type Implications

A developmental perspective encompasses a somewhat predictable sequence of growth, adaptation, and transformation. A general definition of development refers to orderly and sequential changes in characteristics and attitudes over time. Earlier characteristics help shape later characteristics and an understanding of antecedent-consequent patterns is useful to students and to those helping them. It is important to remember that not all change is synonymous with growth or development. Changes can be purely external and do not necessarily imply improvement, maturation, or predictable sequentiality. While developmental change does occur over time, few changes occur simply as a result of time. As Weathersby and Tarule (1980) so articulately put it:

> The dynamics (of development) involve learning that is irreversible and sometimes at the core of our lives. Further, the process of developmental change implies both choice and necessity in interaction with life circumstances. Development is not merely additive; it involves a process of qualitative change. (p. 2)

Many developmental theories relating to late adolescence and young adulthood have been formulated as "developmental tasks," "stages of development," "student typologies," and "needs and problem areas." Some of these had their base in the psychosexual stages of Freud, the psychosocial stages of Erikson, and the cognitive stages of Piaget. More recently, theories of adult development have exploded upon the scene based in part on research with selected groups of adults, some in college and some outside.

Knefelkamp, Widick, and Parker (1978) examined student development theories and clustered them as follows with some of their major proponents:

1. Psychosocial theories—Chickering, Erikson, and Sanford

2. Cognitive development theories—Piaget, Perry, Kohlberg, and Loevinger

3. Maturity models—Douglas Heath

4. Typology models—Roy Heath, Newcomb, and Cross

5. Person-environment interaction models—Holland, Stern, Pace, and Clark and Trow

This chapter cannot address all of these theories or models; however, one major theory, Chickering's psychosocial model of student development, will be explored with implications for psychological type. Perhaps this examination of Chickering's model with type implications can serve as a template for exploring type.

Human development theories have not been systematically related to psychological type. There has been little research to indicate the connection between student development theory and type. What follows, therefore, are some *reasoned speculations* based on our knowledge of type theory and student development theories. The reader should be aware that these are *speculations* and not use them for fact, but be spurred on to conduct research to validate, refine, or disprove these speculations.

Type theory gives the foundation for hypothesizing about the connections between life cycle theory and theories of student development. If we can consider type "the given" for the student, we have enough evidence to know that different types deal with life cycle developmental tasks differently. We also know that different types experience college in different ways. As a foundation for most theories of human development, concepts from life cycle stage theory can also influence our understanding of student development.

Life Cycle Stage Theory

Life cycle theory helps us be aware that students have certain milestones and marker events in which those who are within relatively the same age group may have many commonalities. Life cycle stages form the foundation for much of the adult development literature and provide important concepts for understanding students. Adulthood is not a stable state, but is divided into successive life periods, each with its own learning tasks. Some of the research indicates that most American adults' lives are patterned in predictable sequences with certain key issues and tasks associated with each life stage. Some of the life cycle concepts and their relation to students follows:

1. *Life stage—an age-linked period in which certain issues and adaptive tasks or marker events are paramount.*

Havighurst (1972) conceptualized developmental tasks associated with different life stages. The life phase of "leaving the family" (age 18 to 24) means coping with the major psychic tasks of separating from family, reducing dependence on family support and authority, and regarding one's self as an adult. Marker events for this time according to Neugarten (1968) involve leaving home, developing new roles, and making autonomous living arrangements. Such markers for the young adult might include college, travel, military service, job, education, career plans, and love relationships. The characteristic stance for this life stage is a balance between "being in" and "moving out" of the family.

2. *Developmental tasks—external and internal components required in adjusting to life events.*

Regarding the tasks of adulthood, Freud said that the normal person should be able to do two things well—love and work. Erikson (1959) created a formulation of critical issues to be resolved in eight stages of the life cycle. The stages for early childhood and adolescence involve trust vs. mistrust, autonomy vs. shame and doubt, initiative vs. guilt, and industry vs. inferiority. The stages generally confronting late adolescents and adults are identity vs. role diffusion, intimacy vs. isolation, generativity vs. stagnation, and integrity vs. despair. However, if students reach college and they have not coped with the first four stages, they will have difficulty forming an identity and handling subsequent stages.

If the major developmental task for most 18- to 24-year-olds is "leaving the family," we can predict that different types will experience this phase in different ways. As an example, take John (ISTJ), 18, who may be very practical in moving from home to college. He knows that college is his place to learn and to select his career. He is very planful about selecting specific courses and wants to be sure that he is taking only what is needed to major in his chosen field. When it comes to personal relationships, he has more difficulty in making friends and has not dated much.

Contrast John with Bill (ESFP), 18, who is also leaving home for the first time and sees college as the opportunity to "live it up." He makes lots of friends and becomes involved in sports and student activities. He figures that courses and majors will take care of themselves and that he has plenty of time to make those lifelong decisions.

The major developmental task for persons aged 35 to 45 is coping with the midlife transition. They are adapting to a changing time perspective, revising career plans, and redefining family relationships. Students returning to college at this age have very different purposes and motivations from traditional-aged students (Chickering & Havighurst, 1981).

Consider John and Bill, neither of whom finished college, now at a later period in their lives. John (ISTJ), now 36, has re-examined his career as a supermarket manager. He knows that he worked hard to get where he is, but that there is not much of a future for him unless he finishes college. Although it is a sacrifice for his wife and family, they have decided that it is best for him to return to college and to get his degree in Accounting. This decision will provide greater opportunities for their future.

Bill (ESFP), also now 36, has gone through a difficult time trying to decide on a career. He has moved from one job to another, primarily in sales. He still has lots of friends and fond memories of the "good times" in college, but some regrets that he did not settle down and major in something that would lead to a more substantial future. Upon re-examining his current traveling job in sales, he decided to apply for admission to an external degree program that would give him a credential. His wife gave him encouragement, since it could mean a more secure future for the family. After a few months of studying at night following a full day of sales, Bill recognized that he could not devote as much time to his family and friends as he had in the past. He lost his incentive and dropped out of college again.

We need to examine these hypothetical situations and recognize that, first, John and Bill are *stereotypes* of their types. Nevertheless, we can learn from them. There are consistent themes which prevail, such as both men being practical, with Sensing (S) as their dominant function. There are also several important differences. John is more serious from his Introversion (I), and more planful from his Judgment (J). Bill expresses himself in an open way from his Extraversion (E) and in a spontaneous manner from his Perception (P). A major difference in their types comes from the auxiliary, with John being more logical and objective from his Thinking (T), and Bill being more oriented toward personal values from his Feeling (F).

These type and life cycle differences combined with life circumstances help us better understand students like John and Bill. Recognition that motivations for college are different at age 36 than at age 18 also helps us acknowledge and affirm students no matter what phase they are negotiating in the life cycle. Academic advising, career counseling, and instruction needs to take these developmental task differences into account.

Chickering's Vectors of Student Development

Perhaps the best known and most widely used theory of student development is that conceived by Arthur W. Chickering (1969) in *Education and Identity*. His formulation, based on his own research and on earlier studies of college students, consists of seven areas: competence, emotions, autonomy, identity, interpersonal relationships, purpose, and integrity. He called his seven conceptual clusters "vectors of development" because they seem to have both direction and magnitude.

These seven vectors of student development apply to late adolescents and young adults, and also to most older adults returning to college who find themselves confronted with these important existential issues at a different level (Thomas & Chickering, 1984). Chickering's vectors seem to apply throughout the life cycle. When interviewed recently, Chickering said:

> I think the greatest impact [on the field of student development and adult learning] has come from the major theories of human development and from research that shows how student development tends to be associated with various kinds of educational experiences and environments and how it can be encouraged under the right conditions. This has provided us with a conceptual theoretical base that has been useful to practitioners. (Garfield & David, 1986, p. 490)

Competence. The first vector is competence, which includes three major elements: intellectual competence, physical and manual competence, and social and interpersonal competence. The major focus of most higher education institutions is on intellectual competence. The attainment of intellectual competence, or the lack of such, generally influences professional and vocational alternatives chosen later. Physical and manual competence, important in terms of success in sports, athletics, dexterity, and stamina to pursue life's tasks, takes on high visibility and status in most college environments. Interpersonal competence is necessary because most life tasks require cooperative efforts; effectiveness generally depends upon the ability to work with others. More important is a "sense of competence," which is the confidence one has in one's ability to cope with whatever comes and to achieve successfully what one sets out to do.

Emotions. "Managing emotions" addresses the area of self-control and involves the ability to recognize and to manage sexual and aggressive impulses. Through increased self-awareness and through opportunities for self-expression and feedback, the student can achieve forms of expression more appropriate to the circumstances.

Autonomy. Emotional and instrumental independence, and recognition of one's interdependence are a part of becoming autonomous.

Emotional independence happens when the student is free from the continual and pressing need for reassurance, affection, or approval from parents, peers, and others. Instrumental independence is when students have the ability to initiate activities on their own and to cope with problems without always seeking help. Being autonomous means having the ability to be mobile in relation to one's needs or desires. Recognition and acceptance of interdependence is the capstone of autonomy.

Identity. For the young adult, establishing identity is more than the aggregate of change in competence, emotions, and autonomy. As Erikson (1959) said, identity is "the accrued confidence that one's ability to maintain inner sameness and continuity is matched by the sameness and continuity of one's meaning for others" (p. 135). Identity involves clarifying conceptions concerning physical needs and characteristics, personal appearance, sexual identification, sex roles, and behavior. A solid sense of identity fosters change in the three vectors of interpersonal relationships, purpose, and integrity.

Relationships. This vector of developing freeing interpersonal relationships involves increasing tolerance and increasing capacity to respond to persons for themselves rather than as stereotypes. Friendships and love relationships shift toward greater trust, independence, individuality, and intimacy. Such relationships can survive differences and disagreements.

Purpose. Questions of "Where am I going?" and "Who am I going to be?" are answered with increased clarity and conviction as purpose is developed. Formulating plans and setting priorities that integrate vocational plans and aspirations, avocational and recreational interests, and general lifestyle considerations are a part of developing purpose. As Chickering (1969) concluded, "With such integration, life flows with direction and meaning" (p. 17).

Integrity. By forming a personally valid set of beliefs that have some internal consistency and that provide tentative guides for behavior, integrity is developed. Such development involves the humanizing and personalizing of values, and the development of congruence. Robert White (1958) described the humanizing of values as the shift from a literal belief in the absoluteness of rules and the purposes they are meant to serve to a more relative view, where connections are made between rules and the purposes they are meant to serve. Thus students move from internalizing their parents' values to forming their own. Personalizing of values leads to the achievement of behavior consistent with the values held. Congruence is achieved in the integration of values and the development of one's own standards for living.

Chickering's Vectors and Some Implications for Type

Now let us *speculate* about the ease or discomfort with which different types develop in Chickering's vectors of student development. These comparisons have important implications for education.

Developing competence, especially intellectual competence, is the realm of all types in the college environment. Effective type development can significantly enhance the use of one's intelligence. Myers (1980b) indicated that it could *almost* be a substitute. Academic achievement requires the capacity to deal with concepts and ideas, the main province of Introversion (I) as well as the capacity to work with abstraction, symbols, and theory, the province of Intuition (N). Myers and McCaulley (1985) found that persons who prefer Introversion and Intuition (IN) will show greater aptitude for education than persons who favor Extraversion and Sensing (ES). The latter's gifts lie in the practical world of action. Thus, type theory predicts that Introverted Intuitives (INs) will have a relative advantage, since their preferences more closely match the majority of academic tasks.

Most aptitude tests are designed to measure knowledge and aptitude in the Introverted Intuitive (IN) domain, although there are many interests and capabilities that aptitude tests do not measure. Data from many studies indicate that Introverts consistently score higher than Extraverts on the SAT-Verbal and that Intuitives consistently score higher than Sensing types, with Sensing-Intuition differences being greater than Extraversion-Introversion differences (Myers & McCaulley, 1985).

In general, Thinking-Feeling (T-F) has much less importance than the other preferences in understanding aptitude. However, academic tasks requiring understanding of human motivations favor Feeling types. Perhaps that is why so many students in psychology classes are Feeling types and are often Intuitive Feeling types. With so much of college research being conducted in sophomore psychology courses, type theory would have us question the generalizability of the findings to the entire population. In regards to the JP preference, the Percepton (P) attitude favors a wide acquaintance with many subjects, which can lead to higher scores on aptitude measures. However, the Judgment (J) attitude is related to application and may be more often associated with higher grades. Since grades are the end product of the interaction among aptitude, application, and interest, they are a relevant measure to be considered and a major concern of most students.

More college professors are Intuitives (N) than Sensing (S) types. They also write exams that more frequently fit their own type. Since many college instructors require students in introductory courses to memorize facts and to recall them for tests, students who are Sensing (S) and Judging (J) may have more of a chance than in later courses. As professors require more hypothesizing and give more essay tests, Intuitive (N) students will have more of an advantage. It is well to remember that every type can learn to survive in the academic world if he or she can learn good study skills and apply them appropriately. Readers are encouraged to read the new MBTI *Manual* (Myers & McCaulley, 1985), which includes many studies to corroborate the theory in this area.

Competence in physical and manual skills also can be the domain of every type. However, interest in physical education as a major might generally indicate interest in physical and manual skills. Sensing types who chose this major were significantly overrepresented in the longitudinal study of freshman students at the University of Florida (McCaulley & Kainz, 1974). There are also high correlations for females between Sensing and interest in Office Practices as measured by the *Strong-Campbell Interest Inventory* (Myers & McCaulley, 1985). It is important to ask whether there are cultural expectations and gender role conditioning involved in these type data. Research is needed to explore relationships between successes, or those who persist in different majors, versus dropouts, and type preferences. We need to understand *excellence*, beyond *interest* in majors, careers, and type.

Interpersonal competence can be predicted from type theory to be related to Extraversion and to Feeling. Extraverts focus their attention on the external world of people and action. Feeling types are concerned about the impact of their decisions on themselves and others. Significantly more students with Intuitive Feeling (NF) preferences were enrolled in programs of clinical psychology, counseling psychology, counseling, and social work than were those with other combinations (Myers & McCaulley, 1985). Since awareness is the first step in developing interpersonal relationships, there appears to be an advantage for Feeling types.

Managing emotions may seem like the province of Feeling types because they have more ready access to their subjective judgment. Feeling types, especially EFs, have more practice in expressing themselves verbally and in relying on their subjective values. Their strong need for harmony means they generally take into consideration the impact of their actions on others and themselves.

Since Thinking types do not frequently express their feelings, but rather attend more to logic and objectivity, their emotions may emerge or even explode unexpectedly. Because their focus is not on the Feeling dimension, they may be surprised by sudden emergence of emotions. Their competence lies more in analyzing objective information and events than in evaluating their own and others' subjective responses. With dominant Thinking, emergence of emotions may signal expression of the inferior Feeling function in a primitive, unpredictable way. A dominant Feeling type, on the other hand, under acute emotional stress, may express a primitive inferior Thinking function through inappropriate and cutting criticism.

Managing emotions may be easier for all types who are well developed. Adolescence, late adolescence, and early adulthood are times for learning to express emotions appropriately. When students become overly aggressive or act on their sexual impulses, one might look for inadequate type development. Clinically, I have observed that this behavior might happen more often in the case of Extraverts than for Introverts. Again, one should not assume that Thinking types do not have emotions; it just may be more difficult for them to process their emotions than it is for Feeling types.

Becoming autonomous is a sign of maturity in this culture. Emotional independence may be easier for Thinking types than for Feeling types because they are loyal more to ideas rather than to people, since Thinking types tend to use objective values in their decision making. However as Feeling types mature, they can become freer of the need for constant reassurance and approval from significant others. Their need for harmony will probably always demand that they consider other people in their decision making. Recognizing one's interdependence with others takes great type development. The ability to tolerate and appreciate differences is one of the major goals of professionals using type working with college students.

Establishing identity seems to be related to Jung's concept of wholeness. As we mature, we are moving toward an identity that is consistent, yet that expresses the totality of our personhood. Men and women in college are expected to form an identity that expresses themselves in terms of appearance, gender roles, and sexual preference. Extraverts with their focus on the external world may be more conscious of their appearance and spend more time deciding about clothes and hairstyles than Introverts. Yet a truly sensitive ISFJ can be just as immobilized about issues of appearance as an ENFJ. It may be somewhat more problematic for female Thinking types and male Feeling types to explain themselves because of our cultural stereotypes which identify logic for males and expressiveness for females. This congruency or incongruency may have more to do with the match between the person and the specific institution or specific community environment. For example, our society may make it harder for a gay ISTJ male student than for a gay ENFP male student, who may be more comfortable with an experimental or unconventional lifestyle.

Developing freeing interpersonal relationships calls for increased tolerance of differences and expanded capacity for intimacy. Helping students to understand their own and others' type can promote an appreciation for individual differences. Since Perceptive types are more open and spontaneous, they probably are able to have freer relationships. Some students who have a Judging orientation to the external world may need more help in learning to respond to others for themselves rather than as stereotypes. Because of their need for closure, they often draw conclusions (Judgment) without enough information (Perception).

An appreciation of differences can be enriched through a recognition of the mutual usefulness of opposites. Sensing types can discover what they can use for Intuitives and vice versa, and Thinking types can discover the contribution of Feeling types and vice versa. Myers (1980a) reminded us that the clearest vision of the future comes from an Intuitive type, the most practical realism from a Sensing type, the most incisive analysis from a Thinking type, and the most skillful handling of people from a Feeling type. Success for any endeavor demands a variety of types, each in the place best suited for him or her.

Developing purpose requires students to form plans and to set priorities about educational and career goals as well as about vocational and general lifestyle strategies. Purpose calls for the development of both perception and judgment and the appropriate use of the external and internal modes. Setting priorities may pose difficulties for Perceptive types, while premature closure on career plans often causes problems for Judging types. Providing information about work settings in type terms can help students make more informed choices (Lynch, 1985). With an ethical and informed counselor, a student can explore his or her own type in interaction with distributions of types among various careers. We must remember that predominance of certain types in specific careers still does not tell us who is succesful or happy in those career fields, but only who was attracted to certain fields. Therefore, precautions need to be given to students when sharing these data.

Developing integrity occurs when students form their own personally valid and internally consistent set of beliefs, which they use to guide their behavior. In shifting from a literal belief in the absoluteness of rules to a more relative view, students begin to humanize their values. Intuitives enjoy seeing patterns and possibilities, so they may challenge their parents' beliefs and compare them with their own. Sensing types may tend to accept the rules literally until they reach a point where their parents' rules conflict with their own needs. When students arrive at behavior that is consistent with their own values, they have come to personalize their values.

We should keep in mind that development of the judgment function serves as a yardstick for *choice*. With development comes consistency in the intentional and appropriate use of type to the specific need or situation. Then congruence can truly mean achieving an integration of one's values with one's standards for living. Perhaps congruence and integrity are what Jung meant by the individual's striving toward wholeness.

Recommendations for Intentional Use of Type to Promote Student Development

The following recommendations are based on knowledge of type, student development theory, and current higher education literature.

For administrators:

1. Implement studies of type within the institution. Provide feedback to faculty and student services professionals regarding student profiles according to major, career choice, instructional preferences, and other needs.

2. Provide professional development for interested faculty and staff about psychological type and student development.

3. Provide, within the curriculum, opportunities for students to learn about type, life cycle, and student development, and the implications for learning, educational planning, and career and life choices.

For faculty:

4. Develop awareness of psychological type and how it affects learning.

5. Examine course syllabi and instructional strategies for opportunities to teach in different ways to appeal to different types. Recognize that different types can learn better if they have some chance to exercise their favorite functions. They can also be challenged to grow when they are supported and have opportunities to expand their repertoire of skills.

6. Examine the methods of evaluation currently used, to determine if they favor certain types. Vary tests and other measures of evaluation so that different types are given a fair chance.

7. In advising students, keep in mind that each one is an individual and has unique needs. Type knowledge can help in identifying some consistent patterns of behaviors and needs.

   For student services professionals:

8. Be aware of the implications of type in each of the specialty areas.

   ▪ Career counselors need to learn about type patterns in different occupations, not to steer students whose type matches the predominant type into an occupation, but to provide full information regarding work settings and implications for type.

   ▪ Personal counselors can be most effective in helping students understand their own type, especially when they are having some difficulties in type development.

   ▪ Student activities staff can use type knowledge in varying programming and in helping students to use their co-curricular activities for full development.

   ▪ Residential life staff members can use type in roommate conflict resolution, environmental planning, programming, and staff training.

9. Begin a developmental transcript approach to accompany an academic transcript which will help students recognize that they can use student activities, work, and volunteer experiences in gaining skills and knowledge for future careers.

   For students:

10. Learn about type, life cycle, and student development, to understand what current and future developmental tasks you are

facing. Make intentional use of type in selecting courses, majors, and instructors, and for understanding career and life choices. Remember that you need both support and challenge to grow and develop.

References

Chickering, A. W. (1969). *Education and identity*. San Francisco: Jossey-Bass.

Chickering, A. W., & Associates. (1981). *The modern American college*. San Francisco: Jossey-Bass.

Chickering, A. W., & Havighurst, R. J. (1981). *The life cycle*. In A. W. Chickering and Associates, *The modern American college*. San Francisco: Jossey-Bass.

Erikson, E. H. (1959). *Identity and the life cycle. Psychological Issues Monograph 1*. New York: International Universities Press.

Garfield, N. J., & David, L. B. (1986). Arthur Chickering: Bridging theory and practice in student development. *Journal of Counseling and Development, 64* (8), 483–491.

Havighurst, R. J. (1972). *Development tasks and education* (3rd ed.). New York: McKay.

Jung, C. G. (1923). *Psychological types*. New York: Harcourt Brace Jovanovich.

Knefelkamp, L. L., Widick, C., & Parker, C. A. (Eds.) (1978). *Applying new developmental findings. (New directions in students services*, No. 4.) San Francisco: Jossey-Bass.

Lawrence, G. (1982). *People types and tiger stripes*. Gainesville, FL: Center for the Applications of Psycholgical Type.

Lynch, A. Q. (1985). The Myers-Briggs Type Indicator: A tool for appreciating employees and client diversity. *Journal of Employment Counseling, 22* (3), 104–109.

McCaulley, M. H. (1981). Jung's theory of psychological types and the Myers-Briggs Type Indicator. In P. McReynolds (Ed.), *Advances in personality assessment*. San Francisco: Jossey-Bass.

McCaulley, M. H. (1985). True types. *Bulletin of Psychological Type, 8* (1), 30.

McCaulley, M. H., & Kainz, R. I. (1974). *The University of Florida longitudinal study: First follow-up*. Unpublished study. Gainesville, FL: Center for the Applications of Psychological Type.

Myers, I. B. (1980a). *Introduction to type*. Palo Alto, CA: Consulting Psychologists Press.

Myers, I. B. (1980b). *Gifts differing*. Palo Alto, CA: Consulting Psychologists Press.

Myers, I. B., & McCaulley, M. H. (1985). *Manual: A guide to the development and use of the Myers-Briggs Type Indicator*. Palo Alto, CA: Consulting Psychologists Press.

Neugarten, B. L. (Ed.). (1968). *Middle age and aging*. Chicago: University of Chicago Press.

Provost, J. A. (1984). *A casebook: Applications of the Myers-Briggs Type Indicator in counseling.* Gainesville, FL: Center for the Applications of Psychological Type.

Quenk, N. (1984). The dynamics of type development. *MBTI News, 7* (1), 1, 17.

Quenk, N. (1985a). Conflicts in function development. *MBTI News, 7* (2), 6–7.

Quenk, N. (1985b) Directionality of the auxiliary function. *Bulletin of Psychological Type, 8* (1), 27–29.

Rogers, C. R. (1961). *On becoming a person.* Boston: Houghton Mifflin.

Thomas, R. E., & Chickering, A. W. (1984). Education and identity revisited. *Journal of College Student Personnel, 5* (5), 392–399.

Von Franz, M. L., & Hillman, J. (1979). *Jung's typology.* Irving, TX: Spring Publications.

Weathersby, B. P., & Tarule, J. M. (1980). *Adult development: Implications for higher education.* (*AAHE/ERIC Higher Education Research Report,* No. 4.) Washington, DC: American Association for Higher Education.

White, R. W. (1958). *Lives in progress.* New York: Dryden Press.

DAVE KALSBEEK has used type in numerous institutional research projects since 1979. Currently Dave is Assistant Vice President for Student Development and Director of Student Life Studies at Saint Louis University, where he is using type as part of the institution's approach to enrollment management and analysis. He is a frequent consultant on using the MBTI in institutional research and building information systems to support MBTI use on college campuses. Dave is currently completing his Ph.D. in public policy analysis at Saint Louis University.

CHAPTER 3

Campus Retention: The MBTI in Institutional Self-Studies

DAVE KALSBEEK

THERE IS A clear and valuable role for the MBTI in campus retention efforts. This chapter will illustrate one process for laying the foundation for effective retention strategies, a process which uses the MBTI as a central construct. First, one conceptual model of student attrition is presented and some implications of that model are discussed. Second, the manner in which the MBTI can be integrated in this model through institutional research and analysis is discussed. Effective management of campus MBTI information is presented as a key first step in campus retention awareness and one successful approach to this task is used to illustrate the process.

A Conceptual Model for Understanding Student Attrition

Though retention and attrition are very complex issues with many intervening variables and factors, a theoretical framework or model offers a common ground for discussions, research, and action. In a summary of existing retention models, Bean (1982) explains:

> A model of student attrition is a representation of the factor presumed to influence decisions to drop out of an institution. The model identifies the interrelationships among the various factors and the relationships between these factors and the

dropout decision. The use of any model is based on certain assumptions about what is important in a dropout decision at a particular institution. (p. 18)

As Pascarella suggests in the introduction to the same volume (Pascarella, 1982, p. 8), "Such models can be particularly useful to institutional researchers and others studying the attrition phenomenon, in that the models provide a parsimonious guide to the selection of variables and to their relationships in student persistence/withdrawal behavior."

One such model of student attrition that has been widely cited and tested is that of Tinto (1975). Tinto suggests that when educators begin the task of making sense of retention or attrition patterns at their institution, they focus on meaningful background characteristics of the students matriculating at the institution. Tinto goes on to suggest that the rich diversity of student background characteristics shapes specific commitments students bring to campus; their commitments to educational objectives and to their chosen college or university play a prominent role in the Tinto model.

From their first contact with the institution, students experience the complexity of the college or university environment. Throughout their ongoing encounters with that environment, students continually gauge the degree to which the institution *fits* with their preconceptions, expectations, preferences, needs, values, or their abilities to cope. Tinto suggests that the critical factor in campus retention is the degree of congruence between the needs, interests, abilities, expectations, and commitments of the students and the academic and social systems of the institution with all of the demands, rewards, constraints, and challenges therein. Every student inevitably experiences some degree of integration or "fit" with the environment, both academically and socially. The model suggests that it is this degree of integration experienced by each individual student which leads to a reappraisal of their initial commitment to an educational degree and to a specific institution, which, in turn, is manifested in the student persisting or withdrawing from the institution.

Implications

The Tinto model has several clear implications for those interested in mobilizing campus retention efforts, and particularly retention research. First, if dropout is viewed as a process as the Tinto model suggests, then retention must be viewed as an outcome and not a goal in and of itself.

The appropriate focus of retention efforts is the nature of the interaction of the individual student with the total campus environment. The greater the degree of academic and social integration experienced by the student, the greater the likelihood of his/her continued enrollment. By targeting efforts to maximize the fit students experience with the campus climate, the Tinto model suggests that retention may take care of itself. To view retention statistics (such as freshman dropout rates or five-year graduation rates) as the goal rather than a proxy measure of the quality of students' experiences may launch enrollment management strategies on the wrong foot.

A second clear implication of viewing dropout as a process is that retention is a total campus responsibility. Since the focus of retention efforts is the quality of each student's academic and social experience and the fit students experience with the institution, then everyone who works, teaches, and studies at an institution has a role in that retention effort. The campus security officer, the financial aid secretary, the server in the cafeteria, the chemistry department chairperson, and the dean of students all have the opportunity (and the responsibility) to affect the student's experience at the institution. The responsibility for retention cannot and does not rest with the student affairs staff or with some retention committee. It is a collective challenge to the total college or university community.

A third implication of viewing dropout as the process Tinto suggests is that any attempt to gather useful information about students' enrollment patterns must consider a broad array of student characteristics, not the least of which are their commitments as discussed above. Attrition researchers often investigate the relationship between very traditional but limited student factors such as aptitude measures, race, hometown, or type of high school and persistence patterns. Such research uses rather static student characteristics without attending to those characteristics which may have a dynamic role in the student's interactions and experiences with the campus climate. Retention research must involve much more complex and encompassing student characteristics.

A final implication closely follows the previous one: accepting dropout as a process suggests that meaningful retention research must be longitudinal in nature. Information must be gathered over time about the ongoing nature of the student experience, attempting to monitor the types of integration certain types of students achieve in certain types of academic and social endeavors. To assume that a one-time snapshot of a student population serves to enlighten an institution as to its retention phenomenon may reflect more of an "event perspective" than a "process perspective." The "event perspective" is exemplified in so-called autopsy studies which survey withdrawing students at the moment of their withdrawal from the institution. The Tinto model would suggest that such research is minimally useful and Terenzini (1982) also suggests that such studies do little to explain enrollment phenomena.

The MBTI and the Tinto Model

There is a clear and valuable role for the *Myers-Briggs Type Indicator* in a retention effort based on the Tinto conceptual model. To understand the retention phenomenon at any one institution, it is necessary to understand the way students experience the campus climate in all of its many facets and the way students interact with the many social and academic challenges they inevitably face in their collegiate experience. If, as Tinto suggests, the critical factor in retention is the degree of congruence experienced by individual students with the academic and social dimensions of the campus climate, then it seems imperative to understand the personal processes at work as students negotiate the academic and social system. All that we know about personality type from both the theory and the existing research suggests that the MBTI can be one effective tool in making sense of that interaction. We know that the MBTI presents us with important information about students' natural interests, learning styles, commitments and values, and work habits. Therefore, it seems that the MBTI, in one single profile, may offer a wealth of useful insights regarding students' academic and social integration with specific campus climates. Type theory suggests that student preferences will determine to a large extent the degree of integration they will experience. Such preferences may be directly related to the processes students use as they appraise and reappraise their commitments to educational objectives and the institution.

Not only is the MBTI useful in describing individual students and understanding the nature of their experience, but it also allows educators to describe the prevailing climates of certain social and academic environments. A number of person-environment theorists (Walsh, 1973) suggest that it is the prevailing or dominant characteristics of a group that, in effect, determine the essential nature of the environment. If we can describe a group of students (Nursing majors, floor residents, members of some campus organization, etc.) using type dimensions, we can go a long way toward understanding the experience of students interacting with that group. Understanding the type profile of the faculty in a department may describe in part the academic challenges students in that department may face and the degree of integration or fit they may experience in that department. In short, type profiles offer added insight to both sides of the interaction equation; the MBTI can effectively describe both the individual student and dimensions of the environment encountered by that student.

The remainder of this chapter presents information related to the role of the MBTI in institutional retention research and actual retention efforts. Much of this chapter describes one particular research project which has as its specific objective the use of the MBTI in understanding the enrollment patterns at one university. The research endeavor entitled TRAILS (Tracking Retention and Academic Integration by Learning Style) is guided by the Tinto model and provides information that fits with the assumptions and premises of the model (Kalsbeek, 1986).

The Trails Project

The major goals and objectives of the TRAILS project are:

- to streamline the use of the MBTI by the university community by effectively managing MBTI data with appropriate information technologies;

- to provide educators necessary institutional data on how student characteristics are related to choice of major, academic "aptitude," academic performance in specific curricular areas, and attrition;

- to provide the information infrastructure for specific programs using type concepts in improving the quality of the academic and social experience of students at the university;

- to provide the research base needed to mobilize the university community in retention strategies;

- to allow student development professionals a mechanism for building bridges with academic colleagues in the service of students; and

- to add to the existing knowledge in the field of how type is related to student performance and persistence in higher education.

Each fall semester, a large proportion of the entering freshman class at Saint Louis University completes the *Myers-Briggs Type Indicator*. The MBTI data for each student are then merged with other institutional information such as ACT/SAT scores, high school grade point average, demographic factors like sex and race, etc. Each subsequent academic term, academic data such as major and GPA are entered in the database for each student. By maintaining such records in a computerized database, researchers can readily answer questions such as: What types of students tend to gravitate to certain majors? How well do different types of students do in certain schools? Do some types of learners do better early in their academic work than in subsequent studies? What types drop out at a greater rate than others? A wide variety of statistical and technical procedures are used to maintain and analyze this complex accumulation of information to answer such questions. The practical management and administration of the TRAILS projects is discussed in more depth at the end of this chapter.

Some preliminary findings of the TRAILS research will next be discussed to illustrate one process for using the *Myers-Briggs Type Indicator* in retention research. The following discussion will address the use of the MBTI in addressing these issues:

1. Population descriptions

2. The relationship of type and traditional measures of academic aptitude

3. The relationship of type to academic achievement

4. Type and attrition

Population Descriptions

When using the Tinto model in addressing institutional retention, one must be able to describe both the students and the environments students encounter at an institution. If we use the MBTI to do that, we need to investigate the type distributions of distinct groups of students, recognizing that this distribution tells us much about that climate or environment. Population description becomes the necessary first step.

Fortunately, there is an ever-increasing accumulation of research with the MBTI which describes specific populations. Generally such research is designed to investigate hypotheses about the role of MBTI preferences in choice of academic major, occupation or career, and so on. For example, Myers (1980) presents some research findings using type tables to describe various academic populations. She presents MBTI profiles for engineering students, liberal arts students, finance and commerce students, counselor education students, etc. Likewise, in a major study of type and medical professions, McCaulley (1978) presents numerous type tables for students in a wide variety of medical-related academic pursuits. Articles in the *Journal of Psychological Type* often present type distributions of distinct student populations. The point of such research is that different types of students are disproportionately represented in certain academic disciplines. When one considers any academic major at an institution as an academic and social environment with its own unique interpersonal dimensions, rewards, constraints, challenges, and supports, then the type profile of the students (as well as the faculty) is vitally important environmental information.

Type and Academic Majors

At the institutional level, one needs to identify the type variables that distinguish specific schools or majors in order to make sense of the student-environment interaction which is so basic to Tinto's model. Three type tables from the TRAILS data at Saint Louis University are presented here (Tables 1–3); these tables illustrate the predominant characteristics of several individual colleges and majors at the university. It is important to note that though all 16 types are represented in each college, the self-selection ratio (SSR) shows clearly that certain types are disproportionately represented in certain academic environments. For those unfamiliar with interpreting the type table and the SSR, see the MBTI *Manual* (Myers & McCaulley, 1985).

What the TRAILS data clearly illustrate is that at Saint Louis University the ST types are most overrepresented in Business majors, the SF types are most overrepresented in the Nursing School, and the NT types are most overrepresented in the College of Arts and Sciences. These differences are significant and serve to make one key point: while it is widely acknowledged that differences in certain student characteristics are often manifested in academic and career interests, the MBTI is an effective tool for portraying and understanding those differences. As indicated above, this is the necessary first step in making sense of retention phenomena. Using the MBTI to describe student populations offers educators insight to the peculiar and unique characteristics of key student groups. Knowing that what distinguishes the Business program from others is the predominance of ST types may tell us something very important about the flavor of that environment for students.

Another population of great importance in any retention effort are those undecided about majors. According to the Tinto model, being uncommitted to a specific major or career may put students at risk. Many institutions find that these undecided students are indeed extremely

TABLE 1

All SLU Business Majors, 1982–85
(N = 370)

Sensing Types with Thinking	Sensing Types with Feeling	Intuitive Types with Feeling	Intuitive Types with Thinking			%	SSR
ISTJ N = 35 % = 9.5 ▪▪▪▪▪▪ ▪▪▪ 1.29	**ISFJ** N = 28 % = 7.6 ▪▪▪▪▪▪ ▪▪ 1.15	**INFJ** N = 9 % = 2.4 ▪▪ .64	**INTJ** N = 6 % = 1.6 ▪▪ .56	Introverts Judging	E 63 / I 37	1.27 / 0.73	
					S 58 / N 42	1.12 / 0.87	
					T 43 / F 57	1.13 / 0.92	
ISTP N = 19 % = 5.1 ▪▪▪▪▪ 1.57	**ISFP** N = 19 % = 5.1 ▪▪▪▪▪ 1.10	**INFP** N = 23 % = 6.2 ▪▪▪▪▪▪ .84	**INTP** N = 6 % = 1.6 ▪▪ .43	Perceptive	J 48 / P 52	0.98 / 1.02	
					IJ 21 / IP 18 / EP 34 / EJ 27	1.02 / 0.95 / 1.07 / 0.94	
ESTP N = 17 % = 4.6 ▪▪▪▪▪ 1.11	**ESFP** N = 25 % = 6.8 ▪▪▪▪▪▪ ▪ .91	**ENFP** N = 55 % = 14.9 ▪▪▪▪▪ ▪▪▪▪▪ ▪▪▪▪▪▪ .99	**ENTP** N = 29 % = 7.8 ▪▪▪▪▪▪ ▪▪ 1.50	Extraverts Perceptive	ST 29 / SF 29 / NF 28 / NT 14	1.30 / 0.99 / 0.86 / 0.90	
					SJ 36 / SP 22 / NP 31 / NJ 12	1.13 / 1.11 / 0.97 / 0.68	
ESTJ N = 36 % = 9.7 ▪▪▪▪▪ ▪▪▪▪▪ 1.30	**ESFJ** N = 35 % = 9.5 ▪▪▪▪▪ ▪▪▪▪▪ .89	**ENFJ** N = 16 % = 4.3 ▪▪▪▪ .69	**ENTJ** N = 12 % = 3.2 ▪▪▪ .80	Judging	TJ 17 / TP 19 / FP 35 / FJ 24	0.93 / 1.08 / 0.93 / 0.87	
					IN 12 / EN 30 / IS 27 / ES 31	0.66 / 0.99 / 1.25 / 1.03	

Notes: ▪ = One Percent; Base Population = All SLU Students; N = 1951.

TABLE 2

All SLU Nursing Majors, 1982–85
(N = 164)

Sensing Types		Intuitive Types				%	SSR
with Thinking	with Feeling	with Feeling	with Thinking				

Introverts Judging

ISTJ	ISFJ	INFJ	INTJ
N = 7	N = 11	N = 6	N = 1
% = 4.3	% = 6.7	% = 3.7	% = 0.6
■■■■ ■	■■■■■■	■■■■	■
.58	1.02	.96	.21

Introverts Perceptive

ISTP	ISFP	INFP	INTP
N = 3	N = 10	N = 6	N = 1
% = 1.8	% = 6.1	% = 3.7	% = 0.6
■■	■■■■■■	■■■■	■
.56	1.31	.49	.16

Extraverts Perceptive

ESTP	ESFP	ENFP	ENTP
N = 4	N = 22	N = 32	N = 4
% = 2.4	% = 13.4	% = 19.5	% = 2.4
■■	■■■■■■■ ■■■■■■ ■	■■■■■■■ ■■■■■■■ ■■■■■■	■■
.59	1.80	1.30	.47

Extraverts Judging

ESTJ	ESFJ	ENFJ	ENTJ
N = 17	N = 22	N = 15	N = 3
% = 10.4	% = 13.4	% = 9.2	% = 1.8
■■■■■■ ■■■■	■■■■■■ ■■■■■■■ ■	■■■■■■ ■■■	■■
1.39	1.26	1.45	.45

	%	SSR
E	73	1.20
I	27	0.69
S	59	1.14
N	41	0.86
T	24	0.64
F	76	1.22
J	50	1.02
P	50	0.98
IJ	15	0.74
IP	12	0.64
EP	38	1.19
EJ	35	1.22
ST	19	0.85
SF	40	1.35
NF	36	1.11
NT	5	0.34
SJ	35	1.09
SP	24	1.22
NP	26	0.83
NJ	15	0.89
TJ	17	0.90
TP	7	0.46
FP	43	1.34
FJ	33	1.21
IN	9	0.48
EN	33	1.08
IS	19	0.87
ES	40	1.34

Notes: ■ = One percent; Base Population = All SLU Students; N = 1951.

TABLE 3

All SLU Arts and Science Majors, 1982–85
(N = 1053)

Sensing Types		Intuitive Types					
with Thinking	with Feeling	with Feeling	with Thinking			%	SSR

ISTJ	ISFJ	INFJ	INTJ	Introverts / Judging	E	60	0.96
N = 85	N = 63	N = 28	N = 44		I	40	1.06
% = 8.1	% = 6.0	% = 2.7	% = 4.2		S	49	0.98
▪▪▪▪▪▪▪ ▪▪	▪▪▪▪▪▪	▪▪▪	▪▪▪▪		N	57	1.06
1.10	.91	.70	1.43		T	43	1.13
					F	57	0.92
ISTP	ISFP	INFP	INTP	Perceptive	J	49	1.00
					P	51	1.00
N = 40	N = 37	N = 95	N = 50		IJ	21	1.01
% = 3.8	% = 3.5	% = 9.0	% = 4.8		IP	21	1.10
▪▪▪▪	▪▪▪▪ ▪▪▪	▪▪▪▪▪▪	▪▪▪▪▪		EP	30	0.94
					EJ	28	0.98
1.16	.75	1.21	1.27		ST	23	1.05
ESTP	ESFP	ENFP	ENTP	Extraverts / Perceptive	SF	25	0.87
					NF	32	0.97
N = 46	N = 67	N = 144	N = 59		NT	20	1.23
% = 4.4	% = 6.4	% = 13.7	% = 5.6		SJ	31	0.96
▪▪▪▪	▪▪▪▪▪▪	▪▪▪▪▪▪▪ ▪▪▪▪▪▪▪	▪▪▪▪▪▪		SP	18	0.92
					NP	33	1.05
1.05	.86	.91	1.07		NJ	18	1.06
ESTJ	ESFJ	ENFJ	ENTJ	Judging	TJ	19	1.05
					TP	19	1.11
N = 76	N = 100	N = 65	N = 54		FP	36	0.95
% = 7.2	% = 9.5	% = 6.2	% = 5.1		FJ	24	0.89
▪▪▪▪▪▪▪	▪▪▪▪▪▪ ▪▪▪	▪▪▪▪▪▪	▪▪▪▪▪		IN	21	1.15
					EN	31	1.00
.96	.90	.98	1.27		IS	21	0.98
					ES	27	0.92

Notes: ▪ = One percent; Base population = All SLU Students ; N = 1951.

likely to drop out. Anchors, Gershman, and Robbins (1985) have accumulated type profiles on undecided majors and their data suggest that the types most overrepresented in the undecided group are IPs and NPs. The TRAILS data (Table 4) suggest that the STP combination is overrepresented as "Undecided" compared to the undergraduate population at large.

Type and Faculty Profiles

Student populations are not the only type profiles worth ascertaining in efforts to map out the type characteristics of an academic environment; understanding the predominant characteristics of the faculty is equally important. Table 5 illustrates type distributions for one department's faculty at Saint Louis University. Though the number of faculty is small, some patterns are important to note. The ratios reflect the difference between the faculty and the student percentage distribution in this specific department. Such information is useful in efforts to explore student-faculty interaction and the quality of the educational experience both in and out of the classroom. For example, the fact that the faculty are predominantly Judging types and the students majoring in that department are predominantly Extraverted Perceiving types may suggest a lot about the challenges and frustrations experienced by both students and faculty in that department.

Using the MBTI with Other Enrollment Data Sources

Type distributions are not the only means of describing student groups in such a way as to aid the retention effort. The TRAILS project (or any such institutional database of student type scores) can be effectively related to other institutional data sources so as to provide added insights about the student population. For example, many institutions participate in the Cooperative Institutional Research Project (CIRP), the national freshman survey conducted by Alexander Astin at UCLA and co-sponsored by the American Council on Education. This national survey provides a rich and useful profile of entering freshmen and allows educators to monitor changes in students over time and to compare their freshmen with students entering comparable institutions nationwide. For some institutions, the CIRP is the only concerted and comprehensive effort to ascertain a profile of the student population.

TABLE 4

Ratios of Undecided Students Compared with All Undergraduates

Type	Base Population[a] N	%	Sample Population[b] N	%	Ratio	Type Group	Base %	Sample %	Ratio
ISTJ	143	7.33	17	6.85	0.94	E	60.28	58.87	0.98
ISFJ	128	6.56	14	5.65	0.86	I	39.72	41.13	1.04
INFJ	74	3.79	12	4.84	1.28				
INTJ	57	2.92	7	2.82	0.97	S	51.51	53.63	1.04
						N	48.49	46.37	0.96
ISTP	64	3.28	11	4.44	1.35				
ISFP	91	4.66	12	4.84	1.04	T	38.19	40.73	1.07
INFP	145	7.43	19	7.66	1.03	F	61.81	59.27	0.96
INTP	73	3.74	10	4.03	1.08				
						J	49.05	47.98	0.98
ESTP	81	4.15	15	6.05	1.46	P	50.95	52.02	1.02
ESFP	145	7.43	21	8.47	1.14				
ENFP	293	15.02	27	10.89	0.72	IJ	20.60	20.16	0.98
ENTP	102	5.23	14	5.65	1.08	IP	19.12	20.97	1.10
						EP	31.83	31.05	0.98
ESTJ	146	7.48	18	7.26	0.97	EJ	28.45	27.82	0.98
ESFJ	207	10.61	25	10.08	0.95				
ENFJ	123	6.30	17	6.85	1.09	ST	22.25	24.60	1.11
ENTJ	79	4.05	9	3.63	0.90	SF	29.27	29.03	0.99
						NF	32.55	30.24	0.93
Sum	1951		248			NT	15.94	16.13	1.01
						SJ	31.98	29.84	0.93
						SP	19.53	23.79	1.22
						NP	31.42	28.23	0.90
						NJ	17.07	18.15	1.06
						TJ	21.78	20.56	0.94
						TP	16.40	20.16	1.23
						FP	34.55	31.85	0.92
						FJ	27.27	27.42	1.01
						IN	17.89	19.35	1.08
						EN	30.60	27.02	0.88
						IS	21.83	21.77	1.00
						ES	29.68	31.85	1.07
						ET	20.91	22.58	1.08
						EF	39.36	36.29	0.92
						IF	22.45	22.98	1.02
						IT	17.27	10.15	1.05

[a] Base Population: All undergraduates
[b] Sample Population: Undecided students

TABLE 5

Faculty in Department X, 1985
(*N*=11)

Sensing Types		Intuitive Types				%	Ratio
with Thinking	with Feeling	with Feeling	with Thinking				
ISTJ	**ISFJ**	**INFJ**	**INTJ**	Introverts Judging	E	36	.49
					I	64	2.53
N = 0	N = 1	N = 0	N = 4				
% = 0	% = 9.1	% = 0	% = 36.4		S	18	.33
	▪		▪▪▪▪		N	82	1.84
					T	45	2.10
					F	55	.70
ISTP	**ISFP**	**INFP**	**INTP**	Perceptive	J	82	1.77
					P	18	.34
N = 0	N = 0	N = 2	N = 0		IJ	45	4.09
% = 0	% = 0	% = 18.2	% = 0		IP	18	1.30
		▪▪			EP	0	.00
					EJ	36	1.04
					ST	0	.00
					SF	18	.45
ESTP	**ESFP**	**ENFP**	**ENTP**	Extraverts Perceptive	NF	36	.96
					NT	45	7.07
N = 0	N = 0	N = 0	N = 0		SJ	18	.60
% = 0	% = 0	% = 0	% = 0		SP	0	.00
					NP	18	.63
					NJ	64	4.03
					TJ	45	3.24
ESTJ	**ESFJ**	**ENFJ**	**ENTJ**	Judging	TP	0	.00
					FP	18	.39
N = 0	N = 1	N = 2	N = 1		FJ	36	1.13
% = 0	% = 9.1	% = 18.2	% = 9.1				
	▪	▪▪	▪		IN	55	6.66
					EN	27	.75
					IS	9	.54
					ES	9	.24

Notes: Comparison population = Undergraduate students in department X (*N* = 171).

The TRAILS data were used to investigate relationships between type and student responses on the CIRP and clear patterns were apparent. For example, on one portion of the CIRP survey, students indicate the importance of certain factors as reasons for going to college. The TRAILS project found that some factors were significantly more important to some types of students than to others (Kalsbeek & DeFiore, 1986). Such patterns are important since the Tinto retention model suggests that these initial objectives, commitments, and intentions of students matriculating at an institution are important factors in understanding attrition. By merging type data with other institutional information such as the CIRP, one can embellish an institution's understanding of the freshman population, and thereby glean important insights related to the retention model.

Type and Academic Aptitude

While it is important to recognize that type distributions provide useful information for the retention model, it is equally important to investigate the degree to which type is related to traditional measures of student aptitude. This is important for retention purposes for two reasons:

1. Measures of aptitude are often determining factors in students' sense of competence, and thereby may influence the degree of commitment they have to an institution and to an educational objective. The literature is replete with insights about the power of expectations and the so-called self-fulfilling prophecy; aptitude measures, when used as indicators of the likelihood of students performing successfully, are powerful sources of expectations.

2. Aptitude measures are often used to place students in special academic programs. High scorers are referred to honors programs; low scorers are often conditionally admitted through special "academic support" offices. As such, aptitude scores determine a whole range of academic and social experiences students have upon matriculating at an institution.

It is generally acknowledged that there is some relationship between type preferences and performance on standardized aptitude measures. Myers (1982) and McCaulley and Natter (1980) discuss several reasons why Intuitive types may perform better than Sensing types on certain IQ and aptitude measures and cite some studies which illustrate these

TABLE 6

One-Way Analysis of Variance of Aptitude Score (SAT)
by Learning Style

Group	N	Mean SAT	SD	Scheffe Post Hoc Comparisons				
					IN	EN	IS	ES
IN	148	1110	184.7	*IN*				
EN	312	1052	177.1	*EN*	*			
IS	188	1008	224.1	*IS*	*	*		
ES	250	932	196.1	*ES*	*	*	*	
Total	989	1019	203.6					

F (3,984)= 30.5
p <.001

Note: *denotes p < .05

differences. The argument is often made that Sensing intelligence cannot be measured by paper-and-pencil instruments, and that Sensing students (especially Extraverted Sensors) are at a disadvantage on any timed examination which focuses on the ability to quickly manipulate symbols, see patterns and relationships between words and concepts, and so on. The TRAILS data clearly support these patterns; on both the ACT and the SAT, the IN types scored the highest, followed by the EN, IS, and ES types (see Table 6). These differences are both statistically and practically significant and such patterns have been remarkably consistent across several institutions.

Correlations Using Continuous Scores

The TRAILS data include strength of preference scores in addition to the simple four-letter type scores of individuals. This allows the proper investigation of the linear relationship between variables, to see if, for example, the strength of preference for intuition is related to aptitude measures. Such an approach may provide more insight regarding the relationship between these variables than if one simply compared the aptitude scores of all Intuitives with all Sensors. Table 7 illustrates these relationships and is discussed further below.

The first step was to convert each preference score to a continuous score, with 100 being the midpoint on the scale. An extreme Sensing

TABLE 7

Myers-Briggs Type Indicator and
Academic Aptitude (ACT and SAT)
Results of a Stepwise Multiple Regression

Variable	Greek beta	R^2	F
Sensing-Intuition	.30	.08	22.96**
Extraversion-Introversion	.10	.09	2.86
Thinking-Feeling	- .06	.09	.95
Judgment-Perception	.02	.09	.07

Note: ** denotes $p < .05$

preference then has a score around 59 while an extreme Intuition preference would score around 139. Therefore, the Sensing/Intuition dimension has a single score which reflects both the strength and the direction
of the preference. The researcher, using a multiple regression approach,
can then answer the question: Is it true that the stronger the preference
for Intuition, the higher the aptitude score? What about preferences for
Extraversion vs. Introversion? Preferences for Thinking/Feeling or
Judgment/Perception? The results of such a regression are shown in
Table 7. In other words, the table shows the degree of the relationship
between each MBTI scale and the aptitude measure (which in this case is
the ACT composite score and the SAT combined score) when all MBTI
scales are considered simultaneously in the regression equation.

The Sensing-Intuition scale has the strongest relationship with aptitude test performance and the analysis suggests that the stronger the
preference for Intuition, the higher the aptitude score. The preference for
the Extraversion/Introversion, Thinking/Feeling, and Judgment/Per-
ception dimensions are not related to aptitude scores to a statistically
significant degree.

Implications

These findings are important in the overall attempt to make sense of
retention and to use the MBTI in retention efforts. First, it seems that the
Intuition preference may be advantaged in traditional measures of aptitude; students with this preference may therefore be less likely to be

found in "remedial" or "special support" programs prescribed for students with low aptitude scores. Table 8 shows the type distribution for one such program. The ratios show that ES learners are more than 1.5 times more likely to be found in this group than one would expect from the overall type distribution of the student body.

Given that certain types of learners tend to score lower on aptitude tests than other learners, the trend of declining board scores faced by many institutions takes on new meaning. Available data suggest that an ever-increasing number of Sensing students are entering American colleges and universities and that, contrary to 10 or 20 years ago, the majority of college students today have a sensing preference (Myers, 1980; Davis & Schroeder, 1980). Academic programs which have witnessed a decline in board scores might benefit from investigating shifts in the prevailing learning style of their students via the MBTI.

Finally, knowing this relationship between type preferences and aptitude (as measured by standardized tests) enables us to make better sense of the academic performance of certain types of students in certain curricular areas. As will be shown in the following section, there is evidence that Sensing learners may be the most successful students in certain academic pursuits, in spite of a poor performance on the ACT or SAT. Using such aptitude measures to screen students for admission may be a disservice to some students and also perhaps to the vitality and success of specific academic programs. In a broader perspective, the current trend in public policy to monitor the *quality* of undergraduate programs through comprehensive assessment of student learning outcomes tends to focus on the use of standardized assessment measures (National Governors' Association, 1985, 1986). Data on the relationship of type to aptitude test performance have implications for such policies at both the state and federal levels.

The ultimate utility of these data at any one institution may be their potential for getting the attention of faculty and academic administrators. Because board scores are accepted at many institutions as important indices of quality, any information that can be directly related to aptitude scores and which may help explain shifting patterns in such scores is likely to at least get the attention of key campus personnel. This information thereby becomes a valuable political resource for mobilizing campus retention efforts. Research on the relationship of type data to aptitude test scores may be an effective entree to the campus decision-making structure and in turn may be an effective means of improving the quality of the learning environment for students, and hence improve retention.

TABLE 8

Selection of Students in "High Risk Program"

Type	Base Population[a] N	%	Sample Population[b] N	%	Ratio	Type Group	Base %	Sample %	Ratio
ISTJ	143	7.33	22	14.19	1.94	E	60.28	61.29	1.02
ISFJ	128	6.56	7	4.52	0.69	I	39.72	38.71	0.97
INFJ	74	3.79	4	2.58	0.68				
INTJ	57	2.92	3	1.94	0.66	S	51.51	76.13	1.48
						N	48.49	23.87	0.49
ISTP	64	3.28	10	6.45	1.97				
ISFP	91	4.66	8	5.16	1.11	T	38.19	59.35	1.55
INFP	145	7.43	3	1.94	0.26	F	61.81	40.65	0.66
INTP	73	3.74	3	1.94	0.52				
						J	49.05	59.35	1.21
ESTP	81	4.15	20	12.90	3.11	P	50.95	40.65	0.80
ESFP	145	7.43	8	5.16	0.69				
ENFP	293	15.02	7	4.52	0.30	IJ	20.60	23.23	1.13
ENTP	102	5.23	4	2.58	0.49	IP	19.12	15.48	0.81
						EP	31.83	25.16	0.79
ESTJ	146	7.48	23	14.84	1.98	EJ	28.45	36.13	1.27
ESFJ	207	10.61	20	12.90	1.22				
ENFJ	123	6.30	6	3.87	0.61	ST	22.25	48.39	2.18
ENTJ	79	4.05	7	4.52	1.12	SF	29.27	27.74	0.95
						NF	32.55	12.90	0.40
Sum	1951		155			NT	15.94	10.97	0.69
						SJ	31.98	46.45	1.45
						SP	19.53	29.68	1.52
						NP	31.42	10.97	0.35
						NJ	17.07	12.90	0.76
						TJ	21.78	35.48	1.63
						TP	16.40	23.87	1.46
						FP	34.55	16.77	0.49
						FJ	27.27	23.87	0.88
						IN	17.89	8.39	0.47
						EN	30.60	15.48	0.51
						IS	21.83	30.32	1.39
						ES	29.68	45.81	1.54
						ET	20.91	34.84	1.67
						EF	39.36	26.45	0.67
						IF	22.45	14.19	0.63
						IT	17.27	24.52	1.42

[a] Base Population: All undergraduates
[b] Sample Population: Students in "High Risk Program"

Type and Academic Achievement

Academic achievement has a prominent role in any investigation of retention patterns. At many institutions, the inability of students to perform academically is the single most important factor contributing to attrition. In the Tinto model, academic performance is one measure of academic integration and is an important consideration as students reassess their commitments both to the institution and to their educational objectives. It is necessary to investigate the relationship of type to academic achievement in order to fully integrate the MBTI with the retention model.

One of the more popular institutional efforts to improve retention is the creation of support programs to assist students having academic difficulty. Such programs often intend to provide kinds of support and structure some students need but which are not available in the traditional classroom. Ideally, such programs would be able to identify early in a semester those students likely to experience academic difficulty. However, it is usually difficult if not impossible to predict which students will encounter difficulty in any one course or any one curricular area. The use of aptitude measures is not always the most effective approach and as we have seen, such measures may be related to personality type. The MBTI may be useful in identifying students who are likely to experience difficulty or special challenges in a given academic area and in facilitating a good educational fit between the learner and the instruction.

Correlations with First-Term GPA

It is not uncommon to find MBTI researchers ranking the GPA of the 16 types from high to low in order to understand the relationship between type and academic performance. At other times, researchers may compare the grades of Intuitives to those of Sensors, Extraverts to Introverts, and so on. As indicated earlier, it may be appropriate to investigate the strength of preference to see whether or not the preference on any MBTI dimension leads to better grades. Table 9 illustrates this relationship of strength of preference to first-term GPA at Saint Louis University.

First we see in Section I of Table 9 that there is a relationship between strength of preference on three of the four MBTI dimensions and academic achievement in the first semester. The greater the preference for intuition, the greater the preference for introversion, and the greater the preference for judgment, the better the GPA. There is a slight though

TABLE 9

Four Myers-Briggs Indices and First-Term GPA
Academic Achievement

I.   Results of a Stepwise Multiple Regression—without aptitude SAT

Variable	B	R SQ	F
Extraversion-Introversion	.24	.05	16.71**
Judgment-Perception	-.13	.06	4.47*
Sensing-Intuition	.13	.08	4.15*
Thinking-Feeling	.10	.08	3.00

II.   Results of a Stepwise Multiple Regression—with aptitude SAT

Variable	B	R SQ	F
Aptitude Score (SAT)	.43	.18	67.35**
Extraversion-Introversion	.20	.22	13.85**
Judgment-Perception	-.14	.23	6.68**
Thinking-Feeling	.13	.24	5.73*
Sensing-Intuition	.00	.24	.00

Note: * denotes $p < .05$
      ** denotes $p < .01$

statistically insignificant relationship between Thinking/Feeling and academic achievement in the first term.

Institutional researchers usually investigate the relationship between grades and aptitude measures in order to verify that the use of aptitude measures to screen students in the admissions process and to place students in appropriate course sections is a worthwhile and effective endeavor. Aptitude measures have been found to be somewhat predictive of first-semester academic achievement. But since we know that type preferences are related to both aptitude and grades, what would happen if we rolled all of this information together? Table 9, Section II illustrates that inquiry as part of the TRAILS project.

First we see that aptitude scores are the best predictors of academic performance. We also see that the impact of the Sensing/Intuition preference on grades is lessened once we consider aptitude in addition to MBTI preference scores in predicting GPA. As indicated in Table 7, the preference for Intuition is positively related to aptitude scores. Therefore, once we have rolled aptitude scores together with type scores in the equation for predicting GPA, much of the impact of Intuition is already accounted for in the aptitude measure. Since it seems that these aptitude measures and the MBTI dimension of Sensing/Intuition may in part be measuring the same thing (given the positive correlation), the impact on grades of this one MBTI preference is diminished once we consider aptitude scores.

Such is not the case in the TRAILS findings with the other type dimensions. First of all, Table 7 showed no relationship between the Judgment/Perception dimension and aptitude scores. However, in Table 9 we see that even after considering aptitude, the greater the preference for Judgment, the better the first-term GPA. Therefore, even when considering aptitude, the Judgment/Perception preference adds more insight regarding first-term academic achievement. Also, we found in Table 7 no relationship between the Thinking/Feeling dimension and the aptitude score, while in Table 9 we see that the stronger the preference for Feeling, the higher the grades. Hence, even after considering aptitude, the stronger the preference for Feeling the better the first-term grades at Saint Louis University. Finally, though there was no significant relationship between Extraversion/Introversion and aptitude scores, the preference for Introversion is related to higher first-term grades even after considering aptitude in the regression.

In summary, the preliminary evidence from the TRAILS studies suggests that MBTI preferences are related to first-term academic achievement at Saint Louis University. Preferences for Intuition may be predictive of academic performance in ways similar to the predictive nature of aptitude scores. The data suggest that the stronger the preference for Feeling judgment, the better the first-term grade (though aptitude scores do not correlate significantly with preferences for Thinking/Feeling). We also find that though aptitude tests may favor neither the Judgment nor the Perception preference, the Judgment attitude seems advantageous for academic achievement. Therefore, in predicting first-term academic performance, the Judgment/Perception dimension adds a great deal to aptitude score.

None of this is particularly surprising. The Judgment/Perception dimension tells us much about students' work habits which surely are manifested in academic performance. Many academic expectations and requirements favor the judgment bias towards closure, structure, and order. In addition, many academic measures are structured similarly to the ACT and the SAT, requiring the quick grasp of patterns and relationships of symbols—which is the gift of introversion and intuition. This may explain in part why the ACT and SAT have been moderately useful through the years in predicting students' first-term academic performance, since performance is so often measured in such a way that it taps into those same intuitive gifts measured by "aptitude."

It must be emphasized that these findings are for aggregate data. Such group trends cannot and should not be used to predict any individual student's performance on aptitude tests or in academic achievement. Other chapters in this volume discuss the appropriate use of MBTI scores in counseling or advising students; the same concerns are present in using the results of studies such as these in predicting individual behavior or performance. These group data best serve to enlighten educators about the environmental challenges students face at an institution or in a specific curriculum.

The Relationship of Type to Advanced Academic Performance

The TRAILS data presented above reflect the grades achieved by students in the *first semester* of a rigorous Jesuit, liberal arts curriculum. Students are engaged in philosophy and theology, history, English, and mathematics courses, all of which may indeed favor the intuitive and introverted preferences. Once students engage more directly in studies related to their chosen major, other preferences may be more advantageous. For example, a student with a strong preference for Intuition may find the challenges of pursuing an Accounting major uncomfortable while a student preferring Sensing may excel, contrary to what would be predicted by aptitude measures alone or by their first-term performance in the core liberal arts curriculum. The Nursing curriculum, especially in clinical studies, may favor the Extraverted Sensing students whose natural gifts may give them an advantage in the specifics of patient care.

Table 10 presents preliminary TRAILS findings on the relationship of the MBTI to academic achievement in the sixth semester for students in four colleges: Business, Arts and Sciences, Nursing, and Allied Health. These data are preliminary findings since a sufficient data set is not yet available for analyses of upperclass achievement in specific curricular areas. Using the fall semester GPA for juniors and seniors as the dependent variable and the four "learning style" groups as independent variables, one-way analyses of variance for each school show no significant differences by learning style.

It is important to look back to Tables 7 and 9 and compare these findings with those for first-semester performance. While first-semester performance apparently strongly favors Introversion and Intuition, more advanced study in any of the schools does not demonstrate significant differences between the learning styles defined by these two MBTI dimensions. The implications of these preliminary TRAILS analyses are that personality dimensions which are strongly related to apti-

TABLE 10

Results of Four One-Way Analysis of Variance for Each College:
Mean Upperclass Grade Point Average by Learning Style

Learning Style	Arts/Sciences		Business		Nursing		Allied Health	
	n	mean	n	mean	n	mean	n	mean
IN	64	3.32	15	2.91	5	3.20	17	3.31
EN	82	3.26	42	2.93	23	3.37	30	3.64
IS	68	3.17	35	3.15	12	3.51	12	3.51
ES	75	3.22	42	3.04	25	3.26	37	3.48
Total	289	3.24	134	3.02	65	3.34	96	3.50
F ratio		.53		1.03		.61		1.29
F probability		.66		.38		.61		.28

tude test scores and to first-semester performance may in no way be related to academic achievement in the upperclass curricula.

In summary, the longitudinal, multivariate approach required by the Tinto model is the approach which is maximally useful for understanding how some preferences may place certain learners at an advantage or disadvantage in certain academic pursuits. As we have seen, type concepts richly embellish the Tinto model and tell us more than we could glean from aptitude measures alone about the academic performance of students. Type data also help us understand the differing challenges of the first semester and subsequent semesters. However, though such group data enlighten educators about general trends in students' performance within a given curriculum, educators cannot take such aggregate findings and apply them to each and every individual student's experience. To do so violates the ethical principles of educational research in general and type theory in particular.

Type and Attrition

Comparing persisting populations to those who drop out, while also considering the aptitude and achievement findings discussed previously, is the final objective of this approach to retention research. This chapter has hopefully made the point that any worthwhile investigation of attrition must be longitudinal (following some distinct cohort of students over time through their enrollment experience) and must focus on carefully selected variables pertaining to the interaction of certain learners with certain social and academic environments. The TRAILS project is one step toward this kind of retention research model. Though the project is young (having begun in 1981), some preliminary findings can be presented which illustrate the relationship of type to attrition.

For example, Tables 11, 12, and 13 compare the dropout population with persisting populations in the Nursing, Arts and Sciences, and the Business programs, respectively. Though these data are preliminary, one can see some patterns which may fit well with some common preconceptions about the interaction of types of learners with these academic programs.

The Nursing dropout table (Table 11) suggests a relationship between the Thinking/Feeling dimension and attrition. While students with a preference for Thinking comprise about 26 percent of the Nursing student group as a whole, they comprise 40 percent of the Nursing dropouts. The TJ group is more than twice as likely to drop out than one would expect from the overall type distribution. On the whole, it is the Thinking/Feeling dimension that accounts for most of the dropout phenomenon in Nursing, with Thinking types being most at risk.

In the Business school (Table 12), we see that most of the differences between the proportions of "types" in the persisting versus dropout populations are slight. However, the most definitive TRAILS research to date focuses on neither ratios such as those shown in Table 13 nor on the nonparametric statistics frequently used in MBTI studies (for example, chi-square). Discriminant analyses suggest that the Extraversion/Introversion and Thinking/Feeling dimensions interact to account for significant differences in enrollment patterns in the Business program (DeFiore & Kalsbeek, 1985). Though these analyses are not discussed in detail here, it suffices to say that studies of the relationship of type preferences to attrition may require a complex set of analytic techniques to ensure appropriate interpretation.

TRAILS research shows that in Arts and Sciences there are no overall relationships between any one MBTI dimension and attrition in this school (DeFiore & Kalsbeek, 1985). Table 13 does indicate that Introverts and Intuitives may be more prevalent in the dropout group than one would expect from the overall college distribution. However, given the variety of programs within Arts and Sciences, with majors ranging from Art to Geophysics to Theology, it is not surprising that no clear relationship emerges. Investigating attrition in each major may be a more appropriate approach of this or any liberal arts college.

TABLE 11

Dropout Ratios of Nursing Students

Type	Base Population[a] N	%	Sample Population[b] N	%	Ratio	Type Group	Base %	Sample %	Ratio
ISTJ	7	4.27	2	6.67	1.56	E	72.56	76.67	1.06
ISFJ	11	6.71	1	3.33	0.50	I	27.44	23.33	0.85
INFJ	6	3.66	0	0.00	0.00				
INTJ	1	0.61	1	3.33	5.47	S	58.54	66.67	1.14
						N	41.46	33.33	0.80
ISTP	3	1.83	1	3.33	1.82				
ISFP	10	6.10	1	3.33	0.55	T	24.39	40.00	1.64
INFP	6	3.66	1	3.33	0.91	F	75.61	60.00	0.79
INTP	1	0.61	0	0.00	0.00				
						J	50.00	56.67	1.13
ESTP	4	2.44	0	0.00	0.00	P	50.00	43.33	0.87
ESFP	22	18.41	4	13.33	0.99				
ENFP	32	19.51	5	16.67	0.85	IJ	15.24	13.33	0.87
ENTP	4	2.44	1	3.33	1.37	IP	12.20	10.00	0.82
						EP	37.80	33.33	0.88
ESTJ	17	10.37	6	20.00	1.93	EJ	34.76	43.33	1.25
ESFJ	22	13.41	5	16.67	1.24				
ENFJ	15	9.15	1	3.33	0.36	ST	18.90	30.00	1.59
ENTJ	3	1.83	1	3.33	1.82	SF	39.63	36.67	0.93
						NF	35.98	23.33	0.65
Sum	164		30			NT	5.49	10.00	1.82
						SJ	34.76	46.67	1.34
						SP	23.78	20.00	0.84
						NP	26.22	23.33	0.89
						NJ	15.24	10.00	0.66
						TJ	17.07	33.33	1.95
						TP	7.32	6.67	0.91
						FP	42.68	36.67	0.86
						FJ	32.93	23.33	0.71
						IN	8.54	6.67	0.78
						EN	32.93	26.67	0.81
						IS	18.90	16.67	0.88
						ES	39.63	50.00	1.26
						ET	17.07	26.67	1.56
						EF	55.49	50.00	0.90
						IF	20.12	10.00	0.50
						IT	7.32	13.33	1.82

[a] Base Population: All Nursing undergraduates
[b] Sample Population: Nursing school dropouts

TABLE 12

Dropout Ratios of Business School Students

Type	Base Population[a] N	%	Sample Population[b] N	%	Ratio	Type Group	Base %	Sample %	Ratio
ISTJ	35	9.46	9	11.84	1.25	E	60.81	57.89	0.95
ISFJ	28	7.57	3	3.95	0.52	I	39.19	42.11	1.07
INFJ	9	2.43	2	2.63	1.08				
INTJ	6	1.62	1	1.32	0.81	S	57.84	55.26	0.96
						N	42.16	44.74	1.06
ISTP	19	5.14	4	5.26	1.02				
ISFP	19	5.14	7	9.21	1.79	T	43.24	40.79	0.94
INFP	23	6.22	5	6.58	1.06	F	56.76	59.21	1.04
INTP	6	1.62	1	1.32	0.81				
						J	47.84	46.05	0.96
ESTP	17	4.59	2	2.63	0.57	P	52.84	53.95	1.03
ESFP	25	6.76	4	5.26	0.78				
ENFP	55	14.86	13	17.11	1.15	IJ	21.08	19.74	0.94
ENTP	29	7.84	5	6.58	0.84	IP	18.11	22.37	1.24
						EP	34.05	31.58	0.93
ESTJ	36	9.73	5	7.89	0.81	EJ	26.76	26.32	0.98
ESFJ	35	9.46	7	9.21	0.97				
ENFJ	16	4.32	4	5.26	1.22	ST	28.92	27.63	0.96
ENTJ	12	3.24	3	3.95	1.22	SF	28.92	27.63	0.96
						NF	27.84	31.58	1.13
Sum	370		76			NT	14.32	13.16	0.92
						SJ	36.22	32.89	0.91
						SP	21.62	22.37	1.03
						NP	30.54	31.58	1.03
						NJ	11.62	13.16	1.13
						TJ	24.05	25.00	1.04
						TP	19.19	15.79	0.82
						FP	32.97	38.16	1.16
						FJ	23.78	21.05	0.89
						IN	11.89	11.84	1.00
						EN	30.27	32.89	1.09
						IS	27.30	30.26	1.11
						ES	30.54	25.00	0.82
						ET	25.41	21.05	0.83
						EF	35.41	36.84	1.04
						IF	21.35	22.37	1.05
						IT	17.84	19.74	1.11

[a] Base Population: All Business undergraduates
[b] Sample Population: Business School dropouts

TABLE 13

Dropout Ratios of Arts and Sciences Students

Type	Base Population[a] N	%	Sample Population[b] N	%	Ratio	Type Group	Base %	Sample %	Ratio
ISTJ	85	8.07	21	9.33	1.16	E	58.02	52.00	0.90
ISFJ	63	5.98	8	3.56	0.59	I	41.98	48.00	1.14
INFJ	28	2.66	13	5.78	2.17				
INTJ	44	4.18	8	3.56	0.85	S	48.81	43.11	0.88
						N	51.19	56.89	1.11
ISTP	40	3.80	6	2.67	0.70				
ISFP	37	3.51	9	4.00	1.14	T	43.11	40.89	0.95
INFP	95	9.02	27	12.00	1.33	F	56.89	59.11	1.04
INTP	50	4.75	16	7.11	1.50				
						J	48.91	48.00	0.98
ESTP	46	4.37	6	2.67	0.61	P	51.09	52.00	1.02
ESFP	67	6.36	14	6.22	0.98				
ENFP	144	13.68	26	11.56	0.85	IJ	20.89	22.22	1.06
ENTP	59	5.60	13	5.78	1.03	IP	21.08	25.78	1.22
						EP	30.01	26.22	0.87
ESTJ	76	7.22	12	5.33	0.74	EJ	28.02	25.78	0.92
ESFJ	100	9.50	21	9.33	0.98				
ENFJ	65	6.17	15	6.67	1.08	ST	23.46	20.00	0.85
ENTJ	54	5.13	10	4.44	0.87	SF	25.36	23.11	0.91
						NF	31.53	36.00	1.14
Sum	1053		225			NT	19.66	20.89	1.06
						SJ	30.77	27.56	0.90
						SP	18.04	15.56	0.86
						NP	33.05	36.44	1.10
						NJ	18.14	20.44	1.13
						TJ	24.60	22.67	0.92
						TP	18.52	18.22	0.98
						FP	32.57	33.78	1.04
						FJ	24.31	25.33	1.04
						IN	20.61	28.44	1.38
						EN	30.58	28.44	.93
						IS	21.37	19.56	0.92
						ES	27.45	23.56	0.86
						ET	22.32	18.22	0.82
						EF	35.71	33.78	0.95
						IF	21.18	25.33	1.20
						IT	20.80	22.67	1.09

[a]Base Population: All Arts and Sciences undergraduates
[b]Sample Population: Arts and Sciences dropouts

Of course, not all attrition is problematic or symptomatic of institutional problems. For example, there are multiple explanations for why Thinking types may leave a Nursing program at a higher rate than Feeling types. An argument could be made that students with strong preferences for thinking may not find adequate rewards or support in a nursing career and that it is in their best interest to consider other professional pursuits. In that case, their attrition may be educationally appropriate, and working to reduce that attrition may be inappropriate. Type data can offer an effective mechanism for understanding general trends in attrition and for working with students in making appropriate choices about their educational commitments.

Another example may illustrate the usefulness of such retention data. Recent analysis of the TRAILS data suggest IF types are at risk in the Business program (Kalsbeek & DeFiore, 1986). On the one hand, it may be that their pursuit of other options is an appropriate response to their awareness of the kinds of rewards and challenges of, for example, an Accounting major and/or career. On the other hand, perhaps their attrition is a reflection of the type of social climate characteristic of the Business school at a predominantly commuter campus, where there are few opportunities for personal interaction or affiliation with either faculty or other students. Either way, there are a host of interventions to consider in responding to the students' needs. Relating type data to attrition allows educators to begin to consider the dynamic interactions of types of students with types of academic and social environments, and thereby begin to respond appropriately to enrollment management tasks.

Retention Action Strategies

The Tinto model implies that improving retention is not a goal in itself but rather the outcome of an institution's efforts to increase students' academic and social integration. Any action plan that results from an institution's retention research should attempt to maximize the quality of the student's experience at every point of contact between the student and the institution. This is, of course, easier said than done. Difficult choices must be made about how to make good use of limited resources in such efforts.

Information is the fundamental ingredient in mobilizing any successful enrollment management strategy. In retention programs information without action is empty and action without information is blind. Information management becomes the necessary prelude to any retention program, as well as a necessary ingredient for appropriate assessment and evaluation of enrollment management strategies. This is the value of the TRAILS project, which illustrates one process for building that information infrastructure.

Describing actual retention action strategies using the MBTI, however, is not an objective of this chapter. Using the MBTI to improve an institution's responsiveness to students and its sensitivity to the individual characteristics of students is certainly one means of improving students' academic and social integration within the various environments they encounter at the college or university. A wide variety of avenues exists for using the MBTI for such ends: academic advising and educational planning, career development, environmental management in residence halls, faculty and staff development, and student involvement opportunities. The use of the MBTI in these areas is addressed in other chapters. This chapter has proposed that:

1. investing resources in information systems such as that illustrated by the TRAILS project is necessary for effective broad-based campus change using the MBTI;

2. an information system with the MBTI as the hub facilitates more effective use of the MBTI in the various ways discussed in the other chapters;

3. the MBTI can be one important component in a campus retention strategy, and fits well with the premises of the Tinto model; and

4. to begin to make effective use of the MBTI in campus retention efforts, ongoing research should be conducted to continuously monitor the academic and social integration students may experience in certain environments.

A final and important issue to address in any discussion of attrition research and the TRAILS project is the manner in which the student development staff get the attention and interest of their academic colleagues (advisors, faculty, deans, etc.) in order to introduce the TRAILS data and the value of the MBTI in general. There are certainly no pat answers on the most effective means of building these bridges. The underlying assumptions of the Student Life Studies department at Saint Louis University is that *information* is the key to spanning the traditional boundaries of student affairs in higher education. Information facilitates a synergistic collaboration between student affairs and academic personnel in improving the quality of the experience for all who work, study, and teach at the university (Kalsbeek, 1984; Kalsbeek, MacLean, &

Wallace, 1986). As enrollment issues become increasingly critical for institutions and as pressure mounts for institutions to ensure quality educational outcomes, relevant information becomes an extremely valuable resource. In this sense, information becomes an institution's best investment. The MBTI may be one particularly useful information tool for achieving this dynamic synergism.

Footnote: Operational Details of the TRAILS Project

A frequently asked question is, "How is the TRAILS project actually managed and how are results disseminated in the university community?" Though the purpose of this chapter is to illustrate a *process* for retention-related inquiry with the MBTI as the conceptual focus, some readers may be interested in the pragmatics of the project administration.

The MBTI data are gathered through numerous avenues at Saint Louis University. The Housing office used the instrument in the application process, various academic departments and student service units use it in advising students, and recently the English department began using type concepts in providing writing instruction to undergraduates. The Office of Student Life Studies (the research, evaluation, and information management component of the Division of Student Development) began the TRAILS project in 1981 as an attempt to manage effectively this great volume of MBTI data. A microcomputer-based database of student MBTI data was created initially to compile existing type data and avoid the financial and personal costs (to both students and staff) of redundancy. The database allows the university to avoid having students complete the MBTI numerous times in different contexts.

All student MBTI data are included in the TRAILS database. However, the only records used in the institutional studies illustrated in this chapter are those of the students who chose to sign a statement consenting to having their MBTI profiles included in institutional research projects. Students not consenting are excluded from these studies. In addition, student MBTI profiles are provided to other university offices or services only upon verification of student consent.

Once the MBTI data are compiled in the database, additional institutional data for these students are merged with the MBTI datafile. Aptitude scores (ACT/SAT), demographic data such as gender and ethnicity, and high school grades are obtained from institutional datafiles. Each subsequent semester the student is enrolled at the university, academic information on his/her school of enrollment, major, semester, and cumulative GPA is compiled and merged with the basic MBTI file. This cumulative record for each student completing the MBTI forms the backbone of the TRAILS database.

The system is designed to generate several types of output for use in meeting the project's goals. First, type tables are routinely generated for any subgroup of the student database; type tables for Nursing students, sophomores, students on academic probation, black students, dropouts from Business, and so on, can be requested and generated quite easily. Population comparisons are also generated routinely, allowing investigators to conduct statistical analyses of type distributions between, for example, Nursing students and undergraduates at large. Programs similar to the standard SRTT software provided by CAPT were developed using spreadsheet software.

Secondly, simple listings can be generated for various offices. For example, when the office for Student Volunteer Programs decided to use the MBTI in a leadership workshop, the TRAILS database generated a listing of students in that organization who had already completed the MBTI so that the advisors could plan appropriately, and students were not required to complete the MBTI again. The Counseling Center periodically receives an up-to-date list of all students having completed the MBTI, so that counselors have the information at hand if deemed appropriate in serving students coming to the center for assistance.

Thirdly, the TRAILS database serves as the source of data for the complex statistical analyses briefly introduced in this chapter. Specific datafiles can be generated from the basic TRAILS system and can either be electronically transferred to the university mainframe computer for analysis or used with statistical analysis software on the microcomputer. Any combination of variables can be compiled, or merged for research purposes ranging from simple comparisons of average grades by type to more complex multivariate analyses. Also, as illustrated in the discussion of the relationships of the MBTI to the CIRP data, diverse datafiles can be merged for a wide variety of MBTI-related studies.

Data are prepared for presentation to the university in several ways. Type tables generally serve as the basic resource for TRAILS presentations. Computer-generated color graphics are more effective means of presenting patterns in type distributions and results of the analyses of relationships between preference scores and other variables. A wide variety of graphics software available on the commercial market is used with a color plotter to create striking color transparencies for use with overhead projectors. All TRAILS presentations to the campus community rely almost exclusively on overhead transparencies using either sharp computer-enhanced text graphics or computer-generated bar graphs or pie charts.

Few major written reports are prepared since the data change so frequently; all type tables change twice a year as new data on type and academic performance are obtained. Because of the frequency with which these data change, the preparation of elaborate written reports is not cost-effective. Instead, the only written texts prepared are a series of abstracts, one-page summaries of significant findings, patterns, or implications of the TRAILS study. Abstracts are prepared for very focused audiences, such as Business faculty, student service administrative staff, pre-med advisers, the Faculty Senate, Residence Life staff, or student leaders. These TRAILS abstracts are printed in an easily recognized format on colored paper, and are identical in appearance to the abstracts used by the office of Student Life Studies for reporting findings and conclusions from a wide variety of institutional studies.

Readers interested in more details regarding the structure, process, and findings of the TRAILS project at Saint Louis University and the software used to manage the project should contact the author.

References

Anchors, S., Gershman, E., & Robbins, M. (1986). *Developmental and personality type differences among undecided students.* Unpublished research, University of Maine, Orono. (in press)

Bean, J. P. (1982). Conceptual models of student attrition: How theory can help the institutional researcher. In E. Pascarella (Ed.), *New directions for institutional research:* Vol. IX, No. 4, *Studying student attrition* (pp. 17–33). San Francisco: Jossey-Bass.

Davis, M., & Schroeder, C. (1983). "New students" in liberal arts colleges: Threat or challenge? In J. Watson and R. Stevens (Eds.), *Pioneers and pallbearers: Perspectives on liberal education.* (pp. 71–80). Macon, GA: Mercer University Press.

DeFiore, R. M., & Kalsbeek, D. H. (1985). *TRAILS analyses by school of enrollment,* St. Louis, MO: Studies research report. Saint Louis University, Student Life.

Kalsbeek, D. H. (1986). *Linking learning style theory with retention research: The TRAILS project.* Paper presented at the Association for Institutional Research forum, Orlando, FL.

Kalsbeek, D. H. (1985). *Information utilization and organization development: A review of related literature,* unpublished manuscript.

Kalsbeek, D. H. (1984). *Student development through information management: Spanning boundaries in the information age.* Paper presented at the St. Louis Regional Conference on *Student affairs in the decade ahead,* St. Louis, MO.

Kalsbeek, D. H., & DeFiore, R. M. (1986). *The effect of personality type on student responses in the 1983 cooperative institutional research program survey at Saint Louis University.* Student Life Studies research report.

Kalsbeek, D. H., MacLean, S., & Wallace, D. (1986). *Management information systems versus information management strategies: Two approaches to information utilization in student affairs.* Paper presented at the American College Personnel Association Conference, New Orleans, LA.

McCaulley, M. H. (1978). *Application of the MBTI to medicine and other health professions.* Gainesville, FL: Center for Applications of Psychological Type.

McCaulley, M., & Natter, F. (1980). *Psychological (Myers-Briggs) type differences in education.* Gainesville, FL: Center for Applications of Psychological Type.

Myers, I. B. (1980). *Gifts differing.* Palo Alto, CA: Consulting Psychologists Press.

Myers, I. B., & McCaulley, M. H. (1985). *Manual: A guide to the development and use of the Myers-Briggs Type Indicator.* Palo Alto, CA: Consulting Psychologists Press.

National Governors' Association (1986). *Time for results: The governor's 1991 report on education.* Washington, D.C.: Author.

National Governors' Association (1985). (Hearing of the task force on college quality). *Quality assessment and accountability in undergraduate education.* St. Louis, MO: Author.

Pascarella, E. (1982). (Introduction). In E. Pascarella (Ed.), *New directions for institutional research:* Vol. XXXVI, No. 4, *Studying student attrition* (pp. 1–2). San Francisco: Jossey-Bass.

Terenzini, P. T. (1982). Designing attrition studies. In E. Pascarella (Ed.), *New directions for institutional research:* Vol. XXXVI, No. 4, *Studying student attrition* (pp. 55–71). San Francisco: Jossey-Bass.

Tinto, V. (1975). Dropout from higher education: A theoretical synthesis of recent research. *Review of Educational Research, 43* (1), 89–125.

Walsh, W. B. (1973). *Theories of person-environment interaction: implications for the college student.* Iowa City, IA: The American College Testing Program.

CHARLES SCHROEDER is Vice President for Student Development at Saint Louis University. After earning an Ed.D. in Student Personnel from Oregon State University at Corvallis, he went on to serve as director of a counseling Center, Director of Men's Housing, and Dean of Students. He is currently president of the American College Personnel Association. He has published numerous articles in various student personnel journals as well as contributed chapters to several books in higher education. His type is ESTJ.

SMITH JACKSON is currently Director of Housing at Saint Louis University, where he uses type in matching roommates and promoting individual development. He was first introduced to type at Auburn University where he completed his Ed.D. His dissertation topic was "The impact of roommates on development—a causal analysis of the effects of roommate personality congruence, satisfaction and initial developmental status on end-of-quarter developmental status and grade point average." Smith is an INTP.

CHAPTER 4

Designing Residential Environments

CHARLES C. SCHROEDER and SMITH JACKSON

Overview

As NOTED IN previous chapters, the *Myers-Briggs Type Indicator* is an extremely powerful tool for understanding and facilitating student development. This chapter describes a number of practical and proven strategies for using the MBTI in college and university residence halls. For readers not familiar with some of the inherent challenges in residential living, a brief review is provided. A conceptual framework is then presented as the primary model for utilizing the Indicator to enhance the "fit" between students and their living environments at three different institutions. By following two students, Willard Wilson and Sam Hudson, the reader is subsequently introduced to the role that individual differences play with regard to understanding and resolving roommate conflicts. A variety of practical intervention strategies, along with research findings, are shared which illustrate the efficacy of using the MBTI in pairing roommates for satisfaction and personality development. The chapter concludes with sections on practical administrative considerations and implications.

Inherent Challenges in Residential Living

Colleges and universities have undergone considerable changes in recent years. As the baby boom generation reached college age, enrollments expanded at staggering rates. To cope with the sudden demand for student housing, many institutions launched extensive building programs. Since cost and ease of maintenance were primary design considerations, modern complexes and highrise buildings were constructed with corridor upon corridor of small, cell-like rooms, complete with built-in furniture and institutional decor. A building's long and narrow hallways often house 50 to 60 students and it is quite common for as many as 500 students to occupy one building.

Since many residence halls were constructed without adequate attention to individual needs and interaction patterns, it is certainly not difficult to understand why many students find residence halls a bit overwhelming and, at times, downright aversive. Can you imagine, for example, the predicament of a freshman assigned to a 12' by 14' room with a stranger who is totally different in basic needs and interpersonal style? Or consider the difficulty students experience when they are assigned to live on a hall of 50 students with whom they have very little in common and yet must share a communal bath? Or, what about some of the frustrations students experience because of built-in furniture and institutional policies that prohibit decorating?

Undoubtedly, architecturally hard and interpersonally dense and diverse residential environments present numerous challenges to students and staff alike. In an attempt to meet these challenges, college and university housing programs have changed their goals and priorities. Dormitories are now called residence halls. House mothers have been replaced by highly trained and skilled residence educators. A multitude of organizations and programs proliferate. Developmental programs are offered on assertiveness training, human sexuality, time management, etc.; discipline has become an intervention point to identify and resolve developmental problems through counseling with students; and community development is fostered through students' participation on programming councils, student governance committees, and judicial boards. These efforts have significantly contributed to improving the quality of residential life for many students.

Nonetheless, there is considerable evidence that students continue to become disenchanted with residence hall living within a relatively short period of time. Major reasons for student dissatisfaction include inability to control personal space, lack of privacy, roommate conflicts, forced sociability, and few opportunities to personalize the institutional environment (Heilweil, 1973). Many of these concerns are related to a basic *mismatch* between students and the social and physical environments of their living units. Even though it may not be feasible to tear down buildings and construct new ones or to reduce the interpersonal density in the residence halls by reducing occupancy, it is possible to implement strategies that will help overcome or at least reduce the negative impact of these factors (Kalsbeek, 1982).

The *Myers-Briggs Type Indicator* has proven to be an extremely useful tool for structuring conditions that enhance the "fit" between students and their resident hall environments. The Indicator has been successfully utilized in matching roommates, suitemates, and floormates. These interventions have been beneficial because they have been applied within a conceptual framework which can be adapted and operationalized for particular residential populations. This overarching framework is Sanford's (1966) notion of the relationship between challenge/support and development.

Balancing Challenge and Support: A Conceptual Framework

According to Sanford, the personality does not just unfold according to a plan of nature. Instead, students must be confronted with challenges sufficiently strong to trigger new ways of thinking and behaving. Once motivated, however, students must feel significant support so they may proceed to experiment with new ways of behaving or new ways of thinking. Sanford emphasized that a delicate balance of challenge and support must be achieved before development can occur. If an environment is overly supportive, students may be satisfied but not adequately challenged to grow. On the other hand, if an environment is overly challenging, students may be so overwhelmed and overstimulated that they will not be satisfied and development will not occur. It is particularly important to note that the amount of challenge one can tolerate is a function of the support available. Challenges which might otherwise be maladaptive may become growth inducing when moderated by support.

In order to design residential environments that will allow for student satisfaction and development, the relative degrees of challenge and support that are characteristic of a specific setting in a specific student population must first be assessed (Rodgers, 1980). Since students are most affected by their immediate surroundings, it is best to analyze the smallest social unit possible. If the setting is highly supportive, then more challenge, less support, or both would need to be introduced to achieve a developmental balance. If, on the other hand, the setting is found to be overly challenging, then more support, less challenge, or both would be needed (Kalsbeek, Rodgers, Marshall, Denny, &

Nicholls, 1982). The following section describes how the MBTI has been effectively used to balance the ratio of challenge and support in various residential environments.

Using the MBTI to Balance Challenge and Support in Residence Halls

Humanizing the Environment in a Highrise Complex

At Ohio State University the MBTI was used to balance the challenge/ support characteristics of a highrise residence complex. The complex was assessed as an overly challenging environment as evidenced by exceedingly high damage rates, numerous mental health referrals, and very low retention rates (historically 1 to 4 percent). The complex consists of two 24-story towers with six suites per floor. A suite typically houses 16 students in a cluster of four rooms, resulting in 96 students living on each floor. Beyond the density of students assigned to suites and floors, other challenging factors that were identified included: the developmental levels of the residents; the significant heterogeneity of the students' cultural backgrounds; built-in furniture; and the overwhelming size and complexity of the multiversity itself. Few elements of support were present for mediating the excessive amount of challenge. For example, the student staff to resident ratio per floor was 1 to 96, the professional staff to student ratio was 1 to 900, and there were very few upperclass role models. This particular situation called for an intensification of the degree of support.

Kalsbeek et al. (1982) assigned suitemates according to their degree of similarity on the MBTI. Prior to their arrival in the fall, first-year students desiring to participate in this project were mailed the Indicator. Students were then assigned to suites in the following fashion: (a) they were identical on all processes (Pure Strategy suites); (b) they had their most-preferred process in common (Dominant Strategy suites); (c) they had in common their second most preferred process (Auxiliary Strategy suites); or (d) they had in common the same process they preferred for dealing with the external world (External Strategy suites). In principle, these suites represented different points on a continuum of support, with "degrees of support" being defined by different degrees of commonality on the MBTI. This relationship is depicted in Figure 1 and Table 1. As expected, it was found that the more similar suitemates were in their mental functioning, the more support they perceived in their environment.

The Ohio State intervention suggests that the living group can serve as a source of support and mediate between students and environmental factors. The MBTI was used to foster mutually supportive suitemates, thereby humanizing a complex, impersonal, and challenging setting. Assigning students to floor units according to MBTI functions has produced similar results.

Transforming an Aging Complex into an Exciting Community

At Auburn University, the MBTI was used to pair hallmates and room-mates in the Magnolia Dormitories residential community. In the early 1970s, this complex was operating at an occupancy rate of approximately 80 percent and retention, from spring to fall quarters, was less than 30 percent. Resident behavior was characterized by overt hostility toward the environment as evidenced by considerable damages, numerous roommate conflicts, and a full docket of discipline cases.

Two change strategies were implemented which served to reverse the downward spiral in both the physical and interpersonal environments of the complex. First, residents were encouraged to paint, decorate, and otherwise personalize their rooms and hallways to suit their tastes and needs. Second, roommates were matched on the basis of common personality dimensions using MBTI scores obtained during summer orientation sessions. On some floors students were assigned to the units based upon commonality in dominant MBTI personality functions. One floor unit, for example, was composed of dominant Sensing types, another dominant Intuitive types, and so forth. Housing students

FIGURE 1

Relationship Between MBTI Similarity and
Perceived Support in Suite Housing

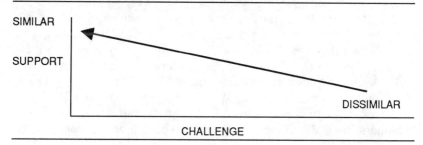

TABLE 1

Degrees of Challenge-Support for MBTI Suitemate Groupings

MBTI Grouping Strategy	Description	Highest Degree of Support/ Lowest Challenge
Pure	All four preferences are identical	
Dominant	Identical dominant personality functions	
Auxiliary	Identical auxiliary personality functions	
External	Identical functions with which one deals with the external world	
Random	Maximum heterogeneity of personality types by random assignment	
		Highest Degree of Challenge/ Lowest Support

together with the same personality function resulted in predictable and stable social environments which could often, but not always, be forecast from type theory.

Not surprisingly, a floor unit composed of dominant Intuitives was found to tolerate a great amount of diversity in behavior without social sanction, to prefer less formal structure and organization in the residence halls, and to be quick to get involved in a multitude of activities. At first glance, however, it might seem curious that the Intuitives, more than any other dominant type grouping, emphasized a traditional social orientation as measured by the *University Residence Environment Scale* (Moos & Gerst, 1974). And yet, the Intuitives initially expected this emphasis, eventually found it in their living unit, and ideally preferred it. It appears that the Intuitives created a social climate emphasizing dating and heterosexual activities. Formal social situations became creative outlets for the collective imagination of the residents. A costume party for Halloween was a sure bet for the Intuitives!

A major advantage associated with grouping floor units by dominant types is that not only does this strategy permit insights into type behaviors, but it also allows developmental programs to be more easily fitted to the living units. For example, many Intuitives tend to be energetic and ambitious and because some of them (particularly NPs) exhibit poor time management, they often feel they have far too much to do. Thus, staff can focus on time management programming to address this particular need of some of the Intuitives.

The overall results of utilizing this strategy in the Magnolia Dormitories were quite dramatic. Within a period of three years, retention from spring to fall quarters increased by 30 percent and damages decreased by 360 percent. Further, occupancy during the same time period exceeded 100 percent each year with many prospective residents being turned away as waiting lists became excessive. Of special interest in this regard were the observed friendship patterns which emerged. When asked to indicate where their friends lived, students living on the MBTI-matched floors had a much higher percentage of their friends living on their same floor than did those students randomly assigned to floors. Thus, grouping students on floors according to the MBTI was an effective strategy for facilitating supportive interactions, friendship patterns, and group cohesiveness (Schroeder, Warner, & Malone, 1980). The same results may also be achieved by encouraging students to self-select into living units. When given the opportunity, students migrate toward residential groups with whom they share personality styles and create interpersonal environments with unique characteristics.

Creating Floors with Unique Characteristics

During the spring semester of each academic year, residents in Saint Louis University residence halls describe the social climates of their floors. These descriptions are compiled into a publication, *Choices*, which is distributed to prospective residents. Residents are also given the opportunity to assign new residents to their floor for the following fall term as a first priority in the assignment process. The description which the residents of "13G" composed was as follows:

> The word that best describes our floor is FUN! Sometimes we may seem pretty disorganized, but when we all want to do something, somehow we all pitch in and it gets done. There are lots of different types of girls on the floor—with different interests and activities, music and friends which make us really interesting! Most of us study and work in the early evenings and do a lot of our considerable socializing in the later evening hours, when doors are often open and popcorn popping. We enjoy playing intramural sports and recently got red sweatpants with "13G"

appliqued on the bottom—which we all wore together to the cafeteria for dinner on the day we got them.

The women assigned to this floor were dominant Intuitives (N). The following year the demand for this floor by Intuitives exceeded many times over the number of spaces available. The current composition of the floor is illustrated in Table 2.

The description the women gave of their floor's personality was predictable from knowledge of the MBTI composition. Since retention in this living unit is so high, the few new residents attracted to and assigned to this floor are paired with roommates with whom they have complementary MBTI types, a roommate matching strategy to be discussed later.

The social climate of another floor in the same building has several parallels yet is distinctively different from that of the women of 13G. The women of 9G described their floor in the following fashion:

Most of us returned to the floor this year and the new girls fit in perfectly. We all contributed to painting our floor in a twilight design with a silhouette and setting sun design (which placed second in the Room Personalization contest). We are mostly Physical Therapy majors and put a big emphasis on our classwork. We often study together as our schedules are similar. We are also athletic as a group, and many of us work out together and several girls work at the Rec Center. We are well on our way to winning the overall women's Dorm League Championship—a hot contest between us and 4 Walsh. We do a lot together and really pride ourselves on our involvement and support.

TABLE 2

MBTI Composition of 13G

Preferences	Percentage	Preferences	Percentage
Extraversion	82	Introversion	18
Intuition	88	Sensing	12
Feeling	83	Thinking	17
Perception	73	Judgment	27

Whereas the women of 13G had a wide range of academic majors, 67 percent of the women living in 9G majored in Physical Therapy and Nursing one year, and 84 percent majored in the same fields the following year. Even though it was primarily the grouping variable of majoring in Physical Therapy which retained and attracted residents to 9G, an after-the-fact view of the current women's MBTI profiles, as displayed in Table 3, is enlightening.

As revealed in Chapter 3, academic majors and academic schools are predominated by students of certain psychological types and thus these settings often create an environmental "press" on an individual's behaviors. It is not surprising then to find that a living unit predominated by students majoring in Physical Therapy would also have a high percentage of Extraverted Sensing Feelers; hence, one would expect that certain behaviors would be valued and perpetuated from year to year. The women of 9G have won the All Sports Dorm League Championship for the past two years and are on their way to a third championship; they have won at least one blood drive competition in each of the last three years of the drive's existence; and they have repainted their hallway each year. Contrasted with the spontaneous, fun-loving atmosphere described by the Intuitives of 13G, the description of 9G portrays a more serious, structured, and achievement-oriented atmosphere. Even though Physical Therapy is a highly competitive curriculum, the interactions and activities described by 9G suggest a supportive living environment. New students to this floor were assigned to roommates as similar as possible in MBTI types in order to further enhance the degree of support exhibited by returning residents.

TABLE 3

MBTI Composition of 9G

Preferences	Percentage	Preferences	Percentage
Extraversion	80	Introversion	20
Intuition	20	Sensing	80
Feeling	90	Thinking	10
Perception	50	Judgment	50

All of the preceding strategies demonstrate that grouping students in floor units or suites according to similar personality styles increases the probability that friendships and a sense of community will emerge in a natural fashion. Since students with similar personality characteristics view a situation (perception) and respond or draw conclusions about it (judgment) in the same manner, they find more support in living groups with whom they share the dominant group interests or personality. The same reasoning also applies to the roommate situation. The behaviors and attitudes of a roommate with a similar personality style can provide the student with evidence that he or she is functioning in a consistent and meaningful manner; the interpersonal environment is perceived as predictable and understandable. If, however, roommates differ radically in their perceptual and response patterns, they may threaten each other, clash frequently, and in general, utilize energy that could be better spent on things they value.

Using the MBTI to Understand and Resolve Roommate Conflicts

The Case Study of Willard and Sam

The role that individual differences play with regard to the quality of student/environment interactions can be further understood by viewing this issue from the perspective of two typical students.

> Two 18-year-old freshmen, Willard Wilson and Sam Hudson, arrive at Any University, USA. Everything has been done for them—they have been assigned to a nice, clean room on the 14th floor of "The Towers," their resident assistant has informed them about various policies and procedures, and they are now ready to embark on their college careers.

> Willard, raised in a rural community 70 miles from the nearest city, is basically an aggressive, practical, analytical type who possesses a great knack for managing facts and details. Willard has already taken great pains to systematically organize his personal belongings—books are neatly arranged on the shelf, clothes are smartly hung in the closet, and his bed is routinely made each morning before he departs for class. To be sure, Willard likes to live his life according to a plan! He manages his time wisely and completes his studying promptly at 10:00 PM each

night, and then retires for a minimum of eight hours sleep. Willard reasons that since he is paying $300 per quarter in room rent, he should be able to sleep and study in a distraction-free environment. For Willard, his room is primarily a work environment—he does his socializing with one or two close friends from a neighboring residence hall.

Sam Hudson grew up in a large city of over three million. He is sociable, outgoing, warmly enthusiastic, and highly creative. Because he prefers to think about imaginative possibilities, he has real difficulty with details and always appears to be disorganized. His bed and study area are cluttered with notebooks, dirty clothes, athletic equipment, half-eaten sandwiches, and candy wrappers—in short, it appears to be pure chaos. Because of his natural tendency to work in bursts of energy, Sam's study habits are erratic. It is not unusual for him to postpone unpleasant tasks, and he may wait until the last minute to complete an assignment. Hence, he frequently pulls "all-nighters." Sam has no trouble with distractions, actually preferring to study with his favorite rock music emanating from a 100-watt stereo. For Sam, his room is primarily a play environment—he enjoys socializing with a wide variety of friends at all hours of the day and night.

Willard's and Sam's relationship begins to deteriorate rapidly. Sam is really beginning to get on Willard's nerves. Willard seems to be constantly studying, but not making the grades he would like—and Sam, who hardly ever puts in any time, is making all "A's." Sam is inviting his friends into the room late at night for parties and other social events.

Willard hopes things will get better but he is pretty convinced they won't. It seems to Willard that he can't even move around his room without bumping into Sam. The built-in furniture and inflexible arrangements seem to force confrontation. Anytime he and Sam write a paper, they have to sit right next to each other at the built-in desks along one wall of their room. When Willard tries to sleep at night, Sam almost invariably has the lights on. Everything is so crowded, so complex, so unpredictable that Willard is really beginning to feel the *stress* of being confined to a tight space with someone much different than himself. He is becoming increasingly nervous, tense, and overtly hostile in his interactions with others.

It doesn't take much imagination to visualize the potential conflicts inherent in Willard and Sam's relationship. From the description of Willard's personal characteristics, one can assume that he has a basic need for *structure*. He prefers to structure his room in ways that demonstrate order, clarity, organization, and predictability. Willard finds freedom in structure; planned, systematic ways of doing things help him feel in control, influential, unrestricted, and important. Because Willard is *naturally* skilled at planning and organizing things, he just can't understand why Sam is so disorganized. Why doesn't Sam clean up his side of the room? Why can't Sam meet deadlines? Why doesn't Sam develop a study schedule? How can Sam study with the stereo on? Why does Sam spend so much time socializing? Maybe Sam is just basically aimless and irresponsible!

From the description of Sam, it appears that his basic needs are opposite and antagonistic to Willard's. Sam has a basic need for *freedom*. He enjoys living life in an independent, spontaneous fashion and flexibly adapts to unexpected changes in his environment. Whereas Willard seeks to structure and control almost every aspect of his environment, Sam would much rather understand than control things. In an attempt to satisfy his need for freedom, Sam avoids uninspired routines and established ways of doing things. He feels a sense of influence and control by living in accord with his spontaneous, imaginative inspirations and prefers to keep his options open by avoiding closure. Because Sam's basic needs are in opposition to those of Willard, Sam cannot understand why Willard has to organize everything or why Willard spends so much time studying. Why doesn't Willard loosen up? He always seems to have his nose to the grindstone, all work and no play! Sam reasons that maybe Willard's basic problem is that he is too rigid, inflexible, and task oriented.

Obviously, Willard and Sam are opposite types—Willard is an ISTJ and Sam an ENFP. According to type theory, they have no mental process in common. They perceive things differently, formulate decisions from different perspectives, and tend to prefer to live their lives in opposite ways. Although Willard and Sam are expressing their *natural differences* in trying to meet their conflicting needs, they probably view each other as purposefully irritating. If, however, someone could help Willard and Sam understand their natural differences, they might not only allow for each other's preferences but perhaps appreciate and benefit from them. The MBTI can be very useful in this regard as it can help us understand in advance many of the basic living style preferences which can limit satisfaction between roommates.

Understanding Basic Living Style Differences
Between Roommates

Some very basic differences in living styles must be overcome before roommates will be satisfied. Three of the most potent dimensions on which roommates must be compatible are study habits, sleeping conditions, and bedtimes. Differences on these dimensions are repeatedly the source of annoyance for roommates, yet are predictable from knowledge of MBTI profiles.

Differences in preferences for sleeping conditions and study habits can readily be explained when roommates' abilities to concentrate or relax with different amounts of background noise—music, talking, TV, etc., are understood. Some students (screeners) are able to "tune out" distractions even in a highly loaded setting such as a residence hall. These are the students who can literally sleep or study in a crowded and noisy bus depot. Other students (nonscreeners) are not able to be selective in what they focus their attention on and are attuned to minor, subtle changes in the environment (Mehrabian, 1976). These students have difficulty in achieving and maintaining necessary levels of privacy in a residence hall. In their attempts to establish desired privacy levels, students like Willard may sometimes appear overly controlling and unfriendly. These students often pay a very high cost for achieving privacy.

The screener–nonscreener dimension is highly related to the MBTI preference for dealing with the outer world in a perceptive or judging way; Perceiving types tend to be screeners and Judging types, nonscreeners. The time that students go to bed is also related to the judgment-perception preference. Perceiving types, particularly NPs like Sam, tend to go to bed later than Judging types both during the week and on the weekends. Since Perceiving types often become consumed in an activity or thought that interests them, it is no wonder they stay up later and, because they are often oblivious to time, may not go to bed according to a schedule. There is even some observational information to suggest that Perceiving types tend to be "late night" people and the Judging types are often "morning" people. It is apparent that differences on the judgment-perception preference could generate difficulties between roommates like Willard and Sam, particularly when they must function in such a tight space as a 10′ x 12′ room.

Another basic living style issue which roommates must resolve is their preferences for neatness. Neat students like Willard prefer neat roommates while clutterers prefer clutterers. This dimension is related to the MBTI preference for extraversion or introversion; Extraverts tend to see their roommates as neat while Introverts often view their roommates as messy (Jackson, 1984). The Extravert, by definition, simply needs a greater amount of external stimulation than the Introvert. Certainly a messy room is more stimulating than a neat one! The Extravert's craving for stimulation has also been denoted in residence halls; Extraverts tend to paint their rooms in highly exciting colors such as Pixie Green and Dark Regal Purple while Introverts often paint their rooms in colors such as Blue Cloud or Lemon Meringue (Jackson, 1983). The way students personalize and keep their living space often reflects whether they prefer to orient themselves to the outer world (extraversion) or toward the inner world (introversion). As with the judgment-perception dimension, roommates who vary greatly in their preferences for extraersion and introversion may find it difficult to feel at home and simply be themselves with one another.

The mental processes, sensing-intuition and thinking-feeling, are also predictive of some disparities for which roommates must accommodate. For example, Feelers tend to be less concerned with boundaries and have a broader range of acquaintances. In contrast, Thinkers tend to be more territorial and have a tighter circle of a few, close friends. While these and the other type-related behaviors associated with roommate conflicts have been verified empirically (Schroeder et al., 1980), residence educators knowledgeable of the MBTI can derive many others. Since a major source of all interpersonal problems is the failure to communicate, the multiple uses of the MBTI as a counseling tool, as presented in Chapters 5 and 7, can be successfully applied to resolving roommate conflicts.

Helping Roommates Accommodate Natural Differences

A proven mechanism for resolving roommate conflicts is for roommates to develop a behavioral contract, a process which can help roommates function effectively regardless of their degree of dissimilarity in personality styles. Important issues to resolve include cleanliness, study habits, sharing personal belongings, bedtimes, where each keeps his/her things, entertaining guests, and attitudes toward social behaviors. Resolution through compromise on these matters would be of great benefit to Willard and Sam. For example, Willard and Sam might agree on certain hours for sleeping, studying, and socializing in thier room. During designated study hours, Sam could use headphones if he wished to listen to music; conversely, Willard might study in the library during the designated socializing hours. Sam could agree to keep his clothes off the floor and in his closet and Willard might agree to cleaning the entire room only twice a week. In addition to these kinds of behavioral accommodations, it might be possible for Willard and Sam to structure their room to further allow for their differences. Willard might find that installing privacy curtains around his bed would allow him to sleep more easily when Sam pulls an "all-nighter." To deal with the noises that interfere with Willard's studying, he might try reading a magazine with a fan running until he becomes so accustomed to hearing the fan that it is no longer distracting. The fan would serve to block out other distractors so that he could focus his attention on study materials. All these efforts should increase the probability that Willard and Sam could accommodate each other's natural differences.

Over time, roommates like Willard and Sam may even be able to understand and appreciate each other's differences. The amount of time and effort required to make this relationship work, however, may leave little time for accomplishing academic, social, and personal goals. Without *any* similarities in interests, values, motivations, and living habits, it would be difficult, if not impossible, for roommates to establish a meaningful relationship. In conjunction with using the MBTI as a counseling tool to help roommates understand each other and themselves, the MBTI can also be used to match roommates on the basis of personality compatibility.

Pairing Roommates for Satisfaction and Development

The MBTI was first used at Michigan State University as a tool for understanding the dynamics in the roommate situation (Eigenbrod, 1969). No attempt was made to assign roommates by personality type. Instead, freshman roommates living in a six-story, coeducational residence hall of 600 students were classified into the following three broad categories of compatibility: (a) compatible—both the perception (sensing or intuition) and judgment (thinking or feeling) functions of roommates were alike; (b) complementary—either the perception or the judgment functions of the roommates were alike; (c) incompatible—neither the perception nor the judgment functions of the roommates were alike. As predicted, the greater the similarity or compatibility between roommates, the greater the expressed satisfaction with not only their roommates but also with their room assignments. Increased satisfaction with the living situation resulted in greater investment and involvement in maintaining and improving the physical condition of the residence hall. Thus, the roommate relationship mediated the quality of students' interactions with both the social and physical environments of the residence halls.

The MBTI has also been used to assign roommates together on the basis of personality similarity. At Auburn University in 1975 roommates in the Magnolia Dormitories were matched according to commonality in dominant mental functions on the MBTI (Schroeder, 1976). The conditions in the community at the time were stable and there were numerous support systems in place. Since the spring to fall retention rate was over 70 percent, there was a high percentage of upperclass role models for the first-year students. In addition, the student population overall was fairly homogenous. Single rooms had been introduced to reduce the density per floor so that most floors did not house more than 30 students. Students were encouraged to personalize their rooms and hallways and, in general, felt very influential and unrestricted in their behaviors. Public areas had been zoned for specific "type" behaviors to accommodate natural differences in environmental preferences. A recreation area with pinball machines, table games, loud music, and exciting colors was created to provide students with easy access to a variety of novel, intense, and complex stimulation; a woodworking shop was provided to encourage various practical, sensing behaviors; other areas were zones for privacy and so forth. Hence the overall residential community was characterized by a high degree of support.

In this setting, matching roommates with the MBTI had an almost startling effect. The first year this strategy was implemented, requests for roommate changes declined by over 65 percent. In addition, 21 of 24 roommate pairs who had self-selected their roommates had the same dominant functions—the *same* assignment criteria the housing staff had employed. These results clearly indicate that matching roommates with similar MBTI functions resulted in compatibility. In such a secure and predictable environment, however, pairing roommates by commonality in dominant functions may have created an overly supportive environment. The students were obviously satisfied with their living situation, but it was never determined whether or not there was sufficient diversity or challenge between roommates to stimulate their development.

A central question in roommate assignments is whether satisfaction and development are mutually exclusive or whether satisfaction is a requisite to development. Most studies of the goals and processes of roommate pairings have assumed satisfaction as the only desired outcome (Garrison, 1973). The prevailing assumption has been that satisfaction is a prerequisite to academic and personality development. Until recently, however, the relationship between satisfaction and development had not been investigated. In a campus-wide study at Auburn University, the interrelationship of variables in the roommate situation which might affect not only satisfaction, but also academic and personality development was recently examined (Jackson, 1984).

After assignment by the university's standard procedures, freshmen were classified according to their degree of similarity in MBTI profiles. Roommates were classified into the following four groups which ranged from "identical" roommate pairs as the most similar to "opposite" roommate pairs as the least similar: (a) identical—roommates with both dominant and auxiliary functions in common; (b) complementary—roommates with the same dominant function and different auxiliary functions; (c) tangent—roommates with different dominant functions and the same auxiliary function, or roommates with the dominant function of one the same as the auxiliary function of the other; (d) opposite—roommates with both the dominant and auxiliary functions in opposition. Based on previous research studies and theoretical considerations, it was expected that similarity between roommates' MBTI profiles would be related to roommate satisfaction. Further, it was expected that a satisfying roommate relationship would provide a supportive context in which development would occur. Thus, it was expected that similarity between roommates' MBTI profiles would lead to satisfaction which, in turn, would lead to development, both academic and personality. The actual results of the study are quite provocative and are illustrated in Figure 2.

Contrary to previous studies, similarity between roommates' MBTI profiles was not related to roommate satisfaction. Roommates' degree of similarity on the MBTI, however, was related significantly to academic performance, as defined by grade point average. Further, roommates with the highest grades had "complementary" MBTI profiles, followed in descending order by roommates whose MBTI profiles were "identical," "tangent," and "opposite." It appears that the "complementary" pairing provided the incongruence in the roommate relationship necessary for stimulating academic development. Consistent with this finding is Schroeder's (1981) notion that roommates sharing the same dominant function are provided with a common basis for understanding and interpreting actions while having different auxiliary functions helps each roommate, through modeling, develop behaviors corresponding to the roommates' auxiliary function.

FIGURE 2

Relationship between MBTI Similarity, Roommate Satisfaction,
Academic Performance, and Personality Development

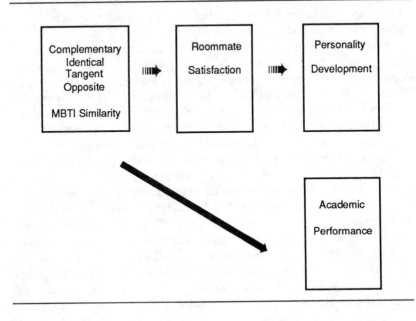

Though roommates' similarity in MBTI profiles was found to be a requisite for academic development, it was not a requisite for personality development. Roommate satisfaction, however, was related significantly to personality development, as defined by selected scales of the *Omnibus Personality Inventory* (Heist & Yonge, 1968). The traditional goal of pairing roommates with the desired outcome of satisfaction was thus confirmed as very worthwhile; the interpersonal environment formed by satisfied roommates provides a medium for personality development.

Collectively, studies of the MBTI in roommate, suitemate, and hall-mate pairings point to the same general conclusion—assigning students to living units according to similarity in MBTI profiles increases the likelihood that students will be compatible and satisfied. Further, the Auburn study (Jackson, 1984) suggests that the MBTI may be promising for creating a dynamic equilibrium in the roommate relationship—one that will not only facilitate satisfaction and thus personality development, but academic achievement as well. While there are different definitions of the degrees of similarity on the MBTI which represent continua of challenge and support, all investigators agree that dominant pairings (presented in Table 4) are effective as assignment criteria. The pairings to the left are identical and become progressively less similar moving to the right. To determine which of the four dominant pairings to use, the practitioner should first assess the relative degrees of challenge and support within the area of assignment (floor or building) and the students to be assigned. When students are in developmental transition, not yet integrated into social groups, and/or the residence hall environment is extremely challenging, students should be assigned as similarly as possible. When students are not in developmental transition, have support groups to help mediate their college challenges, and/or when the residence hall environment allows for a high degree of predictability, students should be paired less similarly. Hence, as previously suggested, the MBTI can best be utilized as a mechanism for balancing the elements of challenge and support in the residential environment. When using the MBTI for various assignment purposes, however, there are a number of practical administrative issues which must be considered.

Practical Administrative Considerations

When using the MBTI for assignment purposes, one of the first issues that must be considered is the most appropriate way to gather type data on resident students, an issue that has been addressed in various ways. At Auburn University, for example, all freshmen students who participate in the summer Pre-College Counseling program complete the MBTI prior to attending one of eight orientation sessions scheduled from mid-June through the last week of July. After the Indicator is scored, the housing staff obtains type scores for incoming freshman from Student Development Services, the department that provides leadership for managing MBTI data.

At Saint Louis University, incoming resident students are mailed the Indicator as part of the housing contracting process. New students are encouraged to complete and return the Indicator within a three- to four-week period during the summer. Once the information is received in the housing office, answer sheets are hand scored by trained student assistants. MBTI type scores, along with academic information and data

TABLE 4

Dominant MBTI Pairings for Each Type

	Identical	Complementary-1	Consonant	Complementary-2
Dominant Sensors				
ESTP	ESTP	ESFP	ISTJ	ISFJ
ESFP	ESFP	ESTP	ISFJ	ISTJ
ISTJ	ISTJ	ISFJ	ESTP	ESFP
ISFJ	ISFJ	ISTJ	ESFP	ESTP
Dominant Intuitives				
ENTP	ENTP	ENFP	INTJ	INFJ
ENFP	ENFP	ENTP	INFJ	INTJ
INTJ	INTJ	INFJ	ENTP	ENFP
INFJ	INFJ	INTJ	ENFP	ENTP
Dominant Thinkers				
ESTJ	ESTJ	ENTJ	ISTP	INTP
ENTJ	ENTJ	ESTJ	INTP	ISTP
ISTP	ISTP	INTP	ESTJ	ENTJ
INTP	INTP	ISTP	ENTJ	ESTJ
Dominant Feelers				
ESFJ	ESFJ	ENFJ	ISFP	INFP
ENFJ	ENFJ	ESFJ	INFP	ISFP
ISFP	ISFP	INFP	ESFJ	ENFJ
INFP	INFP	ISFP	ENFJ	ESFJ

recorded on a "Personal Information Sheet," are then utilized to match roommates. It is important to note that at Saint Louis University, MBTI information generated by the housing office is combined into an integrated database with type scores obtained through freshman orientation, Counseling and Consultation Center testings, and various personal development workshops. The value of integrating this information for retention purposes has been addressed in Chapter 3.

Obviously, there are a number of ethical considerations that must be addressed when using the MBTI to match roommates, floormates, and suitemates. First, students must clearly understand why this approach is beneficial and they must consent to the utilization of the data for matching purposes. At Saint Louis University, this is communicated to incoming resident students when they receive the MBTI booklet and answer sheet. Naturally, all MBTI information generated for matching purposes is handled in a confidential manner. Room assignments are made by trained, professional staff. No information on a student's type is released without his or her expressed, written consent. Students are encouraged, but not required, to participate in the process. Students choose to participate by signing an informed consent form. In addition, the roommate selection and assignment process is highlighted in the following fashion in the SLU Housing Brochure:

> From choice of roommate to selection of a floor unit, you
> have freedom to associate with whomever you choose. Our
> application process provides information which will help you
> choose living arrangements where you will feel most at home. If
> you do not indicate a preference for a particular roommate, the
> information obtained through the application process will be used
> to make assignments.

In applying these strategies at Auburn University, Mercer University, and Saint Louis University, housing staff have utilized type scores for matching purposes—no attention has been given to strength of preference scores. However, since other information (academic goals, living habits, etc.) is combined with MBTI information, the housing director can obtain a fairly accurate picture of a student's personality prior to the actual assignment.

Costs associated with administering an assignment program of this nature include purchasing a supply of MBTI booklets and answer sheets, and mailing and scoring the instrument. Since it is common for 10 to 15 percent of the students to fail to return their booklets and answer sheets, these items must be replaced at additional cost. Similarly, if the Indicator is hand scored, student assistants or clerical support staff must be paid for their time. For housing staff desiring a different scoring option, Consulting Psychologists Press and the Center for Applications of Psychological Type offer a low-cost, rapid, efficient computer scoring service that provides individual scores and profiles. CAPT offers a composite profile by preference for various groups as well.

One final consideration—staff should be aware of the politics associated with using a personality instrument for roommate matching purposes. Unless the program is *effectively* communicated to student affairs staff, faculty, key administrators, and students, the approach could be viewed as a deliberate attempt to manipulate the environment in order to change the behavior of students without their knowledge and consent. We are certainly not advocating such an approach for residence educators. Rather, we are advocating that the MBTI be used to help students understand themselves and others and to avail themselves of the opportunities for development which campus environments offer.

Implications

Throughout this chapter, we have described various strategies for applying the MBTI in residence halls—strategies which, in many cases, have served to improve the quality of life for students. Some of the strategies, however, may challenge the traditional approaches to student development used by many college housing staffs. On most campuses it is quite common for residence hall staff to spend considerable time and energy reacting to problems, mediating roommate conflicts, responding to discipline problems, implementing developmental programs, and working with resident assistants (RAs). Although some of these roles are both necessary and appropriate, they appear to suggest a crises management perspective akin to hospital emergency room treatment. In this chapter we have suggested an alternative role—environmental management—a strategy more akin to preventive medicine. Instead of expecting students to adjust or accommodate themselves to prevailing social environments, residence educators can use the MBTI as one means of structuring environments that respond to the diversity in students' needs and preferences. Hence, we hope that residence educators will recognize the value of environmental management as a principle for promoting student development.

Although the MBTI is definitely not a panacea for all the problems students and staff experience in residence halls, when properly applied it is an extremely useful tool for contributing to conditions in the residence halls that promote various dimensions of student development. Perhaps it goes without saying that any tool must be applied with care; its user must recognize both the possibilities and limitations associated with its application. Almost everyone has witnessed great works produced by knowledgeable and experienced craftsmen using primitive tools and, conversely, inferior products created by novices utilizing sophisticated, state-of-the-art tools. Likewise, the MBTI can be used most effectively when in the hands of a knowledgeable practitioner— one who possesses not only a thorough understanding of the MBTI and how to apply it, but also grasps the complex interactions between students and the physical and social environment of his/her own campus. For example, an MBTI roommate-matching strategy that is effective at a large multiversity, such as Ohio State University, may be totally inappropriate at a small Catholic women's college. Therefore, prior to utilizing the MBTI as an intervention strategy, residence educators should systematically assess sources of challenge and support in their residential settings and then adopt an MBTI strategy for their local circumstances.

Finally, almost all colleges and universities are experiencing a dramatic decline in traditional college-age students, a change resulting in diminished financial resources and steady-state enrollments. In response to this situation, most institutions are being challenged to improve their retention rates. Fortunately, housing officials are in a favored position for impacting the retention of their students. The results of over 20 years of research have clearly shown that the on-campus living experience can mediate students' satisfaction, functioning, and persistence with virtually all aspects of their undergraduate experience (Astin, 1977). While these benefits have always been goals of residential programs, they have infrequently been directly linked to staff interventions. The MBTI can be used to intentionally create conditions in the residence hall which promote student academic achievement, personal growth, and satisfaction—student development objectives related to retention.

Whether by design or by default, residence educators are managers of the social ecology of students. With increasing knowledge that the social environments in residence halls can be purposefully structured, college housing administrators have not only the opportunity for influencing students' development, but also the obligation to reduce or eliminate the inhumane conditions that residence hall environments sometimes create for students. When appropriately applied, the MBTI is a sound, useful, and efficient tool for these purposes.

References

Astin, A. W. (1977). *Four critical years*. San Francisco: Jossey-Bass.

Eigenbrod, F. A. (1969). The effects of territoriality and personality compatibility on identity and security (Doctoral dissertation, Michigan State University). *Dissertation Abstracts International, 30*, 2329A.

Garrison, R. (1973). Roommate selection: A plan for community growth. *The Journal of College and University Student Housing, 3*, 15–18.

Heilweil, M. (1973). The influence of dormitory architecture on resident behavior. *Environment and Behavior, 5*, 377–411.

Heist, P., & Yonge, G. (1968). *Omnibus Personality Inventory* (Form F). New York: The Psychological Corporation.

Jackson, S. (1983). The relationship between psychological type and color preferences. Unpublished manuscript, Saint Louis University, St. Louis, MO.

Jackson, S. (1984). The impact of roommates on development: A causal analysis of the effects of roommate personality congruence, satisfaction and initial developmental status on end-of-quarter developmental status and grade point average. Unpublished doctoral dissertation, Auburn University, Auburn, AL.

Kalsbeek, D., Rodgers, R., Marshall, D., Denny, D., & Nicholls, G. (1982). Balancing challenge and support: A study of degrees of similarity in suitemate personality type and perceived difference in challenge and support in a residence hall environment. *Journal of College Student Personnel, 23*, 434–442.

Mehrabian, A. (1976). *Public places and private spaces*. New York: Basic Books.

Moos, R., & Gerst, M. (1974). *The University Residence Environment Scale Manual*. Palo Alto, CA: Consulting Psychologists Press.

Rodgers, R. (1980). Theories underlying student development. In D. Creamer (Ed.), *Student development in higher education: Theories, practices, and future directions*, (pp. 10–95). Cincinnati, OH: American College Personnel Association.

Sanford, N. (1966). *Self and society: Social change and individual development*. New York: Atherton.

Schroeder, C. (1976). New strategies for structuring residential environments. *Journal of College Student Personnel, 17*, 386–391.

Schroeder, C. (1981). Student development through environmental management. In G. Blimling and J. Schuh (Eds.), *Increasing the education role of residence halls*, (pp. 35–51). *New directions for student services, No. 13*. San Francisco: Jossey-Bass.

Schroeder, C., Warner, R., & Malone, D. (1980). Effects of assignment to living units by personality types on environmental perceptions and student development. *Journal of College Student Personnel, 21*, 443–449.

JUDITH A. PROVOST, Ed.D., is a psychotherapist, writer, and trainer who has incorporated MBTI concepts in her work for the past 13 years. She currently is Director of Personal Counseling at Rollins College and is on the faculties of the Center for Applications of Psychological Type and the Association for Psychological Type. Her research interests in higher education have resulted in several journal articles and a dissertation, "Personality type and leisure satisfaction as factors in college attrition." Other books by Judy are *A Casebook: Applications of the Myers-Briggs Type Indicator in Counseling* (CAPT) and *The Freshman Year—Stress or Success* (PPI). As Chair of the Council for Communication and Education of APT, she sits on the executive board; she also serves as Chair of the Ethics Committee of APT. Her education includes an undergraduate degree from the University of Connecticut, graduate degrees from the University of California at Los Angeles and University of Florida, and extensive training with the Gestalt Institute of Florida. She is an ENFP.

SCOTT ANCHORS is currently Director of Residential Education at the University of Maine (Orono). He has a master's degree in Higher Education from Iowa State University and is currently completing his Ph.D. there. Previous to his current appointment at the university he served as Assistant Dean of Students at Mercer University and worked in the Department of Residence Life at Iowa State University. Scott has served as an academic advisor at both the University of Maine and at Mercer University. He coauthored "Self-selection patterns of college roommates as identified by the *Myers-Briggs Type Indicator*," which was recognized as an outstanding contribution to the college housing field by the Association of College and University Housing Officers-International in 1985. Scott is currently a member of APT and CAPT training faculty. His type is ISFJ.

CHAPTER 5

Student Involvement and Activities

JUDITH A. PROVOST and SCOTT ANCHORS

ANYONE INVOLVED IN student activities programming has observed certain patterns of participation. Not all students participate in academic and social opportunities to the same degree. The same group of students consistently appear at certain kinds of events, while other students are seldom seen. Certain organizations tend to draw certain kinds of students. We all know that some students are not reached by activity programming. Perhaps their needs are not being met by opportunities, perceived or real, within the institution. Personality type can be helpful in understanding some of the aspects of students' extracurricular behaviors and responses to activities programming.

This chapter reviews briefly the importance of Astin's (1975, 1977, 1984), Tinto's (1975), and Chickering's (1969) theories to the topic of involvement and activities. Research studies and data concerning student activity patterns and the MBTI are included to show how the MBTI can help in understanding students' needs and behaviors. From this data some general observations about types and involvement are made with recommendations for those working with student activities and setting institutional policy. The approach used by the University of Maine at Orono illustrates some examples of how one institution has used the MBTI extensively.

Theories of Involvement

Student involvement is a key construct in student development theory. Astin (1984) defines student involvement as the amount of physical and psychological energy that the student devotes to the academic experience. He goes on to state, "Thus, a highly involved student is one who, for example, devotes considerable energy to studying, spends much time on campus, participates actively in student organizations, and interacts frequently with faculty members and other students" (p. 297). Astin's research indicates that the more involved students are, the less likely they are to drop out of college. Other theorists and researchers have also pursued the relationship between involvement and retention.

One of these theorists is Tinto (1975). He correlates the degree of student integration with the retention rate of the college or university. Kalsbeek's Chapter 3 about campus retention research describes this model thoroughly. Tinto distinguished two kinds of integration, academic and social. Both are equally important and interdependent. Social integration indicates involvement in campus activities and relationships. Academic integration includes embracing the educational goals of the institution as well as personal educational goals and participating fully in academic programs offered by the institution.

These concepts of involvement and social and academic integration complement Chickering's vectors described in Chapter 2. Consider the vector of competence as it applies to social and academic integration. Students need to develop social and interpersonal competence, and intellectual and instrumental skills. Without this development, integration will not occur. Chickering emphasized the importance of out-of-class experiences; the "student culture." He saw residence halls and extracurricular activities as providing opportunities for growth within his seven developmental vectors.

We can all, therefore, recognize the importance of involvement and social/academic integration to the individual student and to the institution: for the institution, student retention and a sense of educational community; for the individual student, success and satisfaction in the college experience.

Extracurricular activities provide a way for different types to express themselves and a way for their development to be stimulated. For example, suppose a young ENTJ arrives at college hungry for a leadership role and thrives on the challenge of reorganizing a floundering student organization. She is expressing and developing further her natural interest in leading. In terms of Chickering's vectors, she is developing competence.

Additional value is placed on student activities because of their importance in providing a balance with academics and in providing leisure outlets. Many needs are met through leisure such as relaxation and socialization. Balance and effective use of leisure time can mitigate student stress and enhance well-being.

An example of the importance of balance is the experience of many Extraverted students who channel much of their energies into intramurals and varsity sports, aerobics, and other physical activities. After sitting passively in classrooms and studying, many Extraverted students become restless and unfocused. These activities provide an outlet and balance so they can later return to their studies refreshed and able to focus again.

These theories and what we know about psychological types allow us to speculate about patterns of student involvement and strategies to foster that involvement. However, research is necessary to determine more accurately the needs and appropriate approaches for the 16 types. Some of the basic questions are:

- Which activities appeal to which types?

- Which formats or structures for activities are comfortable for different types?

- How can the reluctant types be encouraged and supported to participate?

- How should programs/activities be "marketed" to appeal to a variety of types or to a targeted group?

- How does the nature of balance between academic and social activities vary because of type?

The following research reflects attempts to answer some of these questions.

Research on the MBTI and Patterns of Involvement

The first research on type and involvement patterns may have been done by Harold Grant (1965) at Auburn University. After obtaining MBTI results, Grant surveyed students about out-of-class behaviors such as frequency of drinking, likelihood of joining a fraternal organization, and frequency of dating. He compared these behaviors to types and found certain patterns. Table 1 shows some of these patterns. The Extraverts, for example, indicated a preference for extracurricular activities that involved social groups. The Introverted Sensing types most frequently reported they would "definitely not join" a Greek organization. In 1967,

TABLE 1

Extracurricular Activities of Auburn University Freshmen
Classified According to MBTI Type

ISTJ	ISFJ	INFJ	INTJ
	Movies		Lectures, Drama, or Music
ISTP Athletic Events	ISFP	INFP Movies	INTP Lectures, Drama, or Music
ESTP Social Events	ESFP Social Groups	ENFP Social Groups	ENTP Social Groups and Athletic Events
ESTJ	ESFJ Athletic Events	ENFJ Movies	ENTJ Athletic Events

Source: *Behavior of MBTI Types* by W. Harold Grant, Auburn University, 1965.

Stalcup continued this kind of inquiry at Auburn University by comparing MBTI type with 229 extracurricular activities. Subjects checked activities in which they participated over the freshman–sophomore years, the term in which they participated, and the average number of hours per week spent at that activity. Stalcup found the largest numbers of nonparticipants among Introverts and a higher frequency of certain activities reported for certain of the 16 types.

Provost (1980) surveyed 73 sophomores, juniors, and seniors to explore possible relationships among type, grade point average, leisure interests, and amount of time spent on academic and paid work. Several statistically significant patterns between leisure interests and type occurred. Extraverts reported significantly higher interest than Introverts in social amusements (going to parties, going to popular music concerts, visiting amusement parks) and in intellectual activities (chess, reading mystery stories, playing guitar). Type theory would predict the higher interest in social amusements but not in intellectual activities. The Perception types reported significantly higher interests than the Judgment types in competitive activities (running races, racquetball, backgammon, handball), in social games (softball, frisbee, volleyball, board games), and in social amusements. Analyses of variance for SP, SJ, NF, and NT groupings revealed significantly higher interest in competitive activities by the SPs.

In terms of work and leisure, the Judgment types were significantly higher in reported hours of academic and paid work. Theory would predict that Judgment types would generally place a higher priority on work completion before engaging in leisure, while the Perception types would be more likely to mix work and play and be open to more leisure experiences. Judgment types tend not to play until work is completed, unlike the Perceptives. Judgment types are more concerned with structured time and completion of tasks before taking on new activities. Thus response patterns of Js and Ps to extracurricular activities tend to differ.

Provost (1982) studied the relationship of type to attrition, grade point average, leisure satisfaction at college, and extracurricular activities pursued. The study involved surveying sophomores; the sample size was 189 (84 male, 105 female). *The Leisure Satisfaction Survey* (LSS) measured student responses on six subscales:

- Psychological—satisfies a need for freedom, enjoyment, involvement, and intellectual challenge.

- Educational—satisfies a need for intellectual stimulation and information about themselves and their environment.

- Social—satisfies a need for rewarding relationships with people.

- Relaxational—satisfies a need for stress reduction.

- Physiological—satisfies a need for physical fitness, weight control, and general physical well-being.

- Aesthetic—satisfies a need for involvements that are pleasing, beautiful, and well-designed.

TABLE 2

College Sophomores: Mean LSS Subscale Scores and MBTI Types
(*N*=189)

MBTI Type	Psychological Mean	SD	Educational Mean	SD	Social Mean	SD
ISTJ	17.45	1.75	16.82	1.83	15.36	2.77
ISFJ	17.14	2.85	17.86	2.27	16.86	2.34
INFJ	15.71	3.15	16.14	2.73	15.86	2.67
INTJ	17.00	2.06	16.11	1.17	15.56	3.78
ISTP	14.67	3.72	13.67	1.86	12.50	1.52
ISFP	14.40	2.12	13.60	3.20	14.80	2.39
INFP	13.73	2.84	14.67	3.02	14.80	2.78
INTP	16.44	3.17	14.56	3.97	15.67	2.29
ESTP	15.38	2.39	15.75	3.28	15.50	3.42
ESFP	15.27	2.52	15.73	2.66	16.13	2.64
ENFP	14.66	2.46	14.47	2.44	15.91	2.87
ENTP	16.00	2.08	16.07	3.27	14.79	2.75
ESTJ	16.87	2.90	16.87	2.90	17.80	1.78
ESFJ	16.90	2.64	16.30	1.70	16.60	1.65
ENFJ	16.00	2.28	15.82	2.86	17.55	1.92
ENTJ	15.20	1.69	16.40	1.78	16.30	1.77
	F Ratio = 2.37**		F Ratio = 2.07*		F Ratio = 2.21*	

* Significant .05.　　　　　　Degrees of Freedom = 15
** Significant at .01.

173

Range of LSS Score = 4–20

Table 2 shows mean scores on each of these subscales for each of the 16 types. Three of the six subscales have significantly different scores for the 16 types. Of the three remaining subscales, Relaxational was above the nationally normed mean for all types, indicating the high need among college students for this type of extracurricular activity. The other two scales, Aesthetic and Physiological, were lower for all types. Age is an interactive factor here, since the sample of 19 to 22-year-olds is less likely than an older population to be concerned with these aspects of leisure.

TABLE 2 (continued)

College Sophomores: Mean LSS Subscale Scores and MBTI Types
(N=189)

MBTI Type	Relaxation Mean	SD	Physiological Mean	SD	Aesthetic Mean	SD	Total Score	SD
ISTJ	16.27	2.28	15.36	3.47	14.82	2.79	96.1	9.8
ISFJ	16.14	4.22	14.29	5.02	16.86	2.54	99.1	15.2
INFJ	18.29	1.80	14.14	3.39	16.43	2.37	96.6	13.0
INTJ	16.89	3.06	13.56	4.50	15.00	2.06	94.1	8.9
ISTP	15.17	2.32	12.00	3.35	12.67	1.51	80.7	5.5
ISFP	15.50	2.76	14.40	2.88	13.90	2.60	86.6	12.8
INFP	16.60	2.92	13.07	2.84	14.40	2.72	87.3	11.6
INTP	15.44	4.33	15.11	2.85	14.33	2.24	91.6	10.5
ESTP	16.25	2.76	15.25	2.76	16.00	2.45	94.1	12.8
ESFP	16.47	2.61	14.80	3.53	14.20	2.34	92.6	12.9
ENFP	15.81	2.44	13.78	3.13	13.88	2.27	88.5	9.4
ENTP	16.57	2.71	15.86	3.35	15.07	2.81	94.4	11.8
ESTJ	18.27	2.12	16.20	3.30	16.13	2.83	102.1	10.9
ESFJ	15.90	1.97	15.40	2.99	15.10	2.81	96.2	10.3
ENFJ	18.82	1.08	14.55	5.84	15.27	2.76	98.0	11.8
ENTJ	16.90	1.66	15.50	2.59	14.80	2.04	95.1	5.6
	F Ratio = 1.78		F Ratio = 1.07		F Ratio = 1.75		F Ratio = 2.59**	

* Significant at .05.
** Significant at .01.

Degrees of Freedom = 15
173

Range of LSS Score = 4–20

Readers can draw their own observations from the data in Table 2, but several patterns are worth noting here. The SJs reported higher satisfaction than other type combinations on the Psychological and Educational subscales and total LSS score. Sensing may be more conducive to identification and utilization of the leisure resources on campus. It also may be that Sensing types are more easily satisfied than Intuitives, who tend to be restlessly anticipating the future rather than experiencing the present. Judging types may be better at organizing their time and following through so that they can be involved in activities. The EJs

TABLE 3

Most Frequently Named Activities of College Sophomores by Type
(N=189)

ISTJ	ISFJ	INFJ	INTJ
Sports	Reading	Sports	Friends
Film	Sports	Playing Piano*	Jogging
	Friends		Writing*
	Volunteer Work*		
ISTP	**ISFP**	**INFP**	**INTP**
Sports	Sports	Friends	Sports
Friends	Sunbathing at	Sports	
	Pool	Playing Guitar*	
ESTP	**ESFP**	**ENFP**	**ENTP**
Sports	Sports	Sports	Sports
Friends	Friends	Greek Activities	Parties
		Friends	Friends
		Sewing*	
		Quiet Time*	
ESTJ	**ESFJ**	**ENFJ**	**ENTJ**
Sports	Sunbathing at	Sports	Sports
Jogging	Pool	Parties	Reading
	Greek Activities		Acting*

*Reported only by this type, but not frequent.

scored highest on Social satisfaction, and the TPs lowest, followed by the IPs. The IPs ranked low on many of the subscales and may have more difficulty than other types in becoming involved in student life.

In the same study sophomores were asked, "Please list the three activities you most like to do in your leisure time at college." Table 3 shows the most frequently reported activities for each type and also those activities reported exclusively by one type.

MBTI patterns of involvement in campus activities were again studied in the same college for the purpose of exploring a possible

FIGURE 1

Activity Patterns by Type

Extraversion

- focus on variety and **doing**
- discharge of energy through physical activity and **action**
- opportunities for multiple interactions with others

Introversion

- opportunity for small group, one-on-one, and individual activities
- space for private leisure (e.g., contemplation)
- opportunities for renewal through solitude, nature, passive activities (e.g., a lecture)

Sensing

- physical activities and sports
- established social structures

Intuition

- opportunities to use imagination and originality
- more naturally see possibilities for activities outside established channels

Thinking

- opportunities for mastery
- development of technical or specialized skills

Feeling

- community service activities
- "cheerleading"/persuasive activities
- interpersonal focus

Judgment

- structured and established activities
- leadership
- concern for time (to get academics done), limit-setting on leisure time

Perception

- spontaneous, unplanned activities and parties
- sometimes overinvolvement without follow-through
- play first, work later?

relationship to attrition and grade point average (Provost, 1985). Types who had the lowest and highest rates of persistence at the college four years after matriculation were interviewed about their college involvements. These seniors were asked about campus activities outside of classes and aspects of the college experience that had been most helpful to them.

The types with the lowest rate of persistence at the college were ISTP, ISFP, ESTP, and ENFJ. The persisting ISPs reported very little involvement during the four years except in intramural sports and small informal gatherings. They were influenced to persist at the college primarily because of personal and informal relationships with faculty, the small campus, and the study/travel abroad experiences they had had. The ENFJs reported being very active in student organizations and to a lesser extent in varsity sports. ENFJs found campus resources (facilities, faculty, and student personnel staff) as most helpful.

The types with the highest rate of persistence were ESTJ, ENTJ, ESFJ, and ESFP. These types all reported heavy involvement in student government and/or the Greek system. Many played varsity sports, and all had had leadership roles. Aspects of the college seen as most valuable to them were Greek organizations, friends, student services staff, and relationships with specific faculty. One ENTJ summed up well the high persister group's attitude, "Getting involved in activities and clubs gives students a reason to stay. Doing something for the college made me feel I had an impact." (Provost, 1985, p. 19)

This last study reflects findings similar to those in the other Provost studies, particularly in regard to IP and EJ patterns of involvement. These patterns are consistent with type theory and suggest that activities programming for the IPs should be different than for the EJs.

Summary of Involvement Patterns

A few general trends among traditional-age college students can be noted by preference, remembering that these trends may not be true for *all* individuals.

Each of the 16 types has some distinctive activity patterns. Some observations of these are clustered under the four attitude combinations. The attitudes seem especially significant to involvement because they shape the level of activity and the dimension of time management/spontaneity.

Introversion–Perception. The types with IP orientation tend to be the least involved in established, structured activities. Their involvements tend to be sporadic. They seem to prefer informal, unstructured, and small group formats. They may not respond to opportunities around them unless "dropped in their laps." The ISPs especially may appear "lost" among the maze of campus activities or may randomly respond to an activity which confronts them. All the IPs respond best to an individualized "marketing" approach.

Introversion–Judgment. The IJ combinations may be no more active than the IPs on campus but are generally more deliberative; they tend to be very selective in their involvements. Completion of academics or other work obligations takes priority over leisure and may result in very little time given over to extracurricular activity, unless this activity is seen as a "responsibility." This attitude about priorities may lead to isolation, especially for the ISTJs and INTJs. The ISJs prefer well-organized and established campus organizations. INJs may welcome the challenge of an intriguing leadership position or other activity that gives them a chance to explore their intuitive interests. IJs will respond best to programs that appear well-organized and time limited and be willing to attend if they know the activity is structured (as opposed to "whatever happens, happens").

Extraversion–Judgment. Students with this combination tend to be most visible in campus organizations in leadership roles. They often choose a variety of activities based on action, for example, community service, or the orientation week task group. They are most attracted to organizations where they can have impact and see results. They will tend to "schedule in" lectures and other cultural events which fit with their motivations and interests.

Extraversion–Perception. Students with this combination of attitudes may have cycles of activity followed by overload, and withdrawal to complete academic work. Many activities may attract them, but they may not be able to follow through on all. They may be selected as leaders by their peers and begin their leadership with flashes of brilliance, only to sputter out when overload sets in. They generally enjoy a high level of activity (physical and social) and may need help in becoming selective, taking work load into account. The ESPs are most attracted to pleasurable experiences such as a party with good food and music. All EPs seem attracted by exciting and/or adventurous experiences that provide multiple stimulation to their perception (either S or N). A cultural event with the format of lively discussion will be more appealing than a structured lecture/presentation.

CIRP Data and Type

The above involvement patterns are reinforced by research through the Cooperative Institutional Research Project (CIRP). This national survey, when correlated with type can reveal some useful and enlightening profiles of entering students. At the University of Maine, Hedland (1985) found significant relationships between anticipated involvement in academics and activities and MBTI preference. Anticipated involvement was measured by entering students' reported intentions to participate in specific academic and social activities. Her research used factor analysis to identify relationships between certain items on the CIRP survey and type.

Student-anticipated involvement was found to correlate with several of the MBTI preferences. In comparing the Extraversion/Introversion preference, she found that Extraverts predicted that they will become more involved in the traditional aspects of campus life, such as living in a coeducational residence hall, having Greek affiliation, and acquiring a bachelor's degree. In contrast the Introverts planned to work while attending the university.

Students with a preference for Sensing maintained a practical posture and were likely to foresee marriage as part of their college experience. The Intuitive students anticipated involvement with academic achievement, career achievement, traditional activities, work, and the possibility of interrupting school for other activities. Perceptive students predicted career exploration and the possibility of dropping out of college. Many of these results are predictable from the type descriptions developed by Isabel Myers (Myers, 1980).

In summary, significant relationships exist in the Hedland study between MBTI types and anticipated involvement in various aspects of college life. More research must be done to sharpen these observations and improve our ability to plan activities for all types of students. The following is an example of the application of type principles to activities planning on one campus.

Program Applications, University of Maine

The University of Maine began administering the MBTI to all incoming resident freshman students in the fall of 1980. Due to the large size of this group (usually over 1600 students) and the lack of an opportunity to administer the MBTI on campus, the MBTI is mailed home with explicit directions on how the results will be used. The confidential nature of the results is emphasized. Return rate on this form of administration has been over 98 percent. To check the accuracy of this procedure, and to assure that parents and others are not influencing the students' responses, several mini-research projects have been conducted to cross-check the accuracy of reported types. Students' agreement with their MBTI description proved to be high (Anchors, 1983). Seventy-eight percent of the students agreed with all four of the preferences on their profile.

At the University of Maine the MBTI is used to match roommates, to design programs, to market programs, to track various types' use of campus programs, and to construct a framework for planning, organizing, and involving students on campus. Following is a review of some of the ways the University has been using type.

Peer Helpers

All peer helpers in Student Affairs at the University of Maine are routinely administered the MBTI. The peer helpers range from resident assistants to peer programmers in the areas of sexuality and personal skill adjustment. MBTI results are often the major tool in helping these students conceptualize who they are, as well as in helping them in their roles as peer counselors/advisors on campus. Type is used with these students as a way to confirm their strengths, and to help them recognize how they may be perceived by others. It is often helpful for peer counselors to view their type distributions as a group compared to the distribution among students receiving their services. For example, resident assistants at the University of Maine are likely to prefer Extraversion, Intuition, and Feeling (von Hoffman, 1986). Knowing that these types are attracted to this campus role has caused the professional staff to structure the recruitment process to attract other types and to assure that these student helpers are able to communicate effectively with peers having different preferences.

Encouraging Freshman Adjustment

Psychological type is used as part of a campus-wide focus to encourage freshman involvement, retention, and adjustment in a variety of activities at the University of Maine. The foundation of this approach is a publication, Row by Row (Stone & von Hoffman, 1986), given to entering freshmen. Row by Row is based on the theories of Jung, Perry, and Chickering. It is an attempt to provide a guided tour of the challenges, activities, and opportunities at the University. The publication is illustrated graphically, with clear directions for Sensing types and opportunities for Intuitives to explore possibilities within a general suggested structure. All preferences were considered in designing the presentation of materials. The publication encourages students in a direct, yet fun manner to get involved in the following: locating classes; understanding learning style; getting acquainted with roommates, and getting prepared for their first vacation home. Self-guided instruction and group experiences are suggested for addressing these issues.

Type is used in facilitating academic adjustment, with special programs for students undecided about majors and careers (see Chapter 6). Those students most attracted to academic support activities, such as selecting a major or career, prefer Introversion, Intuition, Feeling, and Perception. This finding suggests to staff that the marketing of these activities needs to be evaluated to see if the program description may "turn off" or not attract other types.

Health Club

The Hilltop Health Club (Anchors & Arsenault, 1984), located in the basement of a college residence hall, is a comprehensive health facility available to all campus residents, faculty, and staff. The club provides a program that focuses on encouraging the physical development of members through goal setting, assessment, and instruction. The facility houses complete weight-lifting equipment, sauna, steam room, whirlpool, and a variety of aerobic equipment. In addition to individual involvement, over 20 noncredit courses are offered ranging from weight training to stress reduction. The program was recognized in 1982 as one of the "Outstanding Residence Hall Programs" across the nation.

The entire environment of the Health Club is inviting, stimulating, action-oriented, and filled with lots of possibilities for health exploration. Over 67 percent of the members have a preference for Perception, which is proportionally more than that in the larger student body. Forty percent of the members prefer Intuition and Perception, with ESFPs and ENFPs being overrepresented among those who join. These findings are not surprising when viewed within a program that is designed for stimulation and action. A positive consequence of this program has been a reduction in student damage and discipline referrals in the residence halls adjoining the Hilltop Health Club.

Although the MBTI is not used in all aspects of campus life, it has impact on the appreciation of differences campus-wide. The University can approach issues and problems using the MBTI as a research and educational tool.

Conclusions and Recommendations

Student involvement has been stressed as a means to academic retention, student satisfaction, and personal development. Type theory gives some insights into the motivations and behaviors of students in regard to extracurricular activities.

Research should continue to address the questions identified early in the chapter. Higher education professionals would do well to record type distributions within selected activities and organizations and to survey the 16 types to determine what their needs are. These needs may vary from one academic setting to another, because of other variables at play such as socioeconomic characteristics.

All professionals engaged in helping students succeed in college should be sensitive to the importance of balancing academics with leisure/extracurricular activity and should also be aware that "balance" will be defined differently among the 16 types. Some types will need encouragement to experiment with activities, while others will need help in limiting themselves and setting priorities. Professionals can help students evaluate their need for balance, for various kinds of activity (such as physical), and for leisure involvements that foster development. Professionals can apply their skills such as time management, assertiveness training, role play (for reluctant participants), program planning, advocacy, and so forth, to facilitate individual student involvement on campus.

References

Anchors, S., & Arsenault, N. (1984). Hilltop health club: A model program for health education in residence halls. *Journal of College Student Personnel*.

Anchors, S. (1983). (Unpublished research.) University of Maine, Orono, ME.

Astin, A. W. (1975). *Preventing students from dropping out*. San Francisco: Jossey-Bass.

Astin, A. W. (1977). *Four critical years*. San Francisco: Jossey-Bass.

Astin, A. W. (1984). Student involvement: A developmental theory for higher education. *Journal of College Student Personnel, 25* (4) 297-308.

Chickering, A. (1969). *Education and Identity*. San Francisco: Jossey-Bass.

Grant, W. H. (1965). *Behavior of MBTI types* .(Research report, Student Counseling Service, Auburn University.) Gainesville, FL: Center for Applications of Psychological Type.

Hedland, J. (1985). *Entering freshman input at the University of Maine at Orono: A conceptualization of the relationship between personality preferences and motivation, influences, goals/values, and potential involvement*. Unpublished doctoral dissertation, University of Maine, Orono, ME.

Myers, I. B. (1980). *Gifts differing*. Palo Alto, CA: Consulting Psychologists Press.

Provost, J. A. (1980). *Work/leisure patterns of college students, personality, and college students, personality, and college grades*. Unpublished paper, Rollins College, Winter Park, FL.

Provost, J. A. (1982). Personality type and leisure satisfaction as factors in college attrition (Doctoral dissertation, University of Florida).*Dissertation Abstracts*, 4309. (University Microfilm No. 83-02289).

Provost, J. A. (1985). Type watching and college attrition. *Journal of Psychological Type*, 9, 16–23.

Stalcup, D. K. (1967). An investigation of personality characteristics of college students who do participate and those who do not participate in campus activities (Doctoral dissertation, Auburn University). *Dissertation Abstracts*, 28, 4452A. (University Microfilms No. 68-5897).

Stone, G., & von Hoffman, I. (1986). *Row by row*. Orono, ME: Department of Residence Life, University of Maine.

Tinto, V. (1975). Dropout from higher education: A theoretical synthesis of recent research. *Review of Educational Research, 45* (1), 89–125.

von Hoffman, I. (1986). (Unpublished research). Orono, ME: University of Maine.

SCOTT ANCHORS is currently Director of Residential Life at the University of Maine (Orono). He has a master's degree in Higher Education from Iowa State University and is currently completing his Ph.D. there. Previous to his current appointment at the university he served as Assistant Dean of Students at Mercer University and worked in the Department of Residence Life at Iowa State University. Scott has served as an academic advisor at both the University of Maine and at Mercer University. He coauthored "Self-selection patterns of college roommates as identified by the *Myers-Briggs Type Indicator*," which was recognized as an outstanding contribution to the college housing field by the Association of College and University Housing Officers-International in 1985. Scott is currently a member of APT and CAPT training faculty. His type is ISFJ.

CHAPTER 6

Academic Advising

SCOTT ANCHORS

THE ADVISING PROCESS can utilize type information to help students by teaching them a useful framework for decision making and assisting them in the development of perception and judgment. While the MBTI is not the answer to all the challenges advisors face in assisting students, it can serve as a useful tool for guiding students through what is often a frustrating and confusing process. This chapter discusses: the importance of advising, type and decision-making styles, a model program for advising, and the use of type to plan a student's course load.

Importance of Advising

Increased interest in advising has resulted in the creation of a national advising association (the National ACademic ADvising Association) and the proliferation of workshops, seminars, and numerous publications on the topic. The advising process can have a tremendous impact on students, their satisfaction with the institution, their academic performance, and ultimately upon retention.

Despite this heightened interest in advising and its potential value, little has been written about using the MBTI for this purpose. Gordon and Carberry (1984) presented an overview of how the MBTI could be used as a resource for developmental advising. They explained that students can benefit from understanding how they process information, and that the MBTI can be used in group advising to help students understand their reactions in certain situations. Others such as McCaulley (1981) and Laney (1949) have discussed the use of the MBTI in career planning, and its implications for improving academic advising.

The advising relationship should be maximized since it is generally one of the few institutional contacts required of students. This contact has potential to help a student explore a variety of issues that are pertinent to college success. The advisor can use type information to help the student gain greater self-insight and select an appropriate program of study.

How do different students proceed through the process of selecting a program of study? Are there characteristic decision-making styles, and do these styles impact academic choices? The next section will address these questions.

Decision-Making Styles

Students vary tremendously in the way they approach the educational planning process. Patterns can be identified among students who are undecided or decided about a college major related to their types and to the combinations of their attitudes (extraversion/introversion and judgment/perception). These combinations are: extraversion-judgment (EJ), extraversion-perception (EP), introversion-judgment (IJ), and introversion-perception (IP). EJ students, for example, tend to be found more frequently among the decided students, and IP students tend to occur more frequently among the undecided students. Myers and McCaulley (1985) described these combinations of attitudes in the MBTI *Manual*. Anchors, Gershman, and Robbins (in press) in a study of characteristics of undecided students found extraversion/introversion and judgment/perception to be related to students' "sense of purpose." As students' scores on the Developing Purpose task of the *Student Development Task Inventory* (Winston, Miller, & Prince, 1979) increased, so did the strength of their preference for extraversion and judgment. Table 1 shows these intercorrelations in a sample of 946 students who were administered both the MBTI and the *Student Development Task Inventory* (SDTI).

Table 2 shows a trend in relationships between the MBTI attitudes and SDTI scores. On the Appropriate Educational Plans subtask of the SDTI, the EJs ranked first, with well-defined and personally meaningful educational goals. They were followed in descending order by the EPs, IJs and finally the IPs. On this subscale students with high scores are described as goal-oriented and self-directed learners. They seek in-depth educational experiences, enjoy college and take advantage of available resources to enhance learning.

TABLE 1

Pearson Correlations Among the SDTI-2 and MBTI Scales
(N = 946)

Scale	Appropriate Educational Plans	Mature Career Plans	Mature Lifestyle Plans
E I	-.21**	-.21**	-.24**
S N	-.02	.04	-.01
T F	-.05	-.09*	-.01
J P	-.15**	-.12**	-.19**

*P .01
**P .001

Reprinted from: Anchors, S., Gershman, E., and Robbins, M. (in press).

These findings will be elaborated upon through the following detailed descriptions of the four combinations of MBTI attitudes in relation to decision making and the advising process.

Extraversion and Judgment: The Decisive Extraverts

EJs have a Judgment function (T or F) extraverted and dominant, while their Perception function (S or N) is introverted and auxiliary. EJs are characteristically decisive, confident, and enjoy closure and making things happen. Their preference for structure and closure makes deciding on a college major an easier task for them, relative to other types. EJs place high priority on completing the task. One EJ advisee said about selecting a major, "I just want to hurry up and get it over with."

Students with Extraversion and Judgment have dominant Feeling or Thinking. This dominant judging process provides a system of order (Thinking) or a set of personal values (Feeling) that shapes the decision to choose a major. Many EJs progress toward graduation through an orderly sequence of studies and milestones (completion of core courses, etc.) that mark their progress. EJs are often uncomfortable when these markers are absent. The absence of these markers or structures can cause distress. For example, one EJ advisee was filled with anxiety and could

TABLE 2

Mean SDTI-2 Subtask Scores for Attitude Combinations

Mature Lifestyle Plans: The ability to balance vocational, avocational, and family plans (maximum score 20).

			Mean
EJ	73	++	15.94
EP	119	+++++++++++++++++++++++++++++++++++++++	15.57
IJ	65	++++++++++++++++++++++++++++++	14.83
IP	74	+++++++++++++++++++++	14.02
	12	13	14	15	16

Appropriate Educational Plans: A high score indicates the individual has well defined and personally meaningful educational goals (maximum score 20).

			Mean
EJ	73	++++++++++++++++++++++++	14.30
EP	119	+++++++++++++++++	13.54
I J	65	+++++++++++++	13.30
IP	74	++++	12.33
	12	13	14	15	16

Mature Career Plans: Involves a tentative commitment to a chosen field (maximum score 20).

			Mean
EJ	73	++++++++++++++++++	13.76
EP	119	+++	12.20
IJ	65	++	12.18
IP	74		11.67
	12	13	14	15	16

Unpublished research (Anchors, 1985).

not sleep because her master's degree "program of study" could not be approved until her entire committee met together. In her case this meant waiting several weeks to finalize her program.

EJs are the most likely types to make early career decisions. McCaulley (1981), in her research on medical students, found that EJ types were most frequent among those medical professionals who knew they wanted to be a doctor as early as ages 10 to 13. Otis (1972) in other research found that ES types were early deciders about medical specialties and that E, S, T, and J were associated with earlier decisions than I, N, and P.

EJ Potential Pitfalls and Strategies

EJs, as one might predict from type theory, may have difficulty with premature or too early foreclosure. In other words, they may not take enough time to gather information and perceptions, and they may fail to consider the possibilities. They may operate in their dominant function without the benefit of their auxiliary. Although the institution may allow or encourage them to put off their decision for several semesters, their discomfort with this may lead to premature closure. Teaching them the value of brainstorming processes and various information-gathering approaches can be of value. The dominant Ts can be motivated by showing the logic of gathering more information, which will make the formula of selecting a major more complete. Feeling types can be motivated to use their auxiliary by stressing that the resulting decision will be a "better" one for themselves and for others.

When advisors find EJ students who are undecided, they should be alert to the possibility that these students may need help in the development of the thinking or feeling function. Advisors can make an assessment: In general how easy is it for these students to make a decision? What guides them in their decisions (personal values or logic)? Does head or heart rule? These questions can be a useful way to begin the process of identifying one function as a guide in their decision making. Of course the advisor should always consider the possibility that Thinking or Feeling is not actually the dominant function, but the auxiliary. This possibility is suggested by a low preference score on any of the attitude scores (E/I and J/P).

EJs can be assisted to strengthen their dominant Thinking or Feeling through values clarification exercises, force field analysis, and other such focusing processes. EJ students can benefit from learning to introvert through quiet reflection and meditation. Advisors can suggest students ask themselves such questions as: What other majors might exist besides my present one? Will I really be satisfied with engineering as a career?

EJs also can be aided by taking career planning courses that involve a high level of activity, such as student presentations, group projects, and out-of-class experiences. Occasionally I have found career planning courses frustrating to EJ students. The exposure to additional possibilities they receive in these courses can disrupt their already conceived educational plans.

Various programs which can give EJs, especially ESJs, hands-on learning about majors and careers can be very helpful. Traditional work co-op programs, where students are placed in job settings for periods of time, can prove beneficial. These programs ground the student in the real world of work, making work less abstract and conceptual. Since these approaches often require more time than most students have, less time-consuming programs should also be offered. Programs can include visiting work settings, interviewing workers, and other related activities that expose students to new options and perspectives.

Introversion and Perception: The Adaptable Introverts

IPs have a Judgment function (T or F) that is introverted and dominant, while their Perception function (S or N) is extraverted and auxiliary. IPs are often described as reflective and looking inward for guidance and direction. Although adaptable in many areas, they stand firm on issues that are important to them.

IPs have a characteristic style that is radically different from the EJs. While the EJs tend to be the executive decision makers, the IPs are often at the other end of the continuum, hesitant and reflective. Many IPs I advise lack information about careers, rarely obtain information about majors as expediently as their EJ peers, and are generally not comfortable making decisions. Decision making for many IPs can be a confusing and difficult process. Since their dominant function is introverted, and their auxiliary function is extraverted, they may be in a struggle between responding to the outer world and yet being true to their inner world of personal values or logic.

The challenge for IFPs is to select a major that is true to their inner spirit and values. Advisors can help them explore who they are, so they can find a fit with a particular major. As Jung said of Introverted Feelers, "Still waters run deep." They can be difficult to understand because of an inability or reluctance to express what is going on internally. Their judgments are grounded in a self often not easily expressed. Extraverted advisors may have more difficulty drawing out IP advisees. The advisor should allow plenty of time for a response from the introverted student during individual sessions. An advisor might also consider sending the student an informal meeting agenda ahead of time to encourage reflection prior to the meeting.

ITPs need an environment that allows and encourages them to construct their own system for selecting a major. Are there plenty of interesting books available? Has the advisor explained various career development models? One INTP advisee after three years of exploration of self and majors said, "I have finally put it all together into a neat formula that makes perfect sense." The student used a diagram to put together a lot of details that explained his past interests and experiences. The diagram showed how factors had shaped and influenced his college attendance and future direction. Diagramming his past, present, and the future was crucial in affirming his choice of a major. The creation of a logical formula was needed by this student to implement a decision. Although this can be a frustrating and complex process, once this formula is developed, it may continue to serve as the backbone for career decision making for years.

IP Potential Pitfalls and Strategies

Like the EJs, the IPs also have some potential pitfalls. They may put off until tomorrow what needs to be done today. In an academic setting this may result in taking five years to complete a four-year program. Their extraverted auxiliary process (Sensing or Intuition) is continually drawing in new and interesting information. They may have a feeling that there is never enough information or time to explore all of the options. In fact when many of them do decide on a specific program of study, the advisor may have to support them while they mourn all of the majors they might have had.

Occasionally an advisee's dominant judgment process has not had an opportunity to develop. Their reliance on their auxiliary perception function without use of their dominant may cause problems requiring more in-depth assistance than an advisor can offer. (See Chapter 2 to understand the dynamics that may occur in this developmental pattern.) Of all the types, IPs and INFPs in particular, are reported to be the most frequent seekers of career assistance (Myers & McCaulley, 1985). When special advising programs are set up that provide opportunities for support and exploration, INFPs are often first in line to join. This high response by INFPs reflects their interest in programs focused on growth and development.

The same strategies and methods developed by IPs for the selection of a major might be used for other future decisions. Helping them to find a decision-making model that works for them is one of the most valuable advising activities. Lawrence's (1982) zig-zag decision-making model is easy to understand and helps students to use their strengths and weaknesses positively.

The zig-zag model begins with sensing. When presented with a problem, a natural beginning step is the gathering of concrete, relevant facts that can be validated through the senses. The second step is the intentional use of intuition. What do these data mean? What possibilities do they suggest? After intuition, thinking is engaged to analyze and evaluate the logical consequences of acting on the facts and possibilities. Finally we use our feeling to judge how these consequences will affect others, and the effect of the decision on interpersonal harmony and personal values. This model when applied step-by-step uses all four functions to achieve a more complete and informed decision. Feeling types respond positively to this approach because of the gestalt-like quality of the process, and Thinking types appreciate the logic in the model.

One of the difficulties many IPs have in selecting a major comes from distractions and preoccupations with other areas of student life. Thus many can benefit from learning time management and goal-setting strategies. For example one IP said that "to do" lists were frustrating to her. While many people said these lists freed them to work on matters of importance, she said lists were only physical manifestations of what she already knew. The problem, she said, was that the items on the "to do" lists swim around and things get accomplished as they come to the top regardless of their importance. Teaching IPs some simple strategies for goal setting and planning can help prevent a last-minute rush that may not reflect their talent and abilities. Advising on these matters can increase their ability to control the outer world that seems so demanding at times.

The IP, more than the other attitude combinations, may profit from a lower advisor/advisee ratio. They often are more confused about decision making and may need more time. More advising time is offered at the University of Maine through an advising program that utilizes faculty advisors, peer helpers, and a special residential program to be described later.

Introversion and Judgment: The Decisive Introverts

IJs are usually reflective, enduring, and tenacious about plans. Their Judgment function (T or F) is extraverted and auxiliary, while their Perception function (S or N) is introverted and dominant. IJs are likely to base their decisions about majors on a deep, solid accumulation of perceptions. Their depth of conviction may come from their enduring and persistent reflection about issues of concern to them.

The combination of the introverted dominant Perception function with extraverted Judgment often results in an advisee who appears decisive, yet prefers to reflect before acting. Thus they can feel confused if rushed to make a decision. Some IJs report a need for "worry time" when making important decisions. This "worry time" helps them work things out internally before they verbalize. Once something is verbalized, many IJs feel it should be adhered to. Time for reflection gives them a sense of completion and rightness, although this need for time (as with the IPs) can prolong the decision-making process.

IJs who are dominant Sensing types select a college major using common sense and practicality as their yardstick. They may ask themselves: Why should I major in Accounting? Is English going to land me a job?

IJs who are dominant Intuitives may evaluate a major by how well it helps them to achieve their dream or inner vision. They may ask themselves: Does this major provide me with a steady flow of interesting ideas in my life? Is the choice sufficiently complex and filled with opportunities?

Some IJs may appear to be both decisive and hesitant about the same issue. Their introversion encourages reflection and information gathering, while the extraverted judging auxiliary works for closure in the outer world. IJs preference for laying a solid foundation before finalizing decisions often results in a process that is frustratingly slow. Their dominant function, whether S or N, may overload them with perceptions that are conflicting or difficult to sort out. One ISTJ came to me in total confusion about what to select as a major. He was bewildered as to how to sort through all the papers he had collected. He had visited each academic department on campus and organized respective brochures and flyers neatly in cross-referenced folders. Like many ISJs, he had thought that gathering and organizing information was the same as understanding it. He had failed to see the trends and patterns among majors and was only focusing on discrete facts. IJs often are perceptual "sponges," and the advisor can serve an important role in helping them sort out what is really important in the decision-making process.

IJ students can benefit from a variety of strategies. Advisors can help them become aware of their style of making decisions. The zig-zag decision-making model can highlight their strong and weak points. Advisors can help them understand and trust their dominant function. Validation of the importance and the richness of the perceptions IJ students gather gives them new confidence in their decision making.

Extraversion and Perception: Adaptable Extraverts

EPs are characteristically energetic, sociable, adaptable, and searching for new experiences. EPs extravert their perceptive function (S or N) and introvert their judging function (T or F).

EP advisees generally have a wide breadth of interests in subjects, majors, and careers. They generally adapt to most advising approaches and respond enthusiastically. EPs at first appear to be decisive. Although EPs may decide quickly, they are likely to change when their dominant function (S or N) receives more information. These advisees are likely to come regularly into an advisor's office with a new major and/or changing academic interest. Within one week an ENFP advisee told me she had decided upon pre-law, physics, math, and psychology. It was no coincidence that she was also taking these courses during the current semester. ENPs' dominant function can cause them to be enchanted by and drawn to almost any new subject. Most majors hold an element of excitement, surprise, and fun. Although changing majors may cause concern for advisors, parents, and others, it is a very natural and comfortable trial-and-error process for EPs. For many EPs, decisions are not particularly things to live with, but ways of responding immediately to the world.

EP Potential Pitfalls and Strategies

At their worst, Extraverted Intuitives can appear to be "in the clouds," unrealistic, scattered, and changeable in selecting a major. Occasionally unrealistic views of themselves and a major/career can result in the development and nourishment of an inflated notion of their own skills and the demands of a particular major/career. Realistic perceptions can be encouraged by such activities as simply examining a college catalog that describes course requirements, or through interaction with a professor who is demanding of them. For example, an ENFP advisee may take a basic math course and be challenged by the professor to be accurate and use a step-by-step process. This experience can help the ENFP realistically evaluate his/her skill related to this learning activity. While the ENPs may idealize the future, the extraverted Sensing types (ESPs) may fail to consider sufficiently the long-range impact of their decisions about a major. They tend to value short-term results. For example, a student may decide to join the military, but fail to consider how it might impact a family in a few years. The advisor can help this student think through his/her decision by probing the effect of this decision on the future.

Helping EPs through the decision-making process can be one of the most challenging activities for any advisor. While IPs may decide silently, and the EJs may act decisively and firmly, the EP may decide with fanfare, only to change soon after. EPs can truly benefit from the traditional values clarification exercises that many academic advisors use. These exercises challenge them in a fun, playful way to develop their introverted auxiliary judging process while learning to prioritize. They can also benefit by setting deadlines for gathering information. A peer with a dominant judging function can be a useful model; these students can be encouraged to work together.

A word of caution seems appropriate at this time about strategies and approaches academic advisors can use in working with students. Most advisors are not trained as psychologists or therapists. Academic advisors should use their skills in advising and their interest in type as a way to help students conceptualize their decision-making process, and make course selections. Advisors should refer those students to counseling or other appropriate professionals when students appear to have needs which go beyond this advising process.

The following program was designed for freshmen, applying the type patterns just described. The program reflects an integration of type theory, student development theory, and environmental management in the provision of advising to students.

Arts and Science in KNOX (ASK): A Model Advising Program

Some programs and services for advising students have too narrow a focus or approach. The multifaceted program described here attempts to impact the total development of first-year college students. The program is based on the assumption that entering students need a balance between challenge and support (see Chapter 4 on Designing Residential Environments). The designers of the ASK program assume that the residence hall environment is a logical place to address the notion of balancing challenge and support.

ASK was created in the spring of 1983 through the joint efforts of the Department of Residential Life and the College of Arts and Science at the University of Maine. The program was recognized in 1983 by the American College Personnel Associations Commission III as one of the "outstanding residence programs" across the country.

The course goals include: helping students think through why they came to college; providing information about prospective careers and majors; establishing positive advisor-advisee relationships; and using the course to identify potential academic and motivational problems.

Students who take the course are assigned to live together on the same wing of a residence hall. They are assigned to roommates using the complementary strategy in Chapter 4. Students share the same advisor, a common course, a similar roommate and a supportive environment. This approach along with a supportive liberal arts faculty encourages students to use their perception and judgment for good decision making. Students are encouraged in the ASK program to use the first few years of college to gather information (perception) about programs of study and careers.

The success of the FSA class is discussed in Gershman, Anchors, Dryfus, and Robbins (1986). They reported that undecided students participating in the course showed statistically significant progress towards selection of a major after one semester.

Using Type in Guiding Course Selection

The MBTI can be used to help students select a beneficial course load for the academic term. Students need to achieve a balance in the kinds of courses and work load selected in any one term. Examples of course selection issues are: amount of reading required, labs, assigned papers, and teaching format (lecture, discussion, independent study). Students' types should be considered along with interests and abilities. Examples of some of the considerations follow.

Reading

Courses can vary considerably in the amount of reading required. Examples of subjects typically requiring more reading are literature, history, and philosophy. The student who is a slow reader and the student who does not enjoy reading may suffer academically if he or she schedules more than one or two of these courses a term. Myers (1980) pointed out that reading involves translating symbols, and that this process seems to be easiest for Introverts with Intuition. Introverted Intuitive students are generally more comfortable with a heavy load of reading assignments than many of the other types.

For example, Extraverted Sensing students' natural orientation towards action in the practical world may cause the world of words and symbols to be less appealing. ES students may need to consider the amount of reading they can comfortably do in a semester, and the importance of balancing reading and lecture courses with action-oriented courses with labs, discussions, field work, etc. See Chapter 9 for additional information on reading and type.

Writing

With the current emphasis on improving writing skills of students, it is likely that most advisees will be taking courses that stress writing. Research by Jensen and DiTiberio (1983) indicated that the MBTI preferences influence approaches to writing and the nature of writing difficulties. Chapter 9 gives clear examples for the types. The amount and nature of writing required in specific courses should be considered in helping plan academic schedules for different types of students.

Discussion/High Participation

Discussion-centered classes and those requiring active participation and presentation tend to appeal more to certain types than to others. Extraverts often thrive on this kind of learning environment. Some Introverts may find these classes stressful. The advisor can help the student evaluate the learning environment of various classes to make balanced selection. *The goal should not be to avoid all challenges to one's type, but rather to achieve a balance between the number of classes that challenge development of less-preferred areas with courses that allow further development of one's natural strengths and preferences.*

Lectures

Lecture classes may be the mainstay of many students' educational experience. Lectures offer Introverts the opportunity to be quietly receptive and digest material being presented. Morgan (1977) found that Introverts in particular preferred the lecture format because it gave an opportunity to sort things out within themselves. Extraverts may become restless and have difficulty holding their concentration in lecture courses unless these are balanced with more participatory forms of learning.

Knowing the impact of different kinds of classes on different types of students can help advisors guide students in choosing a realistic course load. Of course, caution must be used in applying these general type tendencies to individual students, since there may be wide variations due to degree of type development, previous educational experiences, and so forth. Course selection should consider students' preferences and also challenge development of the other functions and attitudes.

Summary

The MBTI can help the advising process in a variety of ways. It can serve as a useful tool in understanding how students view the college environment, how they gather and process information about course selection and related areas, and how they make important decisions about majors and careers. Knowledge of type can assist advisors in developing rapport with their advisees. Undoubtedly students will feel more relaxed and open if such a relationship is characterized by a sense of understanding.

Developmental advising as emphasized here focuses on understanding students from their own perspective and offers them an appropriate balance of challenge and support so that they can learn to use their unique talents and abilities.

References

Anchors, S., Gershman, E., & Robbins, M. (in press). *Developmental and personality-type differences among first year undecided and decided college students.* Manuscript submitted for publication.

Anchors, S. (1985). Unpublished research, University of Maine, Orono, ME.

Gershman, E., Anchors, S., Dreyfus & Robbins, M. (1986). The effects of differential programming on undecided first year college students. *College Student Affairs Journal, 6,* 39–39.

Gordon, V. (1981). The undecided student: A developmental perspective. *Personnel and Guidance Journal, 59,* 433–439.

Gordon, V., & Carberry, J. (1984). The Myers-Briggs Type Indicator: A resource for developmental advising. *NADADA Journal, 2,* 75–81.

Jensen, G., & DiTiberio, J. (1983). The MBTI and writing blocks. *MBTI News, 5,* 14–15.

Lawrence, G. (1982). *People types and tiger stripes: A practical guide to learning styles.* Gainesville, FL: Center for Applications of Psychological Type.

Laney, A. (1949). *Occupational implications of the Jungian personality function types as identified by Myers-Briggs Type Indicator.* Unpublished master's thesis, George Washington University, Washington, DC.

McCaulley, M. H. (1981). *Applications of the Myers-Briggs Type Indicator to medicine and other health professions—Monograph I.* Gainesville, FL: Center for Applications of Psychological Type.

Morgan, M. (1977). Relating type to instructional strategies. In G. Lawrence, *People types and tiger stripes: A practical guide to learning styles,* (52–53). Gainesville, FL: Center for Applications of Psychological Type.

Myers, I. B. (1980). *Gifts differing.* Palo Alto, CA: Consulting Psychologists Press.

Myers, I. B., & McCaulley, M. H. (1985). *Manual: A guide to the development and use of the Myers-Briggs Type Indicator.* Palo Alto, CA: Consulting Psychologists Press.

Otis, G. (1972). *Types of medical students* (Contract No. 71-4066). USPHS, National Institute of Health.

Winston, R. Jr., Miller, T., & Prince, J. (1979). *Assessing student development: A preliminary manual for the Student Development Task Inventory* (2nd ed.). Athens, GA: Student Development Associates.

JUDITH A. PROVOST, Ed.D., is a psychotherapist, writer, and trainer who has incorporated MBTI concepts in her work for the past 13 years. She currently is Director of Personal Counseling at Rollins College and is on the faculties of the Center for Applications of Psychological Type and the Association for Psychological Type. Her research interests in higher education have resulted in several journal articles and a dissertation, "Personality type and leisure satisfaction as factors in college attrition." Other books by Judy are *A Casebook: Applications of the Myers-Briggs Type Indicator in Counseling* (CAPT) and *The Freshman Year—Stress or Success* (PPI). As Chair of the Council for Communication and Education of APT, she sits on the executive board; she also serves as Chair of the Ethics Committee of APT. Her education includes an undergraduate degree from the University of Connecticut, graduate degrees from the University of California at Los Angeles and University of Florida, and extensive training with the Gestalt Institute of Florida. She is an ENFP.

124

CHAPTER 7

Psychological Counseling

JUDITH A. PROVOST

WITHIN COLLEGES AND universities, there has been an increasing use of the MBTI by counseling professionals. Use by counselors and counseling centers includes outreach, education, consultation, research, prevention, and treatment/intervention. The term "counselor" is used here in the generic sense to include all professionals involved in psychological counseling. Many professionals work within counseling centers, but some are found in less traditional organizational divisions within institutions of higher education. Although organizational structures suggest differing strategies for setting up and implementing programs using the MBTI, the basic processes and programs described here have relevance, no matter what the institutional structure.

This chapter begins by showing how the MBTI fits within the counseling process, and continues with a detailed description of one counseling office's program. Counselors should get an overview of the range of MBTI uses and hopefully be stimulated to further applications. Within the counseling process, the MBTI is used as a tool for establishing rapport, understanding a variety of student problems, setting goals for counseling, and designing interventions or strategies. The description of a comprehensive program using the MBTI, developed by the author while director of Personal Counseling at Rollins College, includes: initiation of the program, procedures for administration and interpretation, identification of potential adjustment concerns through early outreach, developmental considerations, and MBTI uses beyond that of direct counseling.

MBTI Use in Counseling/Therapy

The MBTI as a Conceptual Framework

The MBTI provides a language for student and counselor to discuss strengths, preferences for dealing with the world and one's inner life, less-preferred or weaker areas, communication patterns, and so forth. If the concepts are explained accurately and ethically, this language is an objective or neutral one. The objectivity of the Indicator gives both parties a comfortable reference point from which to look at the student's present life and personal development. These concepts can be referred to throughout the course of counseling. Students will use MBTI concepts to varying degrees depending on their type and priorities. For example, Intuitives generally want to work with the theory more extensively than the Sensing types.

The MBTI validates the individual. When students already have a fairly good sense of who they are, their MBTI results are often experienced as a triumphant restatement of themselves. When students are somewhat unclear about themselves, the MBTI provides a language to explore aspects of themselves that previously were too elusive to name. The MBTI can also validate students' tentative life decisions. If the MBTI is interpreted properly, students invariably go away feeling better about themselves, whether they have further counseling sessions or not.

The MBTI is a conceptual framework which makes a useful map of individual type development. This map indicates preferred and least-preferred functions and the probable sequence of function development. Therefore, this map can guide counselors in assessing functioning and in setting counseling goals consistent with where students are developmentally and with where they are likely to go in their future development.

Multiple Uses in Counseling/Therapy

One of the most valuable applications of type is in counseling new students about adjustment to college. This topic is explored later under the discussion of outreach to freshmen. Another frequent application is self-exploration and personal growth through individual counseling. Students are eager for self-knowledge, and the MBTI is one tool to assist in this process.

Understanding communication patterns of various types is valuable in relationship counseling. Intimacy is one of the critical developmental tasks of the traditional student. Counseling frequently focuses on relationships with roommates, boy/girlfriends, close friends, and groups such as one's sorority or fraternity, as well as with family members. A student's type can be discussed in relation to family conflicts and communication patterns. Often students' families are too distant to participate in family counseling, but through use of *Introduction to Type* (Myers, 1987), *Please Understand Me* (Keirsey & Bates, 1984), other materials, and discussions, students may be able to estimate family members' types. Knowing there are 16 different types with different ways of communicating and approaching issues is a revelation to most young people. Students are often locked into struggles with their families for independence and for their own identities. They are relieved and encouraged by these insights about type. Even when students can't be certain what types their families are, they often acquire a new sensitivity and respect for personality differences. They may be able to look at emotional conflicts in a more objective way. The MBTI thus becomes a tool to improve communication, with the counselor serving as coach and guide.

Counselors employ the MBTI when helping students with self-management. Many students seek help in managing their time and learning to set priorities. They also may lack confidence in making decisions for themselves and need assistance in developing decision-making skills. *Introduction to Type* (Myers, 1987) has a clear description of the importance of using all four functions in making decisions. Counselors can use this description and other strategies based on MBTI concepts to teach this skill. Procrastination and work paralysis, when the student can't function because of fear that the outcome will not be perfect, are other counseling problems where the MBTI can shed some light on the individual's personality dynamics.

Another group of students who seek counseling do so not because of college adjustment problems per se, but because of emotional problems of a more serious nature. Depression, severe anxiety, tension, and acute crises are frequently seen problems. Knowing a student's type suggests possible personality dynamics and strengths that may be engaged by the counselor in the therapeutic process. Type can also suggest counseling approaches and language that may be effective in working with clients.

The term "language" here means word choice, use of metaphor, selection of images and content, and style of speaking. For example, an ESTJ client will relate better to a concrete and concise description of the counseling process with specific examples of what the counselor will do and specified outcomes. An INFP client might be put off by such "language" and prefer a description with a broader, more abstract picture of what might be accomplished in counseling.

Type may suggest areas to probe to determine underlying problems; for example, exploring the quality of a young depressed INTP's intimate relationships. An INTP might not initially reveal relationship concerns; these deeper concerns might not be admitted to the counselor until after many sessions. Certain types are more likely to present specific behaviors when under emotional stress. For example, the EPs may become very excitable and even hysterical in behavior. Space does not permit a more detailed discussion of types and presenting problems in psychotherapy, nor is there a need to duplicate existing materials in print. The chapter references cite these additional resources.

The Counseling Process

MBTI concepts should be brought into the counseling process at the appropriate time, in accordance with a student's needs and readiness. Unless a student has made an appointment expressly to learn about the MBTI, the first counseling session (in the author's practice) is usually one of establishing rapport, gathering information about why the student has sought counseling at this time, and beginning to set some counseling goals. The MBTI is not usually introduced until the second or even later sessions, when it fits into the counseling process. Counselors may have access to students' scores from previous group administration, yet not introduce the MBTI explicitly in counseling. For example, when a student presents a crisis with no expressed interest in counseling beyond solving his/her immediate problem, the counselor may formulate hunches about the student's coping style and possible interventions without explicit mention of the MBTI. Students in crisis or in a fragile state of mind are not asked to take the MBTI; later when they have stabilized, they may take the MBTI if it seems relevant to the counseling process.

If counselors refer to MBTI results obtained several years earlier, they should keep in mind that some students will report change in one or more preferences during their college years. The MBTI *Manual* (Myers & McCaulley, 1985) gives test-retest reliabilities for the four scales and also reports various studies of how many preferences students changed over varying periods of time.

Counselors should explore with students, especially those who had reported slight (1–9) or mild (11–19) preferences, whether they see themselves as the type they reported several years earlier. The basic strategies for establishing "true type" are discussed in the *Manual* and may be employed in these situations.

The 16 types have varying expectations about counseling. Goals and duration of counseling vary also. Over a 10-year period in the author's counseling office, the following general tendencies have been observed:

- The SJs often expect direct intervention and advice from the counselor, who is perceived as the authority and expert. They usually want to complete counseling in a few sessions, unless there is a long-term problem such as an ISFJ with chronic depression. The ESJs are most likely to expect concrete suggestions and a brisk pace.

- The INPs frequently are vague in their expectations and goals but hope that counselors will be patient and take time to help them articulate their thoughts. Instead of looking to the counselor as an authority, they tend to need a guide to help them search out the internal and external meanings. They may be put off by too directive a counselor.

- The NTs tend to watch for signs of competence in the counselor before trusting the relationship. They are skeptical of the counseling process unless the counselor can speak their language and explain the process in terms of logic and expertise.

Many other observations can be made; the point is that different types tend to have different attitudes and expectations about counseling, no matter what the presenting problem. Counselors must make their best efforts to join with students and talk the language of their types, almost as if the counselor "acts" like each student's type. This joining facilitates rapport and trust and assures that counseling goals are appropriate to the student, not just to the counselor. Counselors, and other helping professionals as well, have a built-in bias about what being helpful is all about because of their own types. ENFP counselors tend to talk about counseling in terms of change, self-actualization, connecting with people, etc. The MBTI is a good reminder to counselors that their vision of the world is not the *only* vision. Counselors must guard against imposing their standards of mental health and positive outcomes on their clients. On the other hand, once counselors have joined with students and counseling is progressing, counselors can gradually pull back somewhat to their own style and encourage students to experiment with their less-preferred functions. Where the counselor and student are very different in their preferences, the student may become discouraged about changing in the direction suggested by the counselor. The counselor's behavior may seem too far from where the student is, too far to reach. Counselors need to remember this in modeling behaviors such as assertiveness with clients very different from themselves.

The basic principle remains: start with the client's strengths and work from there. After a few small successes, counselors can then begin to challenge and encourage use of the other functions, working toward a goal of balance between the dominant and auxiliary, and ability to use the function necessary in a given situation. Of course, the latter goal is one that will probably extend long past the counseling experience and perhaps well into middle age.

Examples of Counseling Strategies and Type

College students, especially Intuitives, tend to be overly intellectual and prone to rationalization. Often they try to keep counseling interaction on this level. Therefore, it can be quite productive to use some noncognitive and perhaps nonverbal interventions with them, *after* trust has developed. Gestalt and body work are examples of interventions which may serve to cut through the layer of intellectualization.

Feeling types may need to learn how to use their Thinking function to balance their reactions and decisions. Rational Emotive Therapy or Brief Therapy can offer them a model for developing their Thinking. Again, cautiously introduce these interventions, or the student will be turned off by the "cold, impersonal approach."

Many students have difficulty making decisions and using their Thinking and Feeling judgments. Values clarification strategies; guided imagery such as visualizing "the wise old one who knows"; Gendlin's (1981) focusing technique for inner awareness; and writing assignments are examples of ways to help students access their Thinking and/or Feeling. Counselors should keep in mind whether the function they are trying to encourage is extraverted or introverted, because these functions work differently in these two attitudes. Therefore, the strategies would vary as well. For example, journal writing would be a useful way for a busy ENFP to access the introverted auxiliary Feeling. The student trying to develop extraverted Feeling might prefer some activity involving others in some helpful or expressive way or an "assignment" to request feedback from specific individuals.

A majority of counselors are Intuitives (Myers & McCaulley, 1985) and often favor strategies requiring abstraction and imagination, such as guided fantasy, dream interpretation, and metaphor. When working with Sensing students, counselors should introduce their favorite strategies cautiously, so as not to create more confusion in the student. An ISTJ, for example, has a dominant and introverted Sensing function, and the least-preferred function is Intuition. Using guided imagery to help this student work through some difficult problem might increase confusion and instability because the imagery demands use of the least-preferred function. That function might be quite primitive and emerge in a frightening or exaggerated way. Introverted Sensing is a fascinating and difficult function for Intuitives, especially extraverted Intuitives, to grasp. ISJs and ESJs may respond well to a kind of guided "trip" which is more carefully structured with concrete, sequential instructions so that the student plays out sensory impressions and memories like a projector showing an internal film. This can be a rich experience for the student, yet one where the richness cannot be captured through verbalization. Counselors need to respect the nonverbal quality of the client's experience and not assume that the lack of verbal production indicates a minimal response to the intervention.

In summary, counselors need a repertoire of strategies to work effectively with a variety of students and to stretch students to use not only their favorite function but their less-preferred ones as well. Also counselors need to be alert to the bias of their own type in the selection of counseling goals and strategies.

Suggested Research About Counseling and Type

Numerous studies can be designed to examine aspects of the counseling process, student adjustment and mental health, and type. These projects usually require institutional support and certainly necessitate preservation of students' confidentiality. The following are some basic research questions other counselor-researchers have begun to address, but which need further study and replication.

- Is there a relationship between type and presenting problem?

- Is there a relationship between type and number of sessions seen for counseling?

- Are certain interventions preferred and more effective with certain types?

- Is there a relationship between type and outcomes, perceived and actual, of counseling?

- Do students' types influence their selection of specific counselors and/or other student service assistance?

One Comprehensive Program Using the MBTI

The following pages will describe the comprehensive program for using the MBTI developed by the author through the personal counseling office at a private, residential, four-year, liberal arts college in Winter Park, Florida. Rollins College has an approximate enrollment of 1400 and a traditional student body (ages 17–22). The positive nature of the Indicator and its focus on preferred ways of functioning make the Indicator a versatile tool for education about individual differences, personal and academic adjustment, and counseling intervention.

Beginning a Program for All Entering Freshmen

After using the MBTI with individual students in personal and career counseling for a number of years, it became apparent that a more systematic administration of the Indicator would be valuable to the college. The frequency of types on the campus and within certain subgroups would then be known. Faculty and staff were not likely to attempt changes in the campus environment without data such as type distributions of specific student groups. There was campus-wide concern about reducing the attrition rate and identifying factors influencing students' withdrawal from the college. Previous attrition research had focused on traditional variables, such as SAT scores, distance from home, and nature of the high school attended. None had examined personality factors; the MBTI might identify significant variables. Furthermore, the counseling office could operate more effectively if it had students' MBTI results on file before students requested counseling.

This background illustrates the attitude and prevailing climate in which the proposal was made to administer the MBTI to the entering freshman class during orientation week. The proposal necessitated a budget increase to finance the MBTI materials and scoring. The proposal also necessitated some accommodation in the scheduling of orientation activities. The proposal was made to the chief student affairs officer and to the president of the college. This expanded use of the MBTI was presented as a way to determine what, if any, personality factors influenced attrition patterns. If research revealed a relationship between type patterns and attrition, counselors and other college staff could institute preventive measures. The well-documented uses of the MBTI as a tool for improving reading and study skills and guiding career decisions were emphasized. At this writing, the MBTI has been administered to the freshman class for seven consecutive years.

Other professionals seeking to administer the MBTI to a student body should determine carefully their institution's needs and word their proposals to address those needs. It is useful to include some research data from other institutions demonstrating the validity of the MBTI approach.

Procedures for Administration of the MBTI

Orientation week was chosen for freshmen to take the MBTI because there is no other time when the whole class is easily convened. Plans to convene the class later in the semester would result in a much lower percentage of participation. Other schools may have large freshman classes or other events which could be opportunities for administration. The MBTI is given along with several short placement tests and the national ACE survey. Form F was used the first few years, and form G in subsequent years. About 45 minutes is allowed for answering the questions. Students may take longer if needed.

In two large auditoriums, the counselors introduce the MBTI and counseling services. Freshmen are told that information from the Indicator can be helpful to them in adjusting to college, developing appropriate study techniques, selecting courses and an academic major, exploring careers, and gaining more knowledge about themselves. Students are told that their results will be released to them only and will be kept on file in the counseling office until such time as they make appointments to go over their results. These two points, the usefulness of the information to them and the confidentiality of results, are important to stress in obtaining full cooperation. The standardized instructions on the question booklet are reviewed.

Some students miss this group administration. Transfer students and others take the MBTI on an individual basis as needed through the counseling or career/placement offices. Other students want to retake the MBTI during their four years at the college. These answer sheets are hand scored, in contrast to the group sheets which are computer scored.

Procedures for Interpretation

The counseling office sends out a memo to each freshman after the MBTI has been computer scored. The memos invite students to make appointments at their convenience to learn their results. They are told that their results will be held on file in the counseling office while they are students at the college. The usefulness of MBTI information is restated in the memo. A similar memo is sent to all faculty freshman advisors to inform them that their advisees may benefit from making an appointment with the counseling office to review their results. Advisors may find this step especially helpful in working with advisees with academic difficulties or questions about career directions. Several other key student services staff are notified when the scores are available: those in the learning skills center, career and placement center, and academic advising. This outreach increases the visibility of the counseling office to the faculty and other student personnel and encourages referrals. The procedure remains the same; students working with these other staff must call the counseling office to request that their resultsbe given to the appropriate professional. Because results are kept confidential, they are never given out to faculty, staff, or others without a student's request or persmission.

During the first two months after freshmen receive the memo, appointment requests are very heavy, then taper off. The counseling staff is usually able to provide individual interpretation time of approximately 45 minutes. At the very busy times students are given the choice of joining up to three other students in receiving their results. This small group obviously cuts down on individual time, but is a realistic way to deal with peak demand. The basic concepts are explained to the small group and a few minutes spent on each computer printout. Students are told that they can return for individual follow-up appointments if they would like a more personal and in-depth discussion. Students do not object to this approach and seem to enjoy this informal way to be with several other new students.

Many students do not seek their results until the sophomore year when there is more pressure to declare a major and a career direction. Some wait until their senior year, hoping their MBTI results may give them some idea about how to conduct a job search. Although it may sound like an onerous task to offer interpretation to all freshmen, in reality a large percentage will not make appointments immediately.

Those who do make appointments early in their college career often have a need to make this contact with the counseling office or other student services. There may be hidden agendas or needs beyond obtaining results. Counselors can take the opportunity to explore this possibility. These interpretation appointments give new students a legitimate reason for meeting with a counselor. Appointments are voluntary, not compulsory.

Because the MBTI gives students an easy reason for scheduling an appointment with a counselor, the MBTI program is an excellent outreach device. Another aspect of the outreach is the opportunity to explain the various student services during the appointment. At Rollins this means clarifying the role of personal counselors and giving examples of how they work with students. Other services emphasized are the learning and study skills center, career and placement services, and faculty advisors. Additional college resources can be identified as appropriate. After years of use with college students, counselors become practiced in stressing certain services and information for different MBTI types. Certain types are more likely to have difficulties in given areas, and these can be checked out directly or indirectly as appropriate. In the following section these difficulties are described.

Identifying Potential Adjustment Concerns in New Students

Student development literature describes the psychological, social, and academic tasks of college students, 17–22 years of age. These tasks will differ for the nontraditional, older students. Chapter 2 highlighted developmental issues which provide a context for using the MBTI with college students. There is variation within this developmental pattern, and some of this variation can be explained by personality type differences. After 10 years of observing types on a residential campus and comparing observations with those of counselors on other campuses, some general tendencies the author has observed among types can be noted. The term "general tendencies" is used to mean a set of behaviors more likely to be seen in a specific type than in others, but the term does not mean that certain types *will* have certain adjustment difficulties. Knowing some of these tendencies towards specific adjustment concerns can signal areas to explore in initial counseling sessions, information and resources to offer students, and directions for preventive programming. Some observations for each of the 16 types follow, many of which may be more accurate for the traditional than the older student.

ISTJ

The ISTJs (and ESTJs) are less frequently seen for counseling than many of the other types. Freshman ISTJs who do seek counseling are often concerned about academic performance. Some have expressed perfectionist attitudes about the need to get all A's to consider themselves successful. Others have been extremely frustrated that study techniques employed in high school do not bring desired results with the more abstract, theoretical material in college. Much of the evaluation in college is through papers and essay tests. Most ISTJs report being more comfortable with objective tests and homework problems. These freshmen may study most of the night, memorizing material and painstakingly outlining the text. They study slowly and methodically; they often complain of insufficient time to handle a full course load and be as thorough as they feel they need to be. Those who do not seek counseling have probably adapted their style to the college's requirements, but may need assistance in learning new study approaches and techniques for handling essay tests. The college writing lab can provide support to students like these ISTJs who may be anxious about writing papers. Counseling also includes cognitive restructuring of some of the perfectionist self-talk; for example, "I am a failure if I don't get all A's."

ISTP

The ISTPs who come to the counseling office in their freshman year usually do so in crisis. They express initial concerns about making new friends and fitting in. In counseling they often report difficulty managing their time, getting homework done, handling semester-long assignments, and reading abstract material. They tend to be easily distracted by outside events and other students. This type is one of several that seems to have more difficulty in the four-year liberal arts setting. Those who receive early assistance with time management and study skills and emotional support during the freshman transition seem to do better. They also express a need for recreational and social activities on an informal scale and may shy away from large, highly organized student activities and events. Meaningful extracurricular activities seem crucial to their social adjustment to college.

ESTP

Few ESTPs seek counseling. Some are very curious about their MBTI results because of questions about career direction. For example, after half a term in college, several pre-med students began questioning whether they had the stamina and self-discipline to handle the heavy science and math load. They found the MBTI a helpful framework for exploring their strengths and their goals. ESTPs may also need help with time management and study skills. If they receive some help with goal setting, immediate and long range, they are more likely to be successful in college.

ESTJ

Like the other ST types, ESTJs are not frequently seen for counseling. They do welcome the MBTI information as part of their need to set career and academic goals early in their college careers. Occasionally they are too hasty in formulating these goals without first sampling a variety of courses and learning more about the work world. They tend to be methodical in their studies, like the ISTJs, but usually work faster than the ISTJs. Some help in adjusting to abstract material, written papers, and essay tests may be needed.

ISFJ

Many ISFJs come to the counseling office during their freshman year. They explicitly name concerns about adjusting to the academic life and the separation from home and friends. They, along with the ESFJs, seem to express homesickness more frequently than the other types. Many ISFJs seen in counseling are nonassertive, dependent, and unsure of themselves. These students compare themselves unfavorably with their classmates, thinking they may be "too dumb" to be there. They often have trouble communicating their likes and dislikes to roommates. They seem to struggle more than many of the other types with the transition from dependence to independence. They may be looking for a surrogate parent in the counselor or upperclass resident aide. Emotional support, education about the transition phase (especially focused on moving toward independence), assertiveness training, and other such interventions are well received by these students who are highly motivated to become more comfortable with themselves at college. Since their study approaches tend to be as slow and methodical as the ISTJs, they may need some guidance with study techniques, especially with reading.

ISFP

Freshman ISFPs may have difficulty adjusting to the academic load. Their new friendships and social activities usually take precedence over studying. A comfortable social environment is a top priority before they are willing to invest in academic work. Like the ISTPs, they often need assistance with time management and study skills. They may be alienated by NT professors who do not demonstrate personal warmth and interest. Their motivations are personal; for example, they may be more concerned about failing because of the great disappointment they will cause their parents than from any desire to achieve for themselves intellectually. Counselors can help them identify valid motivators for achieving in college. Counselors can also assist them to select courses with content of personal significance to them and taught by professors who will stimulate them through a personal approach.

ESFP

Few ESFPs make appointments during the first term to learn their MBTI results or for personal counseling. Many young ESFPs on campus have told the author that when they feel "down," they go do something to cheer themselves up or talk to a friend. They don't often consider counseling as a primary solution. These students seem to rely primarily on friends for advice about academics and problems of living. Sometimes professors, frequently Feeling types, have great impact in a mentor or helper role. The ESFPs who do come for counseling during the freshman year usually are struggling with some relationship concern, family or boy/girlfriend. They have difficulty focusing on schoolwork when their relationships are not in harmony. Although many young ESFP students could probably use some techniques in study and time management, their interests and motivations often seem more focused on social adjustment and involvement. They feel they can "get by" academically and generally have confidence that "things will turn out fine."

ESFJ

More ESFJs than ESFPs use the counseling office. They seem to take their "responsibilities" as students more seriously and therefore are more quick to want to "fix" problems and improve their position than the ESFPs. Many of their initial concerns at college involve social adjustment. Getting along with roommates and friends and working out conflicts are essential. Many may struggle overtly with letting go of family and the security of home. They need to ventilate feelings about home and friends left behind and receive support for their feelings. They respond well to information about the developmental stage of leaving home. They may also wish some guidance on course selection and modifying study techniques. Because they tend to be conscientious about doing the best work they can, they can become very frustrated if they don't do as well as they "should" do. A predominance of lecture and abstract courses the first few terms of college can discourage the ESFJ learner. A balanced course load, with some discussion classes and personally meaningful material, is more compatible with the ESFJ learning style.

INFJ

Some general patterns seem to hold for all the IN types. They use the counseling office more than the other types. Their concerns tend to certain themes, with some variation because of the other two preferences. IN freshmen are likely to express a lot of doubt about who they are, why they are at college, whether this is the right college for them, whether they will *ever* find a meaningful relationship with the opposite sex, and so on.

The inner world of INFJs is rich and complex because of dominant, introverted Intuition. They need opportunity to express that inner world to a supportive, interested counselor; this may be their first experience in articulating that inner world. Through expression, INFJs can hear and modify any distortions or inner constructions not founded in reality.

In counseling, INFJ males raised with traditional gender roles are often trying to distinguish family values, especially those of the father, from their own values. If the father has lived the traditional male role and has expected this of the son, the student may be confused about internal glimpses of personal values that don't seem to fit with the father's. The counselor can use values clarification to explore identity issues, goal formation, and career planning. Some of these INFJ males may have interests in design, languages, and the arts. These interests may have been discouraged by family as being "impractical" and "feminine."

If the INFJs are comfortable with themselves, they do not usually need help with academic adjustment.

INFP

Some have called the prime dilemma of the young INFP "working through the existential pain of aloneness." INFPs frequently have many unanswerable questions. They relate well to a counselor who acts as a guide, not an advice giver. Their search is spiritual, social (finding an authentic relationship), and idealistic (a career they can believe in). If their lives are too caught up in their inner realities and questioning, they may have trouble focusing on studies. Organization may be a problem. Like INTPs, they may have serious problems with procrastination. Coming from high school where many assignments were on a daily or short-term basis, the self-directed term-long assignments can create a difficult adjustment. Completing term papers on time tends to be one of the biggest problems. Compounding this procrastination is a kind of perfectionism in which the INFPs have set such high personal standards and expectations for themselves that it is hard to write the first line of a paper. That first line is never good enough, and what if the paper isn't "brilliant"? Although serious procrastination may be spotted in these students early in their freshman year, they may not be ready to engage in efforts to change this pattern until later in their college careers when they have become very tired of this repetitive and destructive pattern. Often it is their professors who make this later referral to the counseling office. Of course, not all INFPs have a problem with procrastination. The more developed the two functions, N and F, and the more balance between them, the less likely there will be a problem with procrastination. In any case, many INFPs make contact with the counseling office early in their college career because of these kinds of issues. They are usually eager to work in counseling, but may need some help articulating the issues because of the vagueness of their searchings and inner questionings.

ENFP

The INFPs and ENFPs are the most frequent types in the student body at Rollins College and at many other liberal arts colleges. ENFPs are generally comfortable with the notion of talking with a counselor. As new students they may face problems with personal organization, focus, the social environment, and new relationships. A common pattern is ENFP freshmen who think they have their academic and career goals set but quickly change their minds the first term. For example, like the ESTPs, they may start a pre-med program and after a few months question whether they have the motivation to do all the sciences and math. They feel like they are "missing out" on the social life of the college because of being in labs "all the time." Their parents are displeased that they want to change from pre-med to English. They want to live up to their parents' expectations and please parents and professors, yet their social needs are also very important. They may feel torn or at least confused. ENFPs may be interested in so many academic and career areas that they have difficulty focusing, and many bounce from one goal to another. They can benefit from early discussions about goals and from comprehensive career counseling later in the freshman year or early in the sophomore year. They may need help in setting priorities among academic and social demands. They may take on too many extracurricular activities before they have gotten a handle on their academics. If they are "burning the candle at both ends," they are likely to develop illnesses such as mononucleosis, strep throat, and colds. ENFPs are often so busy focusing outside themselves that they don't pay attention to internal stimuli about their own physical state. Through counseling they can learn to identify early signs of overload.

ENFJ

ENFJs, with their organized approach, generally take the academic side of college more seriously than ENFPs. When they seek counseling in their freshman year, it is usually because of social adjustment or family concerns, not academic adjustment. Some of the ENFJ female students may express unhappiness at the "meat market" mentality of some males at the large "keg" parties. Their values about authentic relationships and the need to be respected by the opposite sex may be in conflict with parts of the social environment. They may need help in clarifying their concerns and in finding other social outlets and ways of forming relationships. If they are having difficulties settling in at college, they may have unresolved family concerns, such as mediating between two parents in a nonfunctional marriage. There may be a pull to be home where they can "help." ENFJs who seek counseling for family problems eagerly work for change and better understanding.

INTJ

The INTJs tend to have many of the seeking/questioning and perfectionist characteristics often found in the other INs, but seem less patient with themselves than the other INs. They want closure and some measures of progress. They seem to take their performance, whether in social leadership or in academics, more seriously than any of the other types. They are often impatient with themselves for their internal questioning, which they see as getting in the way of their performance. Mastery and competence are high values; measurement of these values through grades, athletic accomplishments, etc. is demanded of themselves. These themes and the resulting inner conflicts may not emerge in the freshman year. As freshmen they may buckle down to serious studying and not allow themselves "the luxury" of focusing on questions of meaning, identity, and so forth, until these questions later force themselves into the foreground. As freshmen they may be concerned that their peers at college are not serious enough about academics and don't live principled lives ("too much superficial partying," etc.). If they judge their peers in this way, they may become alienated. They need to gain a better understanding of their own type and that of others. As a group, they have the highest grade point average of all the types at the college, and have the profile most like that of the faculty. Although often academically successful, they may be struggling with relationship issues or intrapersonal conflicts.

INTP

The INTPs are more likely to make an appointment to learn their MBTI results than to talk about a personal concern. Since they tend to value independence and to believe they can puzzle out issues on their own, they are less prone to seek ongoing counseling. They are often very curious about their MBTI results. This contact for MBTI interpretation is a good opportunity to build a relationship for the future, when personal concerns may cause them to remember the earlier positive experience with the counselor. INTPs, like the other INs, have many complex questions about the world. They bring their questions and doubts with them to college but may be very reserved about revealing these to a stranger.

These students may have gotten through high school with minimal studying. Often they are test-wise and do not need to study as much as others for tests. College may be a shock to them because they will not succeed solely on natural abilities without studying. Since they have not had to develop study techniques up to this point, they may flounder the first year. The shock of this may undermine their confidence in themselves unless they understand this process and the differences between high school and college. There may be a problem of motivation; if they've never had to face a tough academic obstacle, their first response may be to give up or change directions. Like some of the INFPs, they may procrastinate to a painful degree. These issues can be worked through with counseling and study skills assistance.

In the social and relationships arena, INTPs may have unresolved family or relationship issues when leaving home for college. Feeling is the least-preferred function. Some INTPs leave home without confronting feelings of loss and separation, or without expressing their love to family and old friends. Away at college, these feelings come welling up and throw them off balance. They do not have a framework for dealing with these powerful emotions, which refuse to be manipulated in the manner of objective facts and will not stay "shelved." Counselors can assist INTPs in learning how to explore feelings safely and find expression for them.

ENTP

Like the ENFP freshmen, ENTPs may have some difficulties getting focused in college. They may be prone to change majors and career goals frequently. They are usually curious about their MBTI scores and come in readily to learn about themselves. This is an opportunity to probe for their ability to set priorities and organize themselves. ENTPs seen in counseling tend to be restless; the classroom seems too confining to them. They often need the balance of a part-time job, volunteer work, or other outside activity. They must be cautioned not to let these outside activities take up too much time, however. Many ENTPs seen for counseling have eventually flunked out or dropped out to follow enterprises they had begun while students. Counselors can appeal to their future orientation to help them shape goals and manage the frustrations of their current restlessness. Career planning coupled with "real world" experiences, such as job shadowing or internships, can help focus these students. They do not often express social adjustment concerns.

ENTJ

The few ENTJs who seek counseling during the freshman year usually have interpersonal difficulties. Their natural leadership style may be overdone to the point of irritating others with controlling behaviors. They may be puzzled about why people are irritated with them. They may also be troubled by family conflicts that were not resolved before coming to college. They do not have a natural way to process the subjective and emotional data from relationships. Counselors can help them develop a "vocabulary" for talking about and sorting out family relationships. Their energies need to be directed into academic areas where they can be successful and into student organizations where they can express their leadership. They are often quite responsive to their MBTI results. Again this gives counselors a chance to begin building a relationship, which can be valuable to ENTJs later.

Type Development and College Adjustment

These descriptions of potential adjustment concerns for each of the 16 types are meant to be brief. It would take several volumes to do justice to the fascinating variability of each type. Besides variability in life experiences and socioeconomic backgrounds that influence response to the college environment, type development and age are major factors. It is not the intent of this chapter to explain the theory of type development, but rather to show the theory's relevance to college adjustment.

By the time students come to college, they should be comfortable with their dominant function. Many may also be fairly successful in using their auxiliary functions, especially the Introverts who must use their auxiliaries to deal with the external world. One function is used to deal with the outside world, the dominant function for Extraverts and the auxiliary for Introverts, and one function is used to deal with the inner world of self, the auxiliary for Extraverts and the dominant for Introverts.

To function well individuals must relate to both worlds; yet it takes time and maturation for both functions to develop. Eventually there should be a balance between the introverted function and the extraverted function, with the dominant function guiding the individual. Balance does *not* mean both functions are used equally. The two functions are like left and right hands. One hand is favored over the other, but most activities are better performed when both hands are used.

This concept has relevance in considering adjustment issues and other problems students may have. Students with both dominant and auxiliary functions developed appear to be more balanced individuals with more personal resources to draw upon than those who have only developed and favored one function. A good example are the EPs, who have a dominant function in perception, either Sensing or Intuition. Their focus is outward. Without a developed auxiliary in judgment, either Thinking or Feeling, to help them weigh and select from many perceptions, they may be rudderless, moving from activity and stimulus to other externals. They have difficulty focusing or following through on their actions. Therefore, adjustment concerns among unbalanced EPs are more likely than among those with developed auxiliaries. The latter group have learned to select from all their perceptions, prioritize, and evaluate what is important for themselves.

Carrying type development theory further, over a lifetime people also develop some use of their least-preferred functions, the third and fourth or inferior function. Individuals vary considerably in their ability to use these lesser functions; some never approach any comfort in using the third or fourth functions. A developmental goal is to be aware of and comfortable enough with all four functions to be able to use the one appropriate in a given situation. This goal requires ability to extravert and introvert, since some functions are used with the outer world and others with the inner world of self. Naturally, older individuals will have had more opportunity to develop the functions than the freshman of 18. Generally older students have better development and therefore more personal resources than young students. However, this assumption must be checked out in counseling, since there are incidents of unusually well-developed young people and of older students with impeded development.

Additional Applications Through the Counseling Office

Learning and Reading Skills. Rollins College has a separate learning skills center which works with the counseling office in cross-referral.

When counselors identify students with reading difficulties and lack of study skills during the freshman MBTI interpretations, they explain the services of the center and make the referral. Not all students will follow through, but many will at the time of referral, and some will at a later date. Students with a preference for Sensing, especially ISFJs and ISTJs, may be more likely to have reading difficulties. Since most courses require extensive reading, often abstract in nature, improved reading speed and comprehension are important. In the previous section of this chapter several types were identified that tend to have more trouble organizing themselves; these students can benefit from consultation with the learning skills center. Another chapter in this book deals with this subject in greater depth.

At present the counseling office is debating a more aggressive outreach program to those types more likely to have reading and study difficulties. There are some potential problems in a more directed outreach, however. If the wording or other communication with these students is not carefully crafted, these students may get the message that they cannot be successful at the college. The counseling office has guarded against any group of students becoming labeled as potential failures. Because of these concerns, the counselors have used the more general outreach to all freshman and are cautiously considering a carefully designed pilot program to target some students more likely to need help with study and reading skills.

Training in Peer Counseling and Leadership. The counseling office is heavily involved in the training of resident aides, head residents, house managers, rush counselors, and some other ad hoc groups of students. The office also teaches a credit course on interpersonal communications. The MBTI is effective for increasing sensitivity to differences and for inspiring appreciation of the contributions of different types. In a series of workshops students learn how their preferences influence the way they listen, the way they respond, the pace of their responses, the language they use, their values and attitudes, and so forth. This learning is connected to peer counseling techniques. They are encouraged to identify their own biases and "blind spots" and discuss ways of controlling for these.

Resident aides work in teams; the MBTI is helpful in team building. They learn each other's preferences and least-preferred ways of functioning and discuss the implications for the role of resident aide. They explore ways they can complement each other. These same principles are used when working with student organizations which have asked the counseling office to help them with leadership training. Sometimes that help is a response to an organizational crisis. The request may also take the form of a consultation between a counselor and one or several leaders of a group; the MBTI preferences of these leaders may be discussed in light of their concerns. On the basis of such consultation, future workshops may be planned for the organization, sometimes involving the MBTI. Students are usually eager to increase their interpersonal competence and find information about the varying motivations and work approaches of different types especially helpful.

Consultation with Faculty. It takes a great deal of time to establish the trust and respect of an analytical faculty; sometimes misperceptions of counseling functions and methods exist. They tend to be suspicious of personality measures in general, and are initially skeptical about the MBTI. Over the years, faculty have expressed bewilderment and frustration when seemingly capable students do not perform well in the classroom and on tests. Other faculty have referred to counseling students who seem paralyzed about writing papers despite their being very bright. These expressions of frustration by many faculty became the basis for several MBTI workshops presented in the format of faculty colloquia. Faculty were encouraged to take the MBTI prior to the presentations, and most who attended did. After explanation of type theory and MBTI interpretation, the applications to teaching and learning styles were discussed and energetically debated.

It is interesting to note that the predominant type among the faculty at Rollins College is INTJ, the same type among the students with the highest GPA. Yet a large percent of the students are ES. This contrast in faculty and student types, presented in type table form at a colloquium, had the strongest impact on faculty in causing them to reconsider their teaching approaches. A revelation for most faculty was that students who show the most promise on SAT scores often do not have the personality style which seems to perform most industriously (the way faculty desire students to be) at the college. Many faculty began to realize that simply pushing the admissions office to recruit students with higher SAT scores, without looking at other variables such as personality, was not addressing the issue of *how* students managed once they got to college.

These discussions with groups of faculty have led to increased referrals of individual students for MBTI interpretation. Some faculty with freshman classes have requested a presentation about learning styles and group interpretation. In these cases a general explanation of the preferences is given, students estimate their own preferences, and then each is given his/her own results. Sometimes this is followed by class sharing, to the extent that students are comfortable. Faculty may also share their MBTI results.

Another interesting request some faculty have made is for consultation about a problem class. The counseling office has provided a type distribution (without student names) for the class from the class roster. This distribution is examined with the professor in light of his/her own type and teaching methods. The group dynamics are explored and recommendations made. After several years of exposure to the MBTI, some faculty are making additional requests. For example, the basketball coach arranges for the counselors to do team building with the MBTI. The counseling office is exploring the possibility of initiating a training program for faculty freshman advisors to increase their understanding of the MBTI and the implications for their advisees in adjusting to the first year of college.

Research on Attrition.   Since the office of personal counseling has acquired MBTI data on the student body, it seemed logical that this office might investigate whether certain types were more likely to persist or drop out of the college. Two graduating classes have now been tracked, with interesting results. A table showing the persistence rates for one of those classes appears in the Appendix (see Tables 4 and 5). For a thorough discussion of this research see Provost (1985). Chapter 3 also presents a fine discussion of attrition research. This research gives the counseling office a better idea of students at risk and suggests preventive programs. Some of the implications for counseling were included in the discussion about early outreach to freshmen and potential adjustment concerns of the 16 types.

Other research projects can be stimulated and supported by the counseling office. While controlling for the confidentiality of individuals' scores, counselors can provide MBTI data of some designated group, working with faculty of staff researchers. For example, one year the staff member in charge of academic advising provided a list of entering freshmen who had performed poorly on verbal SATs. The counseling office was able to examine the type distribution of this group and identify SJs as overrepresented. The math department has considered using its math placement test (given during freshman orientation) in conjunction with the MBTI to make the appropriate placement in a math course. These are some examples of possible collaborative research projects with others at the college. In addition to the responsibility of protecting the confidentiality of individual scores, counselors should take care that overgeneralizations or labeling do not result from the research.

Conclusion

A detailed description of one couseling office's multiple uses of the MBTI in working with students and the broader college community has been presented. The MBTI has been shown as a useful tool in the counseling process for establishing rapport, identifying counseling goals, and designing appropriate interventions. Programs in other counseling centers indicate wide use of the MBTI and endless possibilities for helping students to become successful in college and to develop as individuals. The counselor can employ the MBTI and type theory to advocate for respecting and accommodating differences among students (and other college community members). MBTI data should be handled appropriately in terms of ethics, confidentiality, and positive application, with special care that type labeling does not occur.

References

Gendlin, E. (1981). *Focusing.* New York: Bantam.

Keirsey, D., & Bates, M. (1984). *Please understand me.* Del Mar, CA: Promethean Books.

Myers, I. B. (1987). *Introduction to type.* Palo Alto, CA: Consulting Psychologists Press.

Myers, I. B., & McCaulley, M. H. (1985). *Manual: A guide to the development and use of the Myers-Briggs Type Indicator.* Palo Alto, CA: Consulting Psychologists Press.

Provost, J. (1985). "Type watching" and college attrition. *Journal of Psychological Type, 9,* 16–23.

Additional Resources

Myers, I. B. (1980). *Gifts differing.* Palo Alto, CA: Consulting Psychologists Press.

Provost, J. (1984). *A casebook: Applications of the Myers-Briggs Type Indicator in counseling.* Gainesville, FL: Center for Applications of Psychological Type.

Quenk, A. (1984). *Psychological types and psychotherapy.* Gainesville, FL: Center for Applications of Psychological Type.

VICTORIA JENNINGS GOLDEN is currently a consultant and director of career development programs at Organizational Renewal Associates in Moorestown, New Jersey. She was previously coordinator of the Counseling and Career Development Center at Santa Fe Community College in Gainesville, Florida. In her 12 years at the college, Victoria used type extensively as both a personal and as a career counselor as well as in her Psychology and Career Development classes. She also had a private practice and conducted workshops in educational and community settings. Victoria was Southeast Chapter Coordinator for APT and was in charge of type talk groups in Gainesville for over three years. Victoria is an ENFP.

JUDITH A. PROVOST, Ed.D., is a psychotherapist, writer, and trainer who has incorporated MBTI concepts in her work for the past 13 years. She currently is Director of Personal Counseling at Rollins College and is on the faculties of the Center for Applications of Psychological Type and the Association for Psychological Type. Her research interests in higher education have resulted in several journal articles and a dissertation, "Personality type and leisure satisfaction as factors in college attrition." Other books by Judy are *A Casebook: Applications of the Myers-Briggs Type Indicator in Counseling* (CAPT) and *The Freshmen Year—Stress or Success* (PPI). As Chair of the Council for Communication and Education of APT, she sits on the executive board; she also serves as Chair of the Ethics Committee of APT. Her education includes an undergraduate degree from the University of Connecticut, graduate degrees from the University of California at Los Angeles and University of Florida, and extensive training with the Gestalt Institute of Florida. She is an ENFP.

CHAPTER 8

The MBTI and Career Development

VICTORIA JENNINGS GOLDEN
and JUDITH A. PROVOST

Each of us can be a so-called gifted person if you identify the gifts you have been given, submit them to whatever training may be necessary and then employ your gifts in work which requires them. (Miller, cited in Mangun, 1982, p. 74)

THE AVERAGE PERSON spends over 100,000 hours during the course of a lifetime involved in some aspect of work or work-related activity. Yet, surprisingly few people develop and apply a solid career decision-making process in planning their future. Our society and the work that supports it are rapidly changing. Jobs that did not exist 10 years ago are in high demand today, and the jobs of today may be in low demand tomorrow. Increasingly the issue becomes not job security but rather employment security. For students this translates into developing the technical, personal, and social skills that will allow them to find a meaningful career and grow through the changes that are sure to occur. Career planning is more important now than ever, and the role of the career counselor is expanding.

Career planning and counseling needs of students have also become more complex because of changes in the postsecondary student population. In the last 10 years, junior and community colleges as well as universities have attracted more minorities, more returning women, more mature men, more students with disabilities (both physical handicaps and learning disabilities), and more international students. Specialized career development programs now target populations such as

151

displaced homemakers (newly divorced or widowed) and nontraditional or nonstereotypic (for gender) students for vocational programs.

There has also been a significant change in student values. The student of the 80s is more goal and success oriented, and as a result, more career oriented. The emphasis in most cases is no longer on knowledge for knowledge's sake, a motto or value of the student of the 60s and early 70s. The majority of students today want to be highly successful and do not want anything to get in the way. Therefore, most want a highly efficient approach to schooling, courses related to their occupational goals and as few "superfluous" electives as possible. Many of these students are more self-oriented versus the 60s and 70s students, who valued a more other-oriented approach. Most students today see college as a means to acquiring a good job and creating a high standard of living.

The *Myers-Briggs Type Indicator* can be one of the counselor's most valuable tools in assisting individuals in their important life decisions. The MBTI provides insight to both the individual and the counselor about the individual's behavioral patterns and problem-solving strengths. Through the MBTI individuals are able to identify their preferences in such a way that a common language and information base is achieved between counselor and counselee. The Indicator can provide a foundation on which to build an understanding of the individual's interests, values, talents, and strengths. Knowledge of type, in conjunction with additional information about an individual, can assist the counselor in making connections between the individual's preferences and certain career fields. The research holds that particular types tend to be attracted to and/or perform well in certain occupations (Myers, 1962; Myers & McCaulley, 1985).

This chapter shows how the MBTI can be incorporated into many of the steps in the career counseling process. Case studies will demonstrate the usefulness of the MBTI in the career planning and decision making of various life stages. Programs in a community college and a four-year liberal arts college will illustrate application of the MBTI in career development.

Psychological Type in Career Counseling

Isabel Myers (1980) stated:

> There is no doubt that a ship needs a captain with undisputed authority to set its course and bring it safe to the desired port. It would never make harbor if each person at the helm in turn aimed at a different destination and altered course accordingly.

In the same way, people need some governing force in their development. They need to develop their best process to the point where it dominates and unifies their lives. In the natural course of events, each person does just that. (pp. 13–14)

The analogy of a ship at sea is very appropriate to the field of career counseling, for each individual is seeking to chart his or her course through often unpredictable seas. Just as every ship needs a captain, so too, does each individual type; type theory identifies the captain as the dominant function. One's dominant function leads the way and sets the principal direction for career attainment. In type theory, the dominant function is the most fully conscious, and thus career counseling should be oriented to the dominant. This means that the career process and work goals for an ISFJ with Introverted Sensing dominant will be different than those for an ENTP with Extraverted Intuition dominant.

Expanding on the ship metaphor to include the other type functions, Golden (1982) says:

It may be useful to envision the type functions as a crew on a ship where the dominant is the captain. The captain sets the course and has the final say in all matters pertaining to the ship. All activities on the ship are in service to the captain. The auxiliary function serves as the chief navigator and is primarily responsible for plotting the course for those ports of destination which have been determined by the captain. The tertiary preference (opposite the auxiliary) can act as an assistant navigator and supplements the strategies worked out by the chief navigator. Last, the inferior function (opposite the dominant) acts as a novice recruit and should be given light duty assignments which benefit the captain. If the inferior/novice recruit is not understood, it can get the whole ship in trouble and even can become a mutineer. An example is the ESTJ (with inferior Feeling) whose explosive outbursts alienate him from peers and result in his being fired. (pp. 1–2)

The metaphor of the dominant as captain and the relevance to career counseling are illustrated in Figure 1. Remember that the dominant function is focused in a particular direction, either extraverted or introverted. With Extraverts the captain is generally readily apparent to others. Introverts' dominant function will be quietly governing affairs from behind the scenes, and initial contact with the counselor may be through their auxiliary function.

In career counseling attention should not only be given to maximizing the expression of the dominant in a particular occupation, but also to

FIGURE 1

Conceptualizing Career Development Counseling by Jung–Myers Type Theory

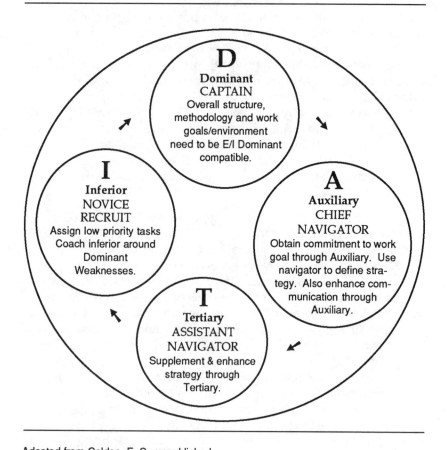

Adapted from Golden, E. S., unpublished.

carefully and accurately assess the risks of occupations or job settings which place high demands on performance of the inferior function. It is often valuable to mention these issues explicitly in counseling. The ESTJ in the example above would probably find little satisfaction and considerable frustration in an occupation which demanded heavy use of the Feeling function, such as a specialty in relationship counseling.

Many individuals who seek career counseling have experienced confusion, roadblocks, rejection, or failure. Many have feelings of inadequacy and identity problems. Others may enter the career counseling process in an emotionally disabled state (for example, following divorce), and it becomes the task of the career counselor to help clients build self-esteem while directing them toward appropriate career fields. Probably the single most valuable aspect of using the MBTI in career counseling is its tremendous ability to enhance self-esteem through a positive description of each type, which can be found in *Introduction to Type* by Isabel Myers (1987). Individuals gain insight as to why some activities have been difficult and others easy; why relationships with some people have been strained and others effortless. The power of psychological type goes far beyond the description of a client's particular type profile and can become a powerful tool for understanding the dynamic world of relationships and work.

A number of years ago the U.S. Department of Labor conducted a study in which the issues of competence and confidence were examined in relationship to hiring and job performance. It was discovered that candidates who possessed greater self-confidence outperformed those who had greater initial competence. The MBTI provides a tool for the development of self-assurance through gaining knowledge and insight of oneself. Many individuals who seek career counseling are not presently functioning at their best, and the MBTI provides insight into who they are and how they can develop.

Counselors using the MBTI need to recognize that many career counseling clients are experiencing problems specific to their own type; for example the Introverted Sensing types who may "retreat, becoming silently absorbed in their inner reactions to sense-impressions" (p. 21) or the Extraverted Feeling types who may "fail to face disagreeable facts" (Myers, 1987, p. 15). These patterns often result from the lack of an adequately developed auxiliary process and may be more common in a younger student population. Myers identifies and describes these behaviors for each type in *Introduction to Type* (1987) and *Gifts Differing* (1980). In such cases the counselor's role may be to help these individuals become aware of their need to balance their lives through development of their auxiliary. For example with an ENFP student who has changed majors three times and still remains undecided, it may be more helpful for the counselor to focus on what the student really cares about (auxiliary F) than on all the possibilities (dominant N). Using type theory in this way the counselor can help initiate personal development through self-knowledge.

Psychological type theory can also be used to select the approach which would be most effective in the career counseling process. If we accept the fundamental hypothesis that type preferences "produce different kinds of people who are interested in different things, are good in different fields, and often find it hard to understand each other" (Myers, 1980b, p. 1), then it becomes incumbent upon career counselors to vary their approaches with different types of individuals or specialize in working with certain kinds of students. Counselors can customize the career counseling approach through adapting to the client's type. For example, with an ISFP student a counselor might start by attempting to establish a personal and trusting relationship (IF) through which the client's values and loyalties (F) could be explored. Following this the counselor could examine the student's experience (S) and work/play attitudes (P). The ISFP student will most likely want a career plan that allows for flexibility and modification.

Linking Type to Work Situations

Myers and McCaulley (1985) outline work situations for each preference scale. Although these lists by preference scale are available elsewhere, it is useful to review them here. These lists can be used to help students clarify their work style preferences and identify individual variation within the preferences. Not all conditions listed will be true for everyone reporting that preference. Sensitivity to individual variation by the counselor and careful exploration with the student can prevent too narrow an interpretation and application to careers.

Extraversion/Introversion

The Extravert-Introvert scale is often the easiest to discriminate when working with the client. Extraverts will tend to favor a quick pace with multiple interactions in their work. Introverts are likely to prefer a quiet, more reflective approach to work. This scale may or may not strongly impact certain career fields. For example, within the field of education there are of course large percentages of both Introverts and Extraverts. The Extravert is more likely than the Introvert to select a consulting/ training role which requires visiting many schools and teachers. The Introvert is more likely to select a research position involving independent effort, the gathering and analysis of data, and the writing of a report. Table 1 indicates other work preferences of Extraverts and Introverts.

Sensing/Intuition

The Sensing-Intuition preference can provide the foundation for an individual's work modality. Sensing types prefer those occupations that deal with concrete, realistic, and operational problems. Intuitive students may be more interested in careers that require complex problem

TABLE 1

Effects of Extraversion-Introversion in Work Situations

Extraversion	Introversion
Like variety and action.	Like quiet concentration.
Tend to be faster, dislike complicated procedures (especially ES types).	Tend to be careful with details, dislike sweeping statements (especially IS types).
Are often good at greeting people (especially EF types).	Have trouble remembering names and faces (especially IT types).
Are often impatient with long, slow jobs.	Tend not to mind working on one project for a long time uninterruptedly.
Are interested in the results of their job, in getting it done, and in how other people do it.	Are interested in the idea behind their job.
Often do not mind the interruption of answering the telephone (especially EF types).	Dislike telephone intrusions and interruptions (especially IT types).
Often act quickly, sometimes without thinking.	Like to think a lot before they act, sometimes without acting.
Like to have people around (especially EF types).	Work contentedly alone (especially IT types).
Usually communicate freely (especially EF types).	Have problems communicating (especially IT types).

From *Manual: A guide to the development and use of the Myers-Briggs Type Indicator*, (p. 79) by I. B. Myers and M. H. McCaulley, 1985, Palo Alto, CA: Consulting Psychologists Press. Copyright 1985 by Peter B. Myers and Katherine D. Myers Reprinted by permission.

solving, tolerance for ambiguity in task and approach, and attention to pattern rather than details. While sensing types may tend to pursue job security, Intuitive types are more likely to follow unconventional and less clearly defined career paths. Within the field of medicine, for example, the specialty of surgeon is more attractive to sensing types, and that of internist to Intuitive types. Table 2 lists other factors.

TABLE 2

Effects of Sensing-Intuition in Work Situations

Sensing	Intuition
Dislike new problems unless there are standard ways to solve them.	Like solving new problems.
Like an established order of things (especialy SJ types).	Dislike doing the same thing repeatedly (especially NP types).
Enjoy using skills already learned more than learning new ones.	Enjoy learning a new skill more than using it.
Work more steadily, with realistic idea of how long it will take (especially IS types).	Work in short bursts of energy, powered by enthusiasm, with slack periods in between (especially EN types).
Are patient with routine details (especially ISJ types).	Are impatient with routine details (especially EN types).
Are impatient when the details get complicated (especially ES types).	Are patient with complicated situations (especially IN types).
Are often not inspired, and rarely trust their inspiration when they are inspired.	Follow their inspirations, good or bad (especially with inadequate type development).
Seldom make errors of fact.	Frequently make errors of fact.
Tend to be good at precise work (especially IS types).	Dislike taking time for precision (especially EN types).

From *Manual: A guide to the development and use of the Myers-Briggs Type Indicator* (p. 80) by I. B. Myers and M. H. McCaulley, 1985, Palo Alto, CA: Consulting Psychologists Press. Copyright 1985 by Peter B. Myers and Katherine D. Myers. Reprinted by permission.

Thinking/Feeling

The Thinking-Feeling preference often is important in terms of individuals' comfort with the technical versus the interpersonal aspects of occupations. Feeling types often choose occupations where they can provide a direct service to people or be in a helping role. They also have a higher need than the Thinking types for a harmonious and supportive work environment. Thinking types are more likely to seek work where logical analysis and evaluation of ideas, numbers, or objects is required. There are, for example, more Thinking than Feeling types in the field of law. Feeling types who go into law find their own niche; for example, an INFP attorney who edits a legal review. Table 3 gives further examples.

TABLE 3
___

Effects of Thinking-Feeling in Work Situations

Thinking	Feeling
Do not show emotion readily and are often uncomfortable dealing with people's feelings (especially IT types).	Tend to be very aware of other people and their feelings (especially EF types).
May hurt people's feelings without knowing it.	Enjoy pleasing people, even in unimportant things.
Like analysis and putting things into logical order. Can get along without harmony.	Like harmony. Efficiency may be badly disrupted by office feuds.
Tend to decide impersonally, sometimes paying insufficient attention to people's wishes.	Often let decisions be influenced by their own or other people's personal likes and dislikes.
Need to be treated fairly.	Need occasional praise.
Are able to reprimand people or fire them when necessary.	Dislike telling people unpleasant things.
Are more analytically oriented— respond more easily to people's thoughts (especially IT types).	Are more people oriented— respond more easily to people's values.
Tend to be firm-minded.	Tend to be sympathetic.

From *Manual: A guide to the development and use of the Myers-Briggs Type Indicator* (p. 81) by I. B. Myers and M. H. McCaulley, 1985, Palo Alto, CA: Consulting Psychologists Press. Copyright 1985 by Peter B. Myers and Katherine D. Myers. Reprinted by permission.

Judgment/Perception

The Judgment-Perception preference relates to orientation in handling tasks, as well as lifestyle. Judging types prefer an organized lifestyle with structure and order. Perceptive types prefer more flexibility and adaptability in their lives and work. Since Judging types tend to be more concerned with issues of control and closure, they are more likely than their opposites to be in management or organizational jobs. Perceptive types are more interested in finding out about the world than in controlling it and are thus more likely to gravitate to jobs requiring adaptation to ever-changing situations, such as in consulting or some form of trouble-shooting. In a wholesale business, for example, it would be more likely to find the Judging type in a production role and the Perceptive type in a marketing or advertising position. Table 4 gives further examples.

TABLE 4

Effects of Judgment-Perception in Work Situations

Judgment	Perception
Work best when they can plan their work and follow the plan.	Adapt well to changing situations.
Like to get things settled and finished.	Do not mind leaving things open for alterations.
May decide things too quickly (especially EJ types).	May have trouble making decisions (especially IP types).
May dislike to interrupt the project they are on for a more urgent one (especially ISJ types).	May start too many projects and have difficulty in finishing them (especially ENP types).
May not notice new things that need to be done.	May postpone unpleasant jobs.
Want only the essentials needed to begin their work (especially ESJ types).	Want to know all about a new job (especially INP types).
Tend to be satisfied once they reach a judgment on a thing, situation, or person.	Tend to be curious and welcome a new light on a thing, situation, or person.

Understanding the four scales and their influence on work motivation and satisfaction is only the first step. Counselors should help students understand the significance of their combination of four preference letters and the 16 types. Earlier the metaphor of the captain of the ship was used to explain the dominant and the role of the other functions. To use this framework with students, counselors must go beyond the four preferences and explain the dynamics of the individual's type: the dominant, the least-preferred, the direction (E or I) the dominant is expressed in, and so forth. This more complete explanation to students allows a broader and more thorough application of the Indicator in all aspects of the career counseling process. That process will now be detailed.

The Career Counseling Process

Where does the MBTI fit into the career counseling process? A comprehensive and systematic process is outlined in Figure 2. This section discusses the use of the MBTI in the various steps of this process.

Student History and Assessment

The counseling interview and the MBTI together serve as the backbone of the assessment process. The MBTI can provide a framework within which to organize other information about the student. *In all discussions of use of the MBTI it is assumed that there has been a careful interpretation and corroboration by the student.* The Indicator's usefulness is only as good as the careful interpretation process; without this process, the results are merely four preference letters amidst a battery of other tests and without assurance of student-perceived accuracy. In cases where much personal data and life experience exists, usually in older students, this data and the MBTI may be sufficient for some kinds of career decision making. For example, consider the case of George, a former minister, now student. George was taking courses in advertising and marketing with the thought of making a career change to fund-raising and promotion of charitable foundations. He was unsure about making such a career leap and sought confirmation of his tentative plan from the career counselor. A thorough interview and MBTI results of ENFP, confirmed by George as true for him, supported his choice.

The MBTI provides understanding of individuals' general characteristics and interests, but in most cases is not sufficiently complete as a single instrument to specify exact career or work targets. The MBTI can suggest general career fields and activities that may be worth consideration, but it is important that counselors do not over-rely on the MBTI as

FIGURE 2

The Career Counseling Process

I. Student History and Assessment
    A. Evaluation of Academic Record, Historic Background
    B. Administration of Appropriate Assessments: *MBTI, Self-Directed Search, Strong-Campbell Interest Inventory,* Values Clarification, Computerized Career Guidance Systems, etc.

II. Counselor-Counselee Discussion
    A. Impact of Past Influences on Career Choices
    B. Career Ideals, Aspirations, and Anxieties

III. Test Evaluation and Interpretation
    A. Instruction and Feedback of Results
    B. Analysis and Comparison of Assessment Data

IV. Examining Potential Occupational Choices
    A. Student's Reaction and Perceptions of Options
    B. Correlations Between Data and Career Fields

V. Student Research
    A. Literature Search of Specific Careers by Students
    B. Interviews with People in Particular Career Fields
    C. Review of Data and Interview Information

VI. Determination of Career Decision
    A. Examination of Choices and Alternatives
    B. Evaluation of Realities
    C. Final Decision

VII. Plan of Action
    A. Academic Recommendations and Preparation
    B. Recommendations for Personal and Career Success

---

their only tool. Psychological type information should be used in conjunction with other assessment approaches. Type provides a means for the interpretation of other assessment data. If, for example, an ESFJ and an INTP both report an interest in art, it does not necessarily mean that they should both seek to become artists, or pursue the same kind of art occupation. It could be that the ESFJ would like to own an art gallery or craft shop, while the INTP might enjoy architecture and design. While this example is perhaps an oversimplification, the point is important. Type provides a set of lenses through which the counselor can more precisely focus on, analyze, and interpret other information about a given client.

Many students will benefit from a more comprehensive evaluation afforded by additional instruments, most commonly an interest inventory such as the *Strong-Campbell Interest Inventory* (Strong) *or Self-Directed Search* (SDS). Interactive computer programs offer values clarification, interests exploration, and career information. In a subsequent section, some correlations and common patterns of MBTI/Strong scores will be discussed.

When suggesting to students that they take the MBTI as part of their assessment, it is important to be clear about what the Indicator can and cannot tell students about career choices. The MBTI *can* indicate:

- preferences and possible strengths which often can be translated into occupational functions

- work environments and activities that might be more and less satisfying

- significant motivators for work

The MBTI *cannot* indicate:

- specific skills and level of competency in the skills

- specific jobs or career fields in which students could be sure to find success

Counselor-Counselee Discussion

After the MBTI has been administered and interpreted, there are several ways the results may be used in counselor-counselee discussions. The counselor may wish to explore the nature of environmental influence on the student's type. The environment may have encouraged or discouraged the development and expression of a student's type; the result might be a student comfortable with self and eager to move forward, or a student unsure, tentative, and confused. The latter student would require more assistance from the career counselor.

One example is a young INFJ student, Tom, who has artistic interests and has always been fascinated by color, design, and aesthetic environments. He comes from a family and cultural background which stress traditional male values and behaviors—tough-mindedness, realism, aggressiveness, and business pursuits. Although Tom has requested career counseling, he exhibits approach-avoidance behaviors in the sessions; he "forgets" appointments, postpones career exploration tasks, and contradicts himself in discussions with the counselor. Helping Tom to gain a deeper understanding of his INFJ preferences may help him resolve some of this conflict.

Another example illustrates the impact of gender roles on type. An INTP woman, Elaine, is very confused about career directions and even admits to sabotaging several experiences that would have brought her small, initial successes. Elaine is a first-generation American whose parents came from "the old country." They have raised her with old-fashioned values about the subservient role of women in the family. Somehow Elaine has managed to get to college without her parents' approval or support, but now that she is here she is quite confused about future directions. As an INTP she is unlikely to be satisfied following a traditional woman's role; she acknowledges her needs for freedom, intellectual stimulation, and challenge. She admits to loving math and theoretical coursework, but becomes flustered when future professional roles are explored. The counselor can give her materials about her type to read and contemplate and work with her to understand the nature of the conflict between her environment and her preferences.

Another major influence can be expectations of parents and significant others. These expectations may or may not be compatible with students' preferences. For example, the ESTJ self-made businessman/ woman may expect an INFP son or daughter to major in Business and eventually take over the family business. The INFP may try to accommodate the parent out of a need for harmony, but may actually have quite different interests and preferences. In another case, a college professor expects her daughter to excel in a liberal arts college and, of course, go on to graduate school. The daughter is an ISFP unhappy with college and unsure of her own capabilities. She would prefer working to going to college.

Previous work or other life experiences can be explored in relation to type to provide more clues to career options. Carolyn, an INTJ, describes in counseling a time when she was completely self-absorbed in a project so that she did not notice that six hours had gone by. She put together a complex model airplane. Carolyn found this curious since she described herself as generally having a short attention span, especially in group activities. This and her other experiences can be related to type and then translated into options to explore, such as architecture.

Test Evaluation and Interpretation

The *Strong-Campbell Interest Inventory* and the *Self-Directed Search* are vocational interest inventories which can provide a powerful addition to the MBTI in career counseling. Both the SDS and the Strong report a student's similarity to John Holland's six General Occupational Themes: Realistic, Artistic, Investigative, Social, Enterprising, and Conventional. *The Dictionary of Holland Occupational Codes* (Gottfredson, Holland, & Ogawa, 1982) offers extensive lists of occupations by these Themes. Studies of the MBTI do show significant correlations between these General Occupational Themes and the MBTI. The *Manual* (Myers & McCaulley, 1985, pp. 195–196) reports the following significant correlations: Artistic with N, P; Social with E, F, J; Enterprising with E, S, J; and Conventional with S, T, J. Readers are encouraged to refer to the *Manual* for more complete information.

Although correlations between the MBTI and the Strong have been documented, a particular individual's scores may not fit these patterns. For example, an ESTJ who scores high on Investigative, Realistic, and Artistic, also scores high on the Occupational Scale, Research and Development Manager, but scores low in Business Management. In this case, the two instruments together sharpen the focus of career options; these are two templates with which to view the individual and identify various relevant dimensions. Another example is an INFJ who expresses high interest in Business Management and Merchandising and scores high on the Enterprising Theme. These patterns, which would not be predicted from type theory, are an example of the variations which often occur within types. However, counselors should carefully explore the nature of discrepancies between expected Strong results (predicted by type theory), unexpected (type theory would predict other scores), and MBTI scores. Discrepancies can signal inaccuracies in measurement, conflict between expressed interests and true nature, conflict between parental expectations or environmental influence and actual preferences in terms of type, or some other intrapersonal or interpersonal tension.

Relationships between the Basic Interest Scales of the Strong and the preferences of the MBTI can be found in the MBTI *Manual* (Myers & McCaulley, 1985, p. 196). Extraverts are, for example, much more likely than Introverts to score high on Public Speaking. However, counselors must take special care with clients who score differently than expected, for some gifted speakers are Introverted. High scores on the Basic Interest Scales should be considered as areas of possible focus for career development and often can be creatively combined to target specific work goals. For example, an ESTP who scores high on Mechanical

Activities, Science, Medical Science, and Sales might consider a career as an engineer specializing in the sales of medical technology. This occupation could provide a high level of extraverted activity under flexible conditions and require attention to equipment, inventory, and appreciation of sensing data. The following are some examples of correlations between the Strong Basic Interest Scales and the MBTI: Adventure with NP; Military Activities with S; Mechanical Activities with T; Mathematics with T, J; Music-Dramatics with N, NF; and Social Service with F, EF.

Examining Potential Occupational Choices

Using the MBTI in conjunction with interest inventories and other tools (for example, computer-based values activities) provides a series of templates to fine-tune career exploration. The MBTI remains the framework which suggests ways of pulling together discrete pieces of information about the student. Within a likely career option the MBTI can suggest work settings, organizational structures, motivators, specialized functions, and subspecialties which would be most likely to satisfy MBTI preferences. For example, an analytical and theoretical INTP interested in chemical engineering might consider research and development within that field, while a practical and action-oriented ESTP might want to specialize in production technology. In this example the specific employers, work settings, functions, and motivators would vary considerably within the career field of chemical engineering.

Appendix D of the *Manual* (Myers & McCaulley, 1985, pp. 243–292) is a valuable tool in identifying specific occupations that the 16 types might find most appealing. In this appendix occupations are listed for each of the 16 types from most frequently occurring to least commonly occurring for each type. The data are reported as the number of a type in an occupation and the percentage in each type making up the total number in the occupation. For example, the most and least frequent careers for INFP are listed in Table 5.

These data show that over 20 percent of the psychiatrists in the database are INFPs. In contrast, less than 1 percent of steelworkers and police are INFPs in this database. The data were collected by Center for Applications of Psychological Type from MBTI answer sheets on which individuals listed their occupations. The listed occupations were then coded using a modification of the *Dictionary of Occupational Titles* code (U.S. Department of Labor, 1977). Caution should be used in suggesting listed careers for specific types because the sample was *not* a random sample. Care should also be taken to point out to students that all 16

TABLE 5

Occupations Attractive to INFPs

Most frequently occurring occupations for INFP

% INFP	N	Occupation
20.59	68	Physician, psychiatry
16.81	113	Editors and reporters
16.42	67	Research assistants
16.35	208	Writers, artists, entertainers, and agents

Least frequently occurring occupations for INFP

% INFP	N	Occupation
1.20	83	Managers, sales, not specified
.95	105	Steelworkers, miscellaneous
.65	155	Police and detectives

From *Manual: A guide to the development and use of the Myers-Briggs Type Indicator* (pp. 278, 280) by I. B. Myers and M. H. McCaulley, 1985, Palo Alto, CA: Consulting Psychologists Press. Copyright 1985 by Peter B. Myers and Katherine D. Myers. Reprinted by permission.

types are represented for each occupation; there is *not* one specific type for any occupation.

The data can be used to help students consider various careers. Students should look at careers listed as most and least frequent for their types and ask themselves:

▪ What are the characteristics of the most frequent careers and how do these relate to my type?

▪ What are the characteristics of the least frequent careers and how do these relate to my type?

▪ Which careers are most appealing and worth further investigation?

Student Research

The counselor should keep in mind the student's type when suggesting specific career research approaches and activities. Extraverts will prefer gathering information through face-to-face conversations with workers and other authorities and through direct experience. Introverts will generally prefer to begin exploration by reading occupational materials. Counselors should not assume that suggesting printed materials to Extraverted students will result in use of this information; counselors will probably have to motivate Extraverts to use these materials. Sensing students may wish to gather many facts either through reading (Introversion) or through direct action (Extraversion). They may benefit even more than the Intuitive types from hands-on experiences such as volunteering, job-shadowing, or interning. Intuitive students may more easily see the patterns between various occupational titles and also be able to see the transferability of their skills and strengths to other related careers. Sensing types may need more help in seeing the connections and may therefore need more direction in this regard. Students with a Thinking preference may enjoy the research aspect involving analyzing facts about occupations, and thus be more patient and thorough with this aspect of exploration. Those with a Feeling preference may become impatient and wish to rely more on personal contacts with select people they admire; their Feeling may influence selective gathering of certain kinds of information and the neglecting of other information. Students with a Judging preference will need to be encouraged to remain open and gather more data; they may have sufficient research. They will require a structured plan for conducting research, and the counselor must explain the necessity of research in a way that makes sense and is motivational to that type. For example, the counselor might say to an ESFJ student:

> Even though you are fairly convinced you want to go into nursing, it would be valuable if you found out a little more about nursing and other related fields before making a final decision. It is important for you to feel satisfied at your work and feel you are doing your best to help others, so you need to do some exploration to make sure this is the best career for you. Let's make a list of other related careers and write out a plan for how you could meet with people in these careers and visit places they work. You can see first hand what their work is like, what they like and dislike about what they do. You can ask them questions about themselves; people generally like to talk about themselves. You can compare what you know about yourself (from assessment) with what you are finding out about these occupations. Then we can get back together and see how what you found out fits with your interests and personality, and decide where to go from there.

On the other hand, students with a preference for Perception or with a dominant Perceptive function may have difficulty knowing when they have gathered sufficient career information. They may like finding out about various careers but avoid making decisions.

The research phase of career counseling has a feedback loop; student and counselor evaluate the student's discoveries and information and help the student integrate this assessment data. The MBTI again can provide the framework for evaluating the data: how does what you now know about this occupation fit with what you understand about your preferences? would this occupation take advantage of your preferences and strengths? would there be certain work settings you would want to seek out and conversely avoid because of your preferences? and so forth.

Determination of Career Decision

The MBTI can suggest to career counselors what decision-making process a student is likely to employ and what areas of the decision-making process are likely to be easier and more difficult. Anchors' discussion of decision-making styles and of Lawrence's "Z method" of decision making in Chapter 6 is very relevant here. The EJ types, for example, are more prone to identity foreclosure, making premature career choices without sufficient information.

Applying the Z method with an ISFJ student, the following example can be given. The first step is to gather facts using Sensing; since Sensing is the dominant introverted function of the ISFJ, the student is likely to be very thorough in this stage of research and decision making. However, the student may be *too* thorough and not move on in the decision-making process; he or she could get bogged down and confused by all the data collected. The next step is to use Intuition to see other possibilities; this could include seeing the transferability of a set of skills or strengths to related careers and work settings, and expanding the choices within an area of interest. Since Intuition is the least-preferred function of the ISFJ, this step would probably be the hardest and require the most assistance from the counselor, and may actually be resisted by the student. The third step is to evaluate the data using Thinking; this is also a less preferred function and might prove difficult for the student. The counselor might have to model how to evaluate the pros and cons and consequences of the various career options. Finally, Feeling is used to evaluate the options in terms of personal values and interpersonal concerns. The ISFJ would probably place a great deal of weight on a career option which helped others.

The MBTI provides counselors with an indication of students' natural decision-making style. Counselors can utilize students' natural strengths in decision making and help them through the more difficult steps, often identified with the least-preferred functions. Students vary in their development of the various MBTI functions, so counselors cannot assume students' competence or lack of it in using a particular function. Counselors must assess ability to use a particular function through the interview process.

Plan of Action

Academic recommendations and preparation should take type information into account. For example, an ENTP may develop a plan to obtain a four-year degree in Marketing with the goal of working in a large New York advertising firm. Many ENTPs become restless in traditional classrooms, and it might be difficult for this ENTP to stick to this goal. The counselor might suggest internships for credit, part-time employment in this field, or other strategies to help the student implement the plan.

Counselors can use their knowledge of type to suggest activities that could stimulate type development and overall personal development to enhance chances for future success. These activities could be extracurricular, volunteer, work-related, or more personal. For example, an ISTJ has decided on a degree and future in business management, yet he has poor writing skills. The counselor might suggest courses to strengthen his writing skills and comfort, since future job success may rest in part on his ability to communicate in writing. The counselor would have to give specific examples of how writing is used in business management to motivate this student to follow through. Another suggestion would be to apply for the position of comptroller in student government, where he could continue to develop his STJ preferences and also challenge development of Feeling through having to work with peers within the organization.

Career and placement counselors can use type information to help students with job search strategies, interviews for graduate school, and related activities. The type concepts of the MBTI give students a language to use in talking about themselves to potential employers or graduate school committees. Students are usually shaky about promoting themselves and may be filled with self-doubt. A thorough discussion of MBTI results can validate students and help them to see themselves as possessing certain strengths which they can develop further. For example, the counselor could suggest that a particular INTP student emphasize his or her strengths in a job interview by saying something like "I've learned that I'm at my best when I'm given a complex problem to solve. I like and am good at investigating all the related issues, gathering and analyzing the data, and pulling it together in written form or on the computer." Because the way students go about their job searches is usually similar to the way they go about making decisions, the previous discussion of type differences in researching career options applies here as well.

Summary of Type and the Career Counseling Process

It is evident that the MBTI is a valuable tool in each step of the career counseling process. Individual preference scales and the interactions between combinations of preferences influence the ways in which students participate in this process. Some of the same observations about types can be made for career counseling as have been made in Chapter 7 for psychological counseling. Individuals with different preferences will come to career counseling with varying expectations for the career counselor and with different strengths to apply to the process. They will prefer differing counseling approaches as well. An ESFJ may expect a concise, focused, almost prescriptive response from the career counselor, while an INFP may need help in structuring career exploration, but the counselor would start by attending to initially expressed needs. The IS student might prefer starting with a computer-based exploration. An IN student might enjoy guided imagery to explore the ideal lifestyle and career of ten years from now, and thus helping to identify values and interests.

Ethical Issues in the Career Counseling Process

Several important points in using the MBTI for career counseling have already been stressed. There are several traps that career counselors may fall into in using the MBTI (or any other instrument for that matter). Often students will ask whether they will be good or successful in a specific occupation because they are a certain type. Type does not predict success, and counselors need to be very clear with students about this. In administering the Indicator, they may want to be explicit about what the MBTI can and cannot do in identifying career options. When students are types rarely occurring in the occupations which they have chosen, counselors should not discourage them from choosing that occupation. Students can be shown type tables and data indicating frequency of their type in certain occupations, and then the implications can be discussed. Perhaps the less frequently occurring types have something special to contribute to that field. But perhaps the student would feel too alienated from other workers in that field and prefer another related field with more of the student's type represented. These are issues to explore with the student, allowing the student to make the final choice.

There are other ethical issues that are more generic, such as preserving confidentiality of students' results and only releasing these with students' permission. Another concern is not forcing the student into a type that the student seems reluctant to accept as true. Scores may not be accurate, and career counselors should not assume that reported scores of any individual are the best fit for that individual. Thus, careful face-to-face interpretation is crucial; if the student merely takes the MBTI on a computer, gets a printout, and leaves, there is no check and further exploration to ascertain the accuracy of these results. This practice is particularly unsound if the student is trying to make a career decision or other choice on the basis of the results.

Case Studies

To further illustrate use of the MBTI in career counseling, several case studies are presented here. Since career counseling may be valuable at various stages over an individual's lifetime, cases are used which show the application of the MBTI in these various career stages. The most frequent application is with young people participating in career planning for the first time and anticipating their first career. Freshmen and sophomores often benefit from a divergent approach, expanding their perceived options beyond one or two obvious occupational choices. The MBTI is an excellent stimulus to brainstorming jobs and settings which would satisfy certain preferences. The two-year community college student selecting a vocational program may find the MBTI helpful in confirming a very specific educational track. Seniors may find the MBTI helpful in converging on specific careers or job settings. The career development process alternates between expansion or divergence and contraction or convergence, and the MBTI is helpful in both these phases. The divergent phase of career development emphasizes the Perceptive function; the convergent phase places more emphasis on the Judging function.

Older students may be re-entering school to complete interrupted education or retraining for a career transition. The re-entry student will probably pass through a divergent phase similar to that of the younger student. Some older students, however, may be seeking confirmation of their tentative career choice and validation of themselves as capable of that goal. Counselors using the MBTI can offer these students a rich experience in understanding themselves and finding patterns in their past experiences and choices.

Beth—A Case of Re-Entry

Beth was a 36-year-old single parent interested in pursuing a college degree. She had initially heard about SIGI, a computerized career guidance system at the community college, and was interested in exploring her career options. It was recommended to her to go through the career counseling program.

Beth, newly divorced, had two main concerns—the support of her 8-year-old child, and the pursuit of education and training for a better position. She had been working as a clerk at a hospital. The pay was low; the stress was high.

She was administered the MBTI, the 16PF, the SDS, and the Strong. She also finished the SIGI values program. Her MBTI results were INTJ. She had strong preferences for Introversion and Thinking. Her highest values on SIGI were Independence, Security, Scientific, and High Income. On both the SDS and the Strong she had consistently high scores on Investigative, Conventional, and Realistic. (Typically, Sensing types have higher scores on Realistic than Intuitive types.) Beth's Social and Enterprising scores were very low, with an average score on Artistic.

The MBTI served as a focal point to assess all the data. Specific relationships were noted: for example, her Introversion on the MBTI was reflected on the 16PF scales Assertive (E-), Reserved (A-), and Apprehension (O+). She reported her strong need for a quiet environment and for working alone, which linked to the 16PF's Abstract Thinking scale, as well as having some correlation with her value of Scientific on SIGI. These patterns related to her high score on Investigative in both the SDS and the Strong. Beth tested high on the 16PF Self-Discipline (Q3+) and Conscientious (C+) scales, which have some correlation with the organized and planful aspects of her Judging preference.

On the Strong, Beth's Occupational Scales were high in Realistic occupations like Architect and Veterinarian, Investigative occupations like Computer Programmer, Systems Analyst, Chemist, Dentist, and Mathematician, and such Conventional occupations as Accountant and Credit Manager.

After careful evaluation of the assessment, and discussions of her interests, preferences, privacy needs, and economic realities, Beth decided to pursue a two-year program in Data Processing. This provided the necessary opportunity for a good paying job in a field of interest and variety that also supported her intellectual and privacy needs. Beth planned on later obtaining an advanced degree.

Gary—A Sophomore Shaping a Career Objective

Gary was a 21-year-old college sophomore near graduation from a two-year college, who was trying to decide whether to major in Banking, Private Finance, Accounting, or Computer Science. He was an average student with some difficulties in English and social science. His favorite subjects were economics, history, and math.

Gary's MBTI results were ESTP, with a slight preference for P. On the Strong the highest Themes were Conventional, Enterprising, and Realistic. Gary's interests were not at all scientific. He did state, however, that he liked working with computers and figuring out math problems with practical application (business math, economics). His Strong Basic Interest Scales also reflected high math and low science and medical science interest.

Gary valued high income and job security. He was very much interested in working with finance and making money. We also discussed his more intrinsic values such as honesty and family security. On the Strong Occupational Scales, Gary's scores did indicate high interest in Credit Manager, Accountant, Investments Manager, Marketing Executive, Purchasing Agent, Computer Programmer, and Enlisted Officer (Army and Air Force).

Gary researched these fields by doing a literature search for information on the various fields and by interviewing various people in each of his top career choices. Gary decided to eliminate both accounting and computer programming due to the degree of Introversion that might be necessary. Accounting might also require more structure (J) than he preferred.

He planned to start his career in banking for experience and then shift into the field of securities sales and investments. As a career objective, this field seemed to match well with Gary's type, interests, and values. Securities sales is a fast-paced, often hectic world where one must be able to adapt rapidly to changing market conditions. One must be able to remember and manipulate great amounts of financial information. This field offers a great deal of financial opportunities as well.

Jackie—A Need to Converge Career Options

Jackie was a 24-year-old college sophomore referred for career counseling. She was bright and energetic, but undecided about her career field.

She had broad interests ranging from music to psychology, making it difficult for her to narrow her choices. She was not doing well academically due to her lack of focus and indecisiveness. She had graduated in the top 10 percent of her high school class. Jackie was administered the MBTI, the 16PF, the Strong, and a values survey.

Her MBTI showed preferences for ENFP with a very clear preference for Extraversion. Her highest values were Freedom, Exciting Life, Social Recognition, Self-respect, Imagination, Independence, Broadminded, and Loving. On the Strong she was very high on the Enterprising, Artistic, and Social Themes. Her lowest Theme was Conventional. On the 16PF she had a high score in Warm, Easygoing (A+), Abstract Thinking (B+), Dominant (C+), Venturesome (H+), and Experimenting (Q1+). The 16PF also indicated Expediency (G-) and Undiscipline (Q2). On the occupational fitness projection of the 16PF she rated high in the Artistic field, and in particular, Musician. Counseling sessions concentrated specifically on Jackie's need to develop greater self-discipline through focusing on developing and executing a career plan. She was encouraged to use her Feeling function to evaluate choices and set both short- and long-term priorities. Jackie focused on a major in Public Relations with emphasis on the music industry. This field would provide conditions compatible with her ENFP preferences: flexibility, creativity, action, and many face-to-face contacts.

Monica—Integrating Art and Leadership

Monica was an 18-year-old freshman who was interested in graphic arts, business, or interior design. Her MBTI showed strong preferences for ENTP. She consistently expressed a need to be in a leadership role. She had high SAT scores and a strong academic record in high school. On administering the 16PF she indicated a high score in Abstract Thinking (B+), Dominance (E+), Venturesome (H+), and Imaginative (M+). On the Strong her scores reflected high Enterprising, Artistic, and Social Themes. Her Basic Interest Scales reflected high scores in Military Activities, Art, Writing, Public Speaking, and Business Management. Specific occupational areas highlighted were Commercial Artist, Photographer, Flight Attendant, Advertising Executive, Public Relations Executive, Buyer, and Marketing Executive.

Because of Monica's strong need for leadership, intellectual stimulation, action, and aesthetic involvement, she decided to pursue a career as an advertising executive where she could use her preference for Extraversion (leadership, sales, multiple and fast-paced interactions), Intuition (imagining possibilities and using creativity for campaigns), Thinking (analyzing ideas and applying logic to evaluate campaigns), and Perception (flexibility, variety, and travel).

Monica's comment was, "This is just what I was looking for: creative challenge, leadership, sales, and an opportunity to do my art and writing."

Evelyn—From Nurse to Counselor

Evelyn came to the women's center of a community college in search of ideas for a career change. She had recently celebrated her 40th birthday. Evelyn was working as a public health nurse but found the work unsatisfying. Now that her four children were in high school and college, she was interested in further education and a new career for herself. She felt that the family situation, with her husband's second income, would allow her to work part-time and go to school part-time. She requested career assessment and was administered the Strong and the MBTI.

She reported preferences for ENFP and for Artistic, Social, and Enterprising on the Strong. As she learned about the MBTI and confirmed her preferences as reported, she became excited at her new understanding of herself. She now had a framework for understanding why nursing had been such a frustration for her—the structure of the hospital setting, the details of medication administration and treatments, and the systematic and procedural tasks. Evelyn realized she had chosen the best specialty within nursing for her type, since as a public health nurse she was able to have more flexibility and educate/counsel people in health matters. ENFPs often report Evelyn's pattern on the Strong. She confirmed several of the occupations within these Themes, in particular those related to counseling, psychology, and the various therapies.

Evelyn had held a secret desire to study psychology. She felt confirmed and encouraged from her assessment results and talks with the career counselor. She decided to obtain a degree in psychology building on her previous college work and then go on to graduate school in counseling if she was still as enthusiastic about school and the field as she currently felt. Evelyn has completed her master's degree in counseling, has a satisfying position, and has become an active leader in her professional organization.

Community College and Four-Year College Applications

A Community College Career Development Center

The optimal use of the MBTI and other assessment instruments in career counseling requires the support and structure of a career center. A career development and counseling center's main purpose is to support the student in clarifying career directions and to provide informational resources and support. The clarification process includes career planning as well as guidance and information on how to reach goals.

A planned system for the career center is necessary to maintain a smooth client flow within a center due to the growing student demands. Student requests for career assistance may be directed into different channels based on need. Students may be interested in gathering information about a particular career, or they may wish to compare several occupations under consideration. They may be unaware of vocational possibilities or of the field for which they may be best suited. General requests for career information (salaries, job outlook, etc.) are met by support staff or student aids who are trained to orient and assist students in locating materials in the career library. Books, journals, career files, and audiovisuals are available in an easy access arrangement.

A large career center, such as the one at the Santa Fe Community College, requires a support staff to assist counselors in screening individual students and in directing them to the appropriate assistance. Students uncertain about a career direction are referred to the counselor for an intake interview. They are also encouraged to use a computerized career guidance system such as SIGI, CHOICES, or DISCOVER. These computer systems enable students to begin exploration before seeing a counselor. The counselor determines the most appropriate assessment approach and instruments. The MBTI is most frequently used in conjunction with the *Self-Directed Search* and the *Strong-Campbell Interest Inventory*, and provides the backbone for the assessment process.

Four-Year Liberal Arts College

The Career and Placement Center at Rollins College is a much smaller operation than that of a public university or community college. It does not offer a large battery of tests or computer-based career exploration. The program emphasizes individual career and placement counseling, outreach in the form of newsletters and mail targeting specific student groups, a comprehensive collection of career materials, and career information programs. Career counseling in a liberal arts setting faces different challenges than in a community college or other institution with many vocational programs. Students who major in History or Greek Classics will probably not apply these studies directly in careers; they will need to expand their thinking beyond the major to careers that tap into broader interests, strengths, and preferences. The MBTI can be valuable here.

The major value of the MBTI is in what the director of the Center terms, "self-assessment."[1] She finds that the MBTI stimulates active participation in the career planning process and empowers students to do self-assessment. The director observes that the MBTI gives students a language to talk about themselves and work conditions and thus empowers them to take responsibility for much of their own career planning. Their accepting responsibility is crucial in a small center and builds skills for after graduation and other career decisions in the future. The students are of traditional age with very little work and life experience. They often can respond more readily to the MBTI concepts of functions and preferences than to the specific occupational titles of many interest inventories.

In addition to the MBTI and counselor interview, other assessment tools may be used, usually the Strong, SDS, and occupational and skills card sorts. The counselors consistently stress the value of the MBTI in affirming clients. This affirmation is particularly important to seniors as they prepare to graduate and interview for jobs or graduate schools. This transition time is anxiety-ridden for most students today, and a thorough MBTI interpretation gives seniors more confidence to go out and talk about themselves in interviews. Knowledge of preferences helps them with decision making about work settings and functions as well. The staff have found Gordon Lawrence's (1982, pp. 28–29) list "I am likely to do my best work . . ." very useful to students in thinking through the career fields and work settings most appropriate for them.

In summary, the director identified three major areas of MBTI application to career counseling: self-assessment, decision making, and preparation for the job search.

Summary

This chapter has shown that the MBTI is a valuable tool at every stage of career counseling, from initial inquiries of young students to the focused questions of midlife career-changing students, from the initial assessment to the job interview. Psychological type theory offers counselors and students a conceptual framework within which to shape understanding of self and the work world and within which to make meaning of many discrete pieces of information (for example, Strong Themes, Basic Interests, and academic performance). The Indicator is only as useful, however, as the counselor who is appropriate and thorough in its administration and interpretation. There are many important cautions

---

1 Interview with Wanda Russell, Director of the Career and Placement Center, Rollins College, February 1987.

in using the Indicator in career counseling, the main one being that individuals should never be discouraged from choosing particular careers on the basis of their types, and the converse that individuals should not be told that they *will* be successful at particular careers because of their types.

Using type the counselor can personalize the career exploration experience for the student, as well as provide a means for looking critically at specific occupations and career paths. One of the most enjoyable parts of using the MBTI is the amazing consistency with which individuals identify with the positive descriptions and potential of their own types. Individuals who receive their MBTI results seem to leave the session with more hope and assurance than when they came in. In closing, it seems that Isabel Myers (1980) said it best:

> Type . . . should lessen the waste of potential, the loss of opportunity, and the number of dropouts and delinquents. It may even help with the prevention of mental illness.
>
> Whatever the circumstances of your life, whatever your personal ties, work, and responsibilities, the understanding of type can make your perceptions clearer, your judgments sounder, and your life closer to your heart's desire. (p. 211)

References

Golden, S. E. (1982). Let your dominant steer your career. *The Type Reporter, 1* (2), 1–2.

Gottfredson, G. D., Holland, J. L., & Ogawa, D. K. (1982). *Dictionary of Holland occupational codes.* Palo Alto, CA: Consulting Psychologists Press.

Lawrence, G. (1982). *People types and tiger stripes: A practical guide to learning styles.* Gainesville, FL: Center for the Applications of Psychological Type.

Mangun, S. L. (1982). *Job search: A review of the literature.* United States Department of Labor, 67–94.

Myers, I. B. (1962). *Manual: The Myers-Briggs Type Indicator.* Palo Alto, CA: Consulting Psychologists Press.

Myers, I. B. (1980). *Gifts differing.* Palo Alto, CA: Consulting Psychologists Press.

Myers, I. B. (1987). *Introduction to type.* Palo Alto, CA: Consulting Psychologists Press.

Myers, I. B. & McCaulley, M.H. (1985). *Manual: A guide to the development and use of the Myers-Briggs Type Indicator.* Palo Alto, CA: Consulting Psychologists Press.

U.S. Department of Labor (1977). *Dictionary of occupational titles.* Washington, DC: U.S. Government printing office.

GEORGE H. JENSEN is an Assistant Professor with the Division of Developmental Studies at Georgia State University. He earned a Ph.D. in English from the University of South Carolina in 1977 and has used the MBTI to teach composition, reading and study skills in a variety of settings. He has published articles in *Proof, MBTLI News, College Composition and Communication*, and the *Journal of Basic Writing*. With John K. DiTiberio, he recently completed the manuscript of *Personality Type and the Teaching of Composition* currently in submission. George's type is INTJ.

CHAPTER 9

Learning Styles

GEORGE H. JENSEN*

THE STUDY OF learning styles is a rather recent phenomenon, and, not surprisingly, the field is replete with the archetypes of an emerging science. At the core of the field are those who feel that their approach to learning styles is a virtual panacea for the current ills of education. At the borders are those who claim that learning styles do not exist, that the varied approaches students adopt to learning are purely random responses to their environment. Caught in between are those educators who sincerely want to become better teachers but who are confused by competing and conflicting paradigms (Kuhn, 1970).

These educators are confused with good cause. Since 1960, approximately 30 instruments of learning styles have appeared. Some of the more interesting and more frequently used are the *Hidden Figures Test* (1962), *Matching Figures Test* (1965), *Group Embedded Figures Test* (1971), *Student Learning Styles Questionnaire* (1974), *Cognititive Style Mapping Inventory* (1975), Kolb's *Learning Styles Inventory* (1976), and Dunn, Dunn, and Price's *Learning Styles Inventory* (adults, 1977; students, 1978). These and other instruments collectively measure about 20 aspects of learning styles (Keefe,1982), but none is comprehensive or clearly superior.

The Myers-Briggs Type Indicator, while it cannot earnestly claim to be comprehensive, has important strengths that are not often found in the rest of these instruments. First, the MBTI is better normed than most instruments of its kind. It was painstakingly developed over a 20-year period. Second, the MBTI is more sophisticated and complex than most learning style assessments. Rather than identify a few "styles," for

---

* The author wishes to acknowledge the assistance of John DiTiberio in writing this chapter.

example, field-dependent versus field-independent, the MBTI can identify 16 types or 16 approaches to learning.

Because of its sophistication, the MBTI can, as Lawrence (1984) has documented, account for most of the traits identified by other widely used instruments. The most significant shortcoming is the MBTI's inability to identify preferences for visual, auditory, and kinesthetic channels of perception and communication (Grinder & Bandler, 1976). Lowen (1982) has hypothesized connections between Sensing and the kinesthetic channel, Thinking and the visual channel, and Feeling and the auditory channel, but his theory remains untested and has yielded mixed results in the clinic and classroom.

What is most striking about the MBTI, and what empowers it, is that the instrument was developed as, and primarily remains, an assessment of personality type. Most learning style inventories assess *how the student is behaving* or *how the student believes that he or she performs best*. With these instruments, teachers can better understand the patterns in a student's learning behaviors, but learning style inventories rarely provide clues as to whether student's behavior is truly their learning style or how they were taught to learn. Rather than assessing behavior, the MBTI assesses personality type. Once the student's type is identified, teachers can make predictions about how that student learns best, which may or may not be consistent with his or her behavior, and suggest alternative methods of study. The MBTI, as will be explained later, allows teachers to penetrate through the veil of behavior to underlying cognitive functions as can few other assessments of learning style.

The MBTI and Learning Styles

In developing fields, terms are often ambiguous or vague, and this is also true of the study of learning styles. "Learning styles" can mean anything from hemisphericity to one's method of sharpening pencils. Lawrence (1984) described four uses of the term "learning styles" as used in connection with the MBTI:

1. Cognitive style in the sense of preferred or habitual patterns of mental functioning: information processing, and the formation of ideas and judgments.

2. Patterns of attitudes and interests that influence what a person will attend to in a potential learning situation.

3. A disposition to seek out learning environments compatible with one's cognitive style, attitudes, and interests, and to avoid environments that are not congenial.

4. A disposition to use certain learning tools and avoid others.

Lawrence states that the MBTI can only predict "preferred or habitual patterns" or "dispositions." As will be explained in the following sections, a student's MBTI results can be used to predict, on a probability model, what kind of behaviors, instructional tools, and environments facilitate or hinder learning for that student. It cannot predict with certainty how that student will read, write, or study. How a student actually behaves will be determined by a number of factors: personality type, parental influence, instruction, learning environment, and maturity. A perfect correlation between personality type and learning style is not possible.

In the following section, a description of the connection between type and learning style is drawn from Lawrence (1982, 1984), McCaulley and Natter (1974), and Myers (1980). See also Figure 1.

Extraversion-Introversion

The E-I dimension can indicate the degree of students' reliance on activity in the learning process and how students become involved in activity.

Extraverted students rely on activity more than Introverts. Since Extraverts tend to use their greatest strength, their dominant process, in the external world, they think best when talking, learn well in groups, and may have difficulty sitting in front of a book for a long period of time. They are usually able to concentrate more fully in classrooms that allow for group discussions or when they take frequent *and active* breaks from the typically solitary tasks of reading and writing.

Since they value active experience so highly, Extraverts tend to leap into academic tasks with little planning or consideration. Once actively involved, they use trial-and-error, which naturally suits their type, to complete the project. They prefer a trial-and-error process because it allows them to think while they are active. Thinking while acting or after acting is how Extraverts think best, which is why Jung referred to them as Epimetheans (Greek for "after-thinkers").

Introverted students, on the other hand, need quiet time for concentration and study, for they think best when alone, or at least when their inner solitude is uninterrupted. They are more comfortable than Extraverts with teacher-centered or lecture-based instruction and long stretches of solitary study, but, unless they anticipate questions before hand, they may perform poorly during in-class discussions. Because Introverts do not alway share what they know, teachers may be slow to appreciate their talents and depth of knowledge.

Jung called Introverts Prometheans (Greek for "fore-thinkers") because they do most of their thinking before they act. They tend to plan extensively, anticipate problems, and develop solutions to these problems before ever becoming involved in a task or activity. If asked a question, Introverts will usually think about their answer, rehearse it, and only then deliver it to their audience. Extraverts, on the other hand, are more likely to begin answering the questions immediately, thinking of what they want to say as they speak.

Sensing-Intuition

In general, the greatest contrast between Sensing and Intuitive students is how they direct their perception. Sensing students tend to focus on the concrete aspects of the here-and-now; they attempt to master first the facts and details of the learning environment. Intuitive students will seek general impressions, or the gestalt of what could possibly be; they will tend to master first the theories and concepts.

Sensing types also like to put into use what they have learned; they are, in general, practical and realistic. Learning for its own sake does not appeal much to them; usefulness does. They like teachers who give clear directions that are concise and to the point, and they tend to be detailed and precise in their own communications. Sensing students can accurately be described as artisans or surgeons. They like to learn a skill or procedure, perfect it, and then practice it without much variation. Thus, they are more likely to complete a task as they have refined it rather than be innovative for the sake of innovation.

Intuitive types are less likely to be patient with routine or overly structured mechanical approaches to learning. They desire and seek the opportunity to let their imaginative instincts work, and thus tend to prefer open-ended assignments. Their greatest strength is a facility for learning concepts and mastering abstract theories; their greatest weakness is a reluctance to observe details and learn facts.

Thinking-Feeling

The T-F dimension is most useful for providing insights into the affective domain of learning styles.

Thinking types tend to perform to the best of their ability when given a clearly presented set of performance criteria. They also want to know that their learning will lead toward a greater understanding of the systematic way that the world works and of the principles that underlie systems. In contrast, Feeling types need to know that what they are about to learn can be put to work for people they are concerned about or in the service of personally held convictions and values. They are best motivated when their hearts are in their work. While all students certainly are at their best when both sets of conditions prevail, thinking types are less likely to complain about dry, uninteresting tasks, as long as they are given a logical reason for doing them. Feeling types, unless given personal encouragement, may find any task boring and unrewarding.

Thinking and Feeling types also differ in how they solve problems and communicate. The talk of Thinking types usually reflects their thought process, which is rule- or principle-based and syllogistic. They often explain their decisions by counting off "reasons" on their fingers: "the first reason is . . . the second reason is . . . the third reason is . . . . " They also frequently punctuate their talk with the markers of an orderly, syllogistic thought: thus, therefore, in conclusion. Their discourse is what Kinneavy (1971, p. 88) calls "thing-centered." They concentrate on content, the message of what is being said, rather than process, how the message is connecting with the audience. They may, as a result, come to their point too quickly, or express it too bluntly.

Since the thought of Feeling types is based more on forming hierarchies of values, their talk is more likely to be expressive, filled with markers like "I feel, " "I believe," or "I like." Their discourse is more "people-centered" (Kinneavy, 1971, p. 88); they are more concerned with how their message is connecting with the audience than with the message itself.

Judgment-Perception

The J-P dimension is most useful for determining whether or not students prefer structured learning environments. Judging types, who tend to gauge their academic progress by their accomplishments, prefer the kind of structured learning environment in which goals and deadlines are set. Judging types can then take pleasure in accomplishing tasks, in writing papers, reading books, or making oral presentations. Perceptive types depend less on accomplishing tasks to feel comfortable with the learning environment. They tend to view learning as a free-wheeling, flexible, and thorough quest which may never end. If in a highly structured classroom, they may feel "imprisoned" and restricted.

Due to their natural desire to reach closure, Judging types tend to be overachievers. They tend to meet important deadlines by keeping

FIGURE 1

Type and Learning Styles

Extraversion (E)

Es learn best in situations filled with movement, action, and talk. They prefer to learn theories or facts that connect with their experience, and they will usually come to a more thorough understanding of these theories or facts during group discussions or when working on cooperative projects. Es tend to leap into assignments with little "forethought," relying on trial-and-error rather than anticipation to solve problems.

Introversion (I)

Since Is may be more quiet and less active in the classroom, teachers may feel the need to press them into taking part in group discussions. Such pressure, however, will often only increase their withdrawal. Teachers need to respect their need to think in relative solitude, for that is how they think best. Is will be more willing to share their ideas when given advance notice. This will allow them time to think about how they will become active in the classroom.

Sensory Perception (S)

Ss learn best when they move from the concrete to the abstract in a step-by-step progression. They are thus at home with programmed, modular, or computer-assisted learning. They value knowledge that is practical and want to be precise and accurate in their own work. They tend to excel at memorizing facts.

Intuitive Perception (N)

Ns tend to leap to a conceptual understanding of material and may daydream or act-out during drill work or predominately factual lectures. They value quick flashes of insight but are often careless about details. They tend to excel at imaginative tasks and theoretical topics.

Thinking Judgment (T)

Ts are most motivated when provided with a logical rationale for each project and when teachers acknowledge and respect their competence. They prefer topics that help them to understand systems or cause-and-effect relationships. Their thought is syllogistic and analytic.

Feeling Judgment (J)

Fs are most motivated when given personal encouragement and when shown the human angle of a topic. Fs think to clarify their values and to establish networks of values. Even when their expressions seem syllogistic, they usually evolve from some personally held belief or value.

Judgment (J)

Js tend to gauge their learning by the completion of tasks: reading "x"-amount of books, writing "x"-amount of papers, or making "x"-amount of reports. They thus prefer more structured learning environments that establish goals for them to meet.

Perception (P)

Ps tend to view learning as a free-wheeling, flexible quest. They care less about deadlines and the completion of tasks. They prefer open and spontaneous learning environments and feel "imprisoned" in a highly structured classroom.

Adapted from McCaulley and Natter (1974) and Lawrence (1984).

commitments limited and focusing on one task at a time. Teachers often view them as being more organized and motivated than Perceptive types. The natural style of Perceptive types, which leads them to over-commit themselves, work on several projects at once, and delay closure until the eleventh hour, may make them appear unmotivated or unorganized. Teachers need to realize that the procrastination of Perceptive types is often as productive as a Judging type's rush to meet a deadline. Perceptive types may delay beginning or finishing projects so that they can more thoroughly conceptualize or research them.

Type and Teaching Style

As any student knows well, teachers too have a style. Extraverts tend to develop student-based classrooms. They prefer very active instruction full of talk, group projects, and experimental learning; they are also more likely to allow students choice about what to study and how to study it. Introverts, on the other hand, tend to develop teacher-based classrooms. They seem to prefer lectures to discussions, and are more likely to structure the learning tasks from the textbook or other instructional materials or from their own plans for the course. Sensing types tend to keep instruction focused on a narrow range of choices, and usually concentrate on factual and concrete questions. Intuitive types are more likely, when students have a choice of assignments, to allow for a wide range of choices. They also tend to focus on questions that involve conjecture, often beginning their questions with "What if . . . ?" Thinking types are more likely to treat a class as a collective, whereas Feeling types are more likely to treat the class as individuals and attempt to attend to each student's needs. Thinking types tend to excel at challenging students, although they may offer little feedback, or at the other extreme, be so critical and harsh that they intimidate rather than motivate. Feeling types are more likely to motivate their students with praise and empathy. Judging types tend to develop orderly classrooms, those with schedules and deadlines. Perceptive types develop more spontaneous classrooms, those with more movement, open-ended discussions, and flexible schedules (Lawrence, 1982).

If students have learning styles and instructors have teaching styles, mismatches are clearly inevitable. What would happen when an ISTJ instructor, who prefers an orderly and quiet classroom, prefers to lecture about facts and details, gives little feedback, and allows for few options on assignments has an ENFP student, who wants to talk about ideas, craves autonomy, wants to work on projects that are personally relevant, and feels imprisoned by structure and deadlines? Not much. The teacher teaches little, probably because he or she finds the ENFP a constant disruption, and the student learns little, probably because he or she is unmotivated, bored, or rebellious. The problem is one that almost every instructor, to some degree and in some fashion, faces with every class; there is always at least one student who seems impossible to reach, who either acts out or drifts off. Something must be done, but what? Should the teacher adapt to the student's learning style, or the student to the instructor's teaching style?

Initially, theorists of learning styles assumed that instructors should adapt their teaching styles to the students' learning styles. More recently, theorists have questioned the practicality and wisdom of this approach (Partridge, 1983). If an ISTJ instructor adapts his or her teaching style to an ENFP student, then what happens to the other students who may be ISFJs, ESFPs, INTJs, and other types? The teacher cannot adapt to a classroom of 30 students who may represent most of the 16 MBTI types. Even if instructors could adapt to a diverse class, some theorists believe that students would be ill served. One purpose of education is to help students grow and mature, to adapt to the adult world. Exposing them to a wide variety of teaching styles, some argue, helps students to develop in ways that they could not if only exposed to the one teaching style that is compatible with their learning style (Partridge, 1983).

Perhaps the greatest condemnation of the matching strategy is that it violates some basic assumptions of type theory: that one's type does not change, that one functions best when acting in accordance with one's type, and that attempting to change one's type has dire consequences. By asking instructors to adapt to their students' learning styles, we are asking them to abandon their preferred behaviors, to hold their strengths in reserve and teach from their weaknesses. Jung felt that many of the failures of education result from instructors who teach from their weaknesses rather than their strengths. An ENTP instructor, whose strength is in leading discussions about concepts and theories, should not be forced to lecture on facts and details. The results of teachers falsifying their type, Jung felt, are "educational monstrosities" (1954, p. 171).

As it is unwise to ask teachers to falsify their type, so too is it unwise to ask students to learn in a process and environment that is foreign to their nature. Yet, if teachers are true to their style and students true to theirs, how can learning occur? How can an ISTJ teach an ENFP?

Without attempting to falsify their type, or abandon their preferred teaching style, instructors can be more flexible in how they teach. Even though Introverted teachers may prefer to lecture, they can allow some time for class discussion. Even though Sensing teachers may prefer to teach facts and details, they can discuss some theories and concepts. Even though Thinking teachers may like to challenge students, they can also give a student a needed pat on the back. Even though Judging teachers like the structure of goals and deadlines, they can also allow for unstructured learning and open-ended assignments. Instructors may not be able to restructure the classroom to meet the needs of each individual, but they can try to include a broad enough range of activities and approaches so that no one type of student feels completely left out.

When students perform poorly, instructors can also use MBTI results to reach an understanding of what that student needs to improve. For example, if an INTP's theoretical lectures bewilder an ISTP student, the instructor might arrange for the student to receive computer-assisted instruction on the topic. Or, when the ISTP student asks for a clarification of some point made in the INTP's lecture, the teacher can explain the theory again, this time including several concrete examples.

Finally, type theory can be useful in establishing contact with that student. To quote an educational aphorism, "You have to reach them to teach them." Whenever dealing with an individual student during tutorials, when answering an individual student's question, or when giving written feedback, instructors can attempt to establish contact with students as an orator establishes contact with an audience. Instructors do not have to match their teaching styles completely to their students' learning styles, as an effective orator does more than simply tell the audience what they want to hear. Rather, instructors can adapt their teaching style to a particular student's learning style long enough to make contact, establish common ground, and pique interest. Instead of asking an Intuitive instructor with predominately Sensing students to teach facts, we can advise him or her to teach some facts as an entree to teaching concepts and theories. The Intuitive instructor can say, "Let me teach you some facts so that I can interest you in my ideas." Figure 2 can aid instructors in establishing contact with students of different types, as an example will illustrate.

Doug (an INFP) wrote the following essay, the first for a remedial composition course, on what bugs him about life:

There are many things in my life that I disapprove of. Not only do they affect my personal being, but also affect everyone in some way. Personally my biggest dislikes are ignorance and hatred towards each other. Everywhere you look you find good examples of this type of behavior. The situations range from something as simple as inconsiderate drivers of cars, to the superpowers of the world threatening each other. The single largest fault of people is that they won't accept each other. If everyone would try to work with human nature and understand it, then there would be a lot less chaos on this planet.

FIGURE 2

Strategies for Making Contact with Students

Extraversion (E)

Making contact: The best way to make contact with Es is through their preferred channel of communication: talk. They usually respond better to oral than to written feedback. Since they value experience, they respond well to compliments about the vitality of their writing.

Words that appeal to Es: experience, vitality, lively, action

Introversion (I)

Making contact: Is will respond better to any situation when given advance notice and when not expected to "think on their feet." Before talking to Is, it is best to tell them what you want to talk about and then schedule an appointment. This will allow them time to think about what they may want to say. Is often respond well to teachers who acknowledge that they have more to say (or write) than they have offered. Is will talk (or write) more when they trust the teacher and when they are not forced to share their ideas.

Words that appeal to Is: thoughtful, serious, sincere

Sensory Perception (S)

Making contact: Ss prefer to process information inductively and attend better to communications that begin with the concrete. Facts, concrete examples, and practical solutions appeal to them. They respond well to compliments about being accurate, reliable, and precise.

Words that appeal to Ss: practical, realistic, solid, concrete, sensible, here-and-now, reliable, accurate

Intuitive Perception (N)

Making contact: Ns prefer to process information deductively and attend better to communications that begin with concepts, theories, or inferences. They love sentences that begin with "What if . . . ?" They value being innovative, original, and theoretical.

Words that appeal to Ns: innovation, possibilities, hunches, inspiration, fantasy

Adapted from McCaulley and Natter (1974) and Lawrence (1984).

Unless instructors are tuned into the student's type, they would probably respond only to the faults in the essay. They might scrawl across the margin of Doug's essay: "You need better organization," "You need to develop your ideas," or "You need paragraphs." Doug's instructor, however, chose to use a knowledge of type theory to make contact with Doug:

FIGURE 2 (continued)

Strategies for Making Contact with Students

Thinking Jugment (T)

Making contact: Ts value being logical and objective. They react most favorably to logical rationale and analytical thought. The prefer criticism that is to the point rather than criticism that is softened or indirect.

Words that appeal to Ts: objective, analytic, logical, valid, systematic

Feeling Judgment (F)

Making contact: Fs tend to respond best to communication after personal contact has been made. They prefer to chat informally before getting down to business. They respond well to any acknowledgment of them as individuals: learning their name, asking about their interests and values, a smile, a pat on the back, etc. They often respond well to an instructor saying that he or she enjoyed reading their essays.

Words that appeal to Fs: beliefs, values, personal, heart-felt, touching, interesting, us, we, together, share

Judgment (J)

Making contact: Js are particularly concerned about the passage of time, and usually respond well to compliments about how efficient, expedient, or punctual they are. Js also value being decisive. They tend to view their work, once it is submitted, as finished, and prefer to hear comments about how they can improve the next essay than about how to improve this essay.

Words that appeal to Js: complete, finished, decisive, hardworking, punctual

Perception (P)

Making contact: Ps are usually most concerned about being thorough, so they tend to view their work as ongoing. They prefer to hear about how to improve this essay rather than about how to improve the next essay.

Words that appeal to Ps: thorough, complete, extensive, in-progress, ongoing

Adapted from McCaulley and Natter (1974) and Lawrence (1984).

Doug,

    I get the idea, very clearly, that there are some things about the world we live in that bug you. Me, too! The thing I like most about this essay is that sense of strong values you have, your feeling that there is something wrong out there. But I think that the paper is weak in one major way: you feel the need to mention all the things that bug you. I appreciate your need to be complete, but I think I would understand your feelings even better if you just selected one gripe and developed it more. Then I could get more connected with your values.

With a knowledge of Doug's type, the instructor was able to connect with him by acknowledging and accepting Doug's "strong values," which evolve from his preference for Feeling judgment. Once contact was made, the instructor could suggest a revision, that Doug be less inclusive and further develop one or two ideas. Even when suggesting a revision, the instructor acknowledged the values or strengths behind the process that produced a weak text. Doug's being a Perception type led to an overinclusion of ideas. The instructor said that he appreciated Doug's "need to be complete" before suggesting a change. The instructor closed with another appeal to Doug's preference for Feeling judgment by saying, "Then I could get more connected with your values." Since Feeling types want to be connected with their audience, the comment should provide additional motivation for change.

The effective use of type theory in the classroom, then, entails a seemingly contradictory application. Instructors should remain true to their type, teaching from their strengths, but instructors should also be flexible enough to allow students to employ their preferred approaches to learning. Instructors must not be asked to change their teaching styles, but they should be shown how to make contact with their students.

Program Example: Division of Developmental Studies, Georgia State University

The Division of Developmental Studies at Georgia State University offers instruction in reading, composition, math, and study skills to students who are marginally prepared for college. The teaching is challenging since the students are placed into the program for diverse reasons and have a range of needs. Some of the students are capable but unmotivated; others are capable but the products of poor school systems. Some are motivated but have poor skills; others are motivated but not exceptionally capable. Several of the composition faculty have found the MBTI useful in meeting the needs of this population, as will be explained after some background is provided.

Even though composition theorists agree that writing should be taught as a process, they are unable to agree on what sort of process should be taught. For example, Rohman (1965) and others (see Young,

1976) believe that students should be taught prewriting strategies, which are typically questioning heuristics such as the "five Ws" of journalism. They feel that, if students decide what they want to say before writing, then the process of putting words on paper will be easier and the finished text will embody more sophisticated thought. In direct opposition, Macrorie (1970), Murray (1978), and Elbow (1973) believe that writers should leap into writing with little planning and discover what they want to say as they put words on paper.

One might think that such obvious disagreements among theorists would lead to an uncertainty among teachers, but not necessarily. Of course, some well-informed instructors are uncertain of what to teach and thus give rather permissive advice. They might tell their students, "Some like to outline, others don't." Or, "Some like to think everything out before they write, others don't." Intuitive types generally find such open-ended advice satisfactory, but Sensing types usually want more direction and may become distressed, confused, and even paralyzed by a variety of options. Many teachers are seemingly unaffected by disagreements of theorists. They continue to issue "rules" of writing: "You must write an outline." Or, "You must develop a thesis before you write." The unfortunate end result of such dogma is the development of writing anxiety. As students are forced to write in a process that is incompatible with their personality type, writing becomes less natural, more laborious, and more stressful (Jensen & DiTiberio, 1983). As Jung has stated, whenever individuals are forced to function contrary to their type, to falsify their type, they will usually experience stress, acute exhaustion, or even neurosis (1921, p. 332).

The instructors in the Developmental Studies program are faced with the results of both the permissive and dogmatic approaches to teaching composition. Sensing types who were not given adequate direction in high school enter college feeling that there are definite ways to approach writing but that these have been hidden from them; that if only a teacher would tell them how to write then they could do it and do it well. These students generally perform better with more guidance, as long as the guidance is compatible with their personality type.

Students of all types who were taught dogmatically that they must write in a prescribed process enter college suffering from writing anxiety. Their anxiety can be relieved if they realign their writing process, and if they begin to write in a process that is more suited to their personality type. The Developmental Studies program instructor, then, needs to provide these distressed or misled students with guidance, but the kind of guidance that is appropriate for each individual student. It is in individualizing advice and instruction that the MBTI is particularly useful.

Jensen and DiTiberio (1984) have shown that composition teachers can use results from the MBTI to make some assumptions about how individuals will tend to write best. Extraverts tend to generate ideas best when talking and prefer to leap into writing with little planning; Introverts, on the other hand, need solitude to think best and prefer to plan extensively—both what to say and how to say it—before writing. Sensing types tend to prefer prescribed organizational patterns, detailed directions, and factual topics; Intuitive types prefer original organizational patterns, general directions, and imaginative, abstract topics. Thinking types think best when they write from very patterned structures, while Feeling types tend to write best when they just follow the flow of their thoughts. Judging types, in their rush to meet deadlines, often shorten the research phase and minimize revision. Perceptive types, in their need to keep discovering more about the topic, extend the research phase and revise extensively. For more information about this, see Figure 3.

Developmental Studies instructors use MBTI results to formulate a working hypothesis of how individual students tend to write best and use this hypothesis to individualize instruction. For example, an Extraverted student may be having difficulty writing because he feels that he must, as he was taught to do in high school, develop an outline before writing. Knowing that Extraverts usually write better when they leap into writing, the instructor can use the theory of Macrorie (1970), and Murray (1978), and Elbow (1973) to show the student how to write without outlines or extensive planning. If an Introverted student is having difficulty developing ideas, the instructor, using the theory of Rohman (1965) and others, might suggest that she use prewriting strategies to clarify her ideas before writing. The MBTI, then, can be used to both resolve apparent contradictions in theory and to individualize instruction, usually with positive results. As students develop a more effective and healthy writing process, writing becomes easier, and the quality of their finished texts improves.

One word of caution should be issued. Even when instructors have their student's MBTI scores, they should not assume that a student who tests as an Extravert will necessarily write as Extraverts typically do. The measurement of type is not always accurate, and, as stated above, people do not always act consistently with their type. It is best, therefore, to give advice carefully. If teachers have an Extravert who plans extensively before writing, they should not dogmatically insist that the student change his or her writing process. A teacher might say: "You might find writing easier if you just leap into it and just do your thinking as you

FIGURE 3

The MBTI and Individual Writing Process

Extraversion (E)

Es generate ideas best by talking about the topic, interviewing people, or actively experiencing the topic. They tend to leap into writing with little anticipation and then write by trial-and-error. They tend to develop a great deal of material as they write. As a result, their in-class essays and first drafts may reflect confusion in early paragraphs and clarity in later paragraphs. If they perform traditional prewriting strategies (such as outlining), they can often do so more easily after writing a first draft. Discussing drafts with others helps them to understand the need for revision and what needs to be revised. Some Es (esp. if also J) may not revise at all unless they receive oral feedback.

Introversion (I)

Introverts plan before writing and want most of their ideas clarified before putting words onto paper. When they begin to write, they stop frequently to anticipate the direction of the essay and where their ideas are leading them. They usually spend more time than extraverts between drafts because they like to have time to consider their revisions. Throughout the writing process, they tend to write alone, asking for advice only from close friends or teachers that they trust.

Sensory Perception (S)

Sensing types prefer explicit, detailed, and specific directions. Their first drafts reflect their inductive thought and are often filled with facts that have not yet been related to a central idea or theme. They feel more comfortable when following a pattern prescribed by the teacher or one that is tried and true, one that they have used in the past. Even during a first draft, they may closely attend to mechanics (grammar, spelling, etc.). They may regard revising as merely correcting or proofreading.

Intuitive Perception (N)

Intuitive types tend to write best when given general directions that allow their imagination to work. Developing a unique approach to the topic is an important part of their prewriting phase. At their best, they tend to write quickly, letting one idea trigger another and paying little attention to mechanics. They tend to innovate organizational patterns. In their first drafts, they may present generalities without examples or concrete support.

From Jensen and DiTiberio, "Personality and Individual Writing Processes," *College Composition and Communication, 35* (October 1984), 285–300.

FIGURE 3 (continued)

The MBTI and Individual Writing Process

Thinking Judgment (T)

Ts tend to select topics that can be written about with emotional distance rather than self-involvement. They tend to make organizational decisions by following a structure, such as an outline. When writing, they tend to focus on content rather than on how the message is affecting the audience. As a result, they may sometimes be overly blunt.

Feeling Judgment (F)

Feeling types prefer topics that they can care about; they often complain about topics that are dry or "boring." When writing, they tend to draw upon personal experience; for example, their introductions often begin with a personal example. They rely less on structure than Thinking types; they usually begin with a sentence and then follow the flow of their thoughts. They also tend to make organizational decisions by anticipating the audience's reaction to their text.

Judgment (J)

Js tend to limit their topics quickly and set goals that are manageable. They also tend to limit their research so that they can begin writing more quickly and complete the project. Their first drafts tend to be short and underdeveloped with ideas stated emphatically and often without qualification.

Perception (P)

Ps tend to select broad topics and dive into research without limiting them. Topics will usually be limited only as the deadline approaches. They want to thoroughly research or analyze a topic, often without a clear focus, before beginning to write and may feel that there is always one more book or article to read. Their drafts tend to be long and thorough. Their writing may ramble because they are inclusive of ideas and data.

From Jensen and DiTiberio, "Personality and Individual Writing Processes," *College Composition and Communication, 35* (October 1984), 285–300.

write. I'd like you to try this approach and see if it works better for you." After the student tries the approach, the teacher should talk to the student and assess whether or not the new approach was actually more comfortable and efficient.

As the MBTI provides insight into individual students, so too can it provide insight into particular coteries of students. Since at least the 1950s, composition theorists have been trying to classify the kind of college students found in programs similar to Developmental Studies at

Georgia State. These students have been labeled as sub-freshmen, remedial writers, basic writers, unskilled writers, and developmental writers; they have been described as being concrete (Lunsford, 1979), unreflective (Pianko, 1979), and overly concerned with "error-hunting" (Perl, 1979). Even though these researchers feel that they are describing the same category of students, one should not assume that the description of "basic writers" (the most commonly employed label) at one university is similar to that at another university (Shaughnessy, 1976). Descriptions of basic writers are usually inaccurate when applied to the students in a particular program at a particular university or college (Jensen, 1986).

A type table of the students in an instructor's class or in an entire program can provide data for refining the crude characterizations found in professional literature. Table 1 is a type table of 188 composition students in the Developmental Studies program. The table shows that the program seems to have a roughly equal distribution of Extraverts and Introverts, but significantly more Sensing types, Thinking types, and Judging types. From this data, one might predict that the typical student in this program is a very structured learner, which is generally true of STJs and consistent with instructors' "hunches" about their students. Should, then, the instructors in this program teach to the typical students? Should they, for example, have all students write on the kind of concrete, detailed, and structured writing topics that appeal to STJs?

The type table, again, provides useful information. If the instructors teach primarily to the STJs, what would happen to the Intuitive students? The Intuitive types are definitely a minority, but 30 percent of the population is a sizeable minority that would be ill served if instructors relied only on their "hunches" about the student population, or descriptions of basic writers in professional literature. By compiling type tables, the instructors in the Developmental Studies program can both understand the typical student *and* appreciate the diversity of the population. Table 1 shows an overrepresentation by STJs, but all of the 16 types appear.

In the Developmental Studies program, these data have been used to make program-wide decisions, such as the selection of topics for an exit essay exam, which all students must pass in order to enter regular English classes. Since the students are predominately Sensing types, the instructors are careful to develop topics that are concrete and detailed, as below:

When you receive this month's MASTERCARD and VISA bill, you notice, much to your horror, that you have been erroneously

TABLE 1

Students in Developmental Composition, Georgia State University
(Eleven Classes from Fall 1982 to Winter 1985)

	Sensing Types		Intuitive Types	
	withThinking	with Feeling	with Feeling	withThinking

ISTJ N=40 %=21 ▪▪▪▪▪▪▪▪ ▪▪▪▪▪▪▪▪ ▪▪▪▪▪▪▪▪ ▪▪▪▪▪▪▪ ▪▪▪▪▪▪▪▪	**ISFJ** N=12 %=6 ▪▪▪▪▪▪▪▪ ▪▪▪▪▪	**INFJ** N=2 %=1 ▪▪▪▪	**INTJ** N=4 %=2 ▪▪▪▪	Introverts Judging
ISTP N=12 %=6 ▪▪▪▪▪▪▪▪ ▪▪▪▪▪▪	**ISFP** N=9 %=5 ▪▪▪▪▪▪▪▪ ▪▪	**INFP** N=4 %=2 ▪▪▪▪	**INTP** N=14 %=7 ▪▪▪▪▪▪▪▪ ▪▪▪▪▪▪	Perceptive
ESTP N=16 %=8 ▪▪▪▪▪▪▪▪▪ ▪▪▪▪▪▪▪▪▪	**ESFP** N=5 %=3 ▪▪▪▪▪	**ENFP** N=10 %=5 ▪▪▪▪▪▪▪▪ ▪▪▪	**ENTP** N=7 %=4 ▪▪▪▪▪▪▪▪	Extraverts Perceptive
ESTJ N=24 %=11 ▪▪▪▪▪▪▪▪▪ ▪▪▪▪▪▪▪▪▪ ▪▪▪▪▪▪▪▪▪	**ESFJ** N=16 %=8 ▪▪▪▪▪▪▪▪▪ ▪▪▪▪▪▪▪▪	**ESFJ** N=6 %=3 ▪▪▪▪▪▪	**ENTJ** N=9 %=5 ▪▪▪▪▪▪▪▪	Judging

E = 48% (n=91)
I = 52% (n=97)

S = 70% (n=132)
N = 30% (n=56)

T = 66% (n=125)
F = 34% (n=63)

J = 62% (n=117)
P = 38% (n=71)

Note: ▪ = 1 student.

charged with $3,400 worth of merchandise that you did not purchase. Rushing to check your wallet, you are relieved to discover your credit card secure. Now, you can assume that the credit card company has made an error, or that someone has duplicated your credit card number. Write a letter to the credit card company notifying them of this serious error. You do not have to mention every item, but you should argue why it was impossible for you to make some of the following purchases:

- $400 worth of clothing from Davison's on April 4th

- $1600 vacation to the Bahamas from Delta Airlines on April 5th

- $230 worth of make-up from J.C. Penney's on April 6th

- $170 worth of tires from Firestone on April 8th

- $500 videotape machine from Rich's on April 5th

- $60 worth of fishing equipment from K-MART on April 10th

- $42 dinner at Po'Folks on April 14th

- $350 stereo from Radio Shack on April 18th

- $47 worth of harp music records from Turtles on April 17th

But since a sizeable minority of students are Intuitive types, the instructors also develop more conceptual and open-ended questions, as below:

John Boulton, who recently lost his job as a welder, was walking down the sidewalk in Cabbage Town carrying a dufflebag when a police car pulled up beside him and two officers got out and demanded to see what was in the bag. They examined the contents and found nothing but his clothes. After explaining that there had just been a robbery down the road, they sped away in their car. Write a letter to William Daniels, Chief of Police, in defense of this man's rights *or* defending the policemen's actions. Before writing, you may want to imagine how Boulton looks and acts, and how the police actually treated him.

By being aware of the diversity of the students in the Developmental Studies program, the instructors are better able to serve the needs of *all* students.

Program Example: The Academic Skills Program, Counseling Service, University of Illinois at Chicago (Health Sciences Campus)

The Academic Skills Program, a division of the Counseling Service of the University of Illinois at Chicago, provides both group and individual instruction in reading, composition, and study skills. Since its clientele are predominately students from the health sciences, the staff in the program more frequently deal with skills at the other end of the spectrum than do the instructors in the Developmental Studies program. The clients of the Academic Skills program are generally bright and highly motivated; they also tend to have been successful students. Once they are faced with the pressures of a health sciences curriculum, however, they find that their skills, which may have been adequate in high school or in undergraduate school, must be improved or refined. The setting of the Academic Skills program is also different. The Developmental Studies program is an academic unit, the Academic Skills program is a clinic. In a clinic, staff are able to spend more time diagnosing the causes of each student's difficulties and developing individualized interventions, and the MBTI can be a useful diagnostic tool.

Most of the Nursing students at the University of Illinois are capable and dedicated students. They are able to master course content with hard work, but they often have difficulty demonstrating their knowledge on objective tests. At many universities, staff may attempt to improve students' test-taking skills by giving what is ultimately platitudinous advice (for example, "look for key words") or by teaching guessing techniques (for example, "if in doubt, pick the longest alternative"). Such interventions can be helpful, but they hardly address the fundamental problems that students have with taking tests. To move beyond mere advice and guessing techniques, one must obtain as many insights as possible into the thought process behind answering test questions. In the Academic Skills program, the staff have students "think aloud" as they read sample test questions. These protocols, when coupled with a knowledge of the student's type, can provide useful glimpses into how a particular student analyzes test questions. The following examples of how Cheryl (an ISTJ Nursing student) misread questions will illustrate this.

Nursing students must learn from two important media: lectures and clinical experience. For Sensing types, the clinical experience often assumes hegemony over the theory of a lecture, leading them to misread questions like:

FIGURE 4

The S-N Dimension and Test-Taking

Sensory Perception (S)	Intutive Perception (N)
When Ss read test questions, they often have hunches as to the correct answer, but they rarely trust their hunches. Frequently, they begin to reread the questions repeatedly, looking for a concrete clue (a fact, underlined, something that relates to their experience, etc.). They often reread a question until they misread it. They may also answer theoretical questions with lived experience, fail to grasp the big picture or system behind the question, and generally lose points by changing answers.	Intuitive types tend to read test questions quickly, at times carelessly, trust their hunch and then move on to the next question. Because they trust their hunches, they are often better test-takers than Ss, but they can often pick up points by checking for careless errors. Their misreading of questions is usually due to a faulty inference, a line of thought that begins with "What if . . .?" A single inference is usually appropriate, but Ns often make inferences from inferences and stray too far from the core of the question.

Note: Only the S–N dimension has been included because the effects of other dimensions on test-taking appear to be marginal.

1. It would be appropriate to explain to a patient on a restricted diet why he or she cannot eat certain foods in order that he or she:
    1. does not think his or her diet restrictions are punitive
    2. will not eat incorrect foods appearing on his or her tray
    3. can continue dietary patterns after discharge
    4. feels that he or she has an active role in his or her care
        a. 1 & 2
        b. 2, 3, & 4
        c. 1, 2, & 4
        d. all of the above

When Cheryl read this question, she felt that all possible alternatives were correct except number three. She eliminated number three because in her clinical experience, she had seen very few patients have restricted diets after leaving the hospital. While number three may have seemed irrelevant to the facts of her experience, it is nonetheless compatible with nursing theory. Cheryl's reliance on the facts of her experience (S), as well as her inability to accept number three as something that might possibly occur (which would be more typical of Ns), led her to select "C" rather than "D," the correct answer.

At other times, Cheryl's inability to view the "big picture" (typical of immature Ss) led her astray, as with the question below:

2. Mr. S. is an 85-year-old man admitted to the hospital with arteriosclerosis (increasing rigidity of the blood vessels). Knowing these facts, you would expect to find:

   1. decreased pulse rate
   2. rise in systolic pressure
   3. decrease in diastolic pressure
   4. rise in pulse pressure
   5. no change in pulse pressure
      a. 1 & 5
      b. 2, 3, & 4
      c. 1, 2, 3, & 5
      d. 2 & 4
      e. 1, 2, & 4

After reading the question, Cheryl felt that number one was a correct response. She reasoned that, since Mr. S.'s blood vessels were rigid, then less blood would be able to flow through them. The result would be a decreased pulse rate. Cheryl's thought process was basically logical, but she made the mistake of analyzing a question on histology, which is a science of body systems, too logically and specifically. While it is true that hardened vessels allow less blood to pass, the cardiovascular system still demands the same amount of oxygen. Therefore, in order to meet the body's demand, the heart must pump faster to supply the same amount of oxygenated blood through a rigidly narrow vessel.

Protocols, or "thinking aloud," can provide valuable information about how students are reading test questions, but instructors can make more sense of a student's spoken thoughts if they use a knowledge of type to interpret them. As the MBTI is useful in diagnosing how students misread test questions (see Figure 4), so too is it useful in diagnosing their difficulties with reading (see Figure 5), study skills (see Figure 1), and time management (see Figure 6).

Conclusion

As stated earlier, the MBTI is not a panacea for the ills of education, but it is certainly a very powerful and useful instrument. It can be a catalyst for helping students to understand how they learn best, for helping

FIGURE 5

The MBTI and Reading

Extraversion

Es may have difficulty concentrating on reading for long stretches of time. They often understand texts better if they process them orally.

Introversion

Although Is may be able to concentrate for longer stretches of time, they may sometimes lose concentration because they begin to contemplate what they read and become lost in a daydream.

Sensing

When learning to read, Ss may have difficulty learning the code of written language. Sometimes, they benefit from the language-experience approach, phonics instruction or other techniques that can help to break the "code." Even when mature, Ss may focus on the facts of a text and neglect the concepts.

Intuition

Since they tend to have a greater facility for symbols, Ns usually learn to read with less difficulty and tend to be more "bookish." Even when mature, they may focus on the concepts of a text and neglect the facts.

Thinking

Ts often focus so fully on the message of a text that they may neglect the style or tone. They often have a greater tolerance for "dry academic treatises." They also tend to be more critical of what they read.

Feeling

Fs tend to be very sensitive to tone and style. They may enjoy an author simply because they like his or her style. They often become bored with texts that do not engage their personal values.

Judgment

Js may be too quick to interpret a text, sometimes on only a cursory reading, and then have difficulty rethinking the text on subsequent readings.

Perception

Ps tend to more thoroughly read and process texts. This may cause them to read more slowly or become bogged down in research.

teachers understand why certain students are performing poorly, and for helping teachers make contact with their students. Many learning styles instruments can offer similar aid, but the MBTI does more. It can also help teachers to move past behaviors to cognitive processes, to better understand the thought processes of students quite different from themselves.

FIGURE 6

The MBTI and Time Management

Extraversion

Es are most motivated when approaching active tasks and may neglect more typically introverted tasks like reading and studying. They sometimes work inefficiently because they leap into tasks without planning and work by trial-and-error. They need to learn that tasks can sometimes be completed more efficiently if they attempt to plan a bit before acting.

Introversion

Is may have longer attention spans for reading and studying, but they often avoid more typically extraverted tasks, e.g., scheduling meetings, returning phone calls, etc. They naturally like to contemplate a task before beginning it, but they may think too long before acting. It is often more efficient to simply leap into a task.

Sensing

Ss often avoid more theoretical tasks and can sometimes spend more time on the details of a task than necessary. Ss may also become locked into their routine approaches to tasks, even when these approaches are inefficient.

Intuition

Ns often have to redo tasks because they neglected important details; they also tend to avoid routine chores. They may want to complete each task (even if it is writing a memorandum) in a unique way, which may be more time consuming.

Thinking

Ts tend to schedule what they feel are the most important tasks first, even if these tasks are the most unpleasant ones. The unfortunate consequence is that Ts sometimes never get around to more rewarding and relaxing activities.

Feeling

Fs tend to schedule the tasks about which they care the most, whether or not these are the most pressing ones. They may avoid tasks that are not connected to their personal values.

Judgment

Js tend to be natural time managers, with one important caveat. They are good at making schedules and sticking to them, but they are not always flexible. They need to learn how to "plan to be spontaneous." They need to plan to stop at key intervals and re-evaluate their schedules.

Perception

The more spontaneous Ps are often reluctant to make schedules. When they do, they often fail to follow them or conveniently lose their "list of things to do." Ps may also overcommit themselves and have trouble meeting important deadlines. Ps need to learn how to prioritize and concentrate on the most important tasks.

References

Elbow, P. (1973). *Writing with power*. New York: Oxford.

Grindler, J., & Bandler, R. (1976). *The structure of magic II*. Palo Alto, CA: Science and Behavior Books.

Jensen, G. H. The reification of the basic writer. *Journal of Basic Writing*, (in press).

Jensen, G. H., & DiTiberio, J. K. (1983). The MBTI and writing blocks. *MBTI News*, 5, 14–15.

Jensen, G. H., & DiTiberio, J. K. (1984). Personality and individual writing processes. *College Composition and Communication, 35*, 285–300.

Jung, C. G. (1921). *Psychological types*. Princeton, NJ: Princeton University Press.

Jung, C. G. (1954). *The development of personality type*. Princeton, NJ: Princeton University Press.

Kinneavy, J. L. (1971). *A theory of discourse*. Englewood Cliffs, NJ: Prentice-Hall.

Keefe, J. W. (1982). Assessing student learning styles: An overview. In *Student Learning Styles and Brain Behavior*. Reston, VA: National Association of Secondary School Principals.

Kuhn, T. S. (1970). *The structure of scientific revolutions* (2nd ed.) Chicago: Chicago University Press.

Lawrence, G. (1982). *People types and tiger stripes: A practical guide to learning styles*. Gainesville, FL: Center for Applications of Psychological Type.

Lawrence, G. (1984). A synthesis of learning style research involving the MBTI. *Journal of Psychological Type, 8*, 2–15.

Lowen, W. (1982). *Dichotomies of the mind: A systems science model of the mind and personality*. New York: John Wiley & Sons.

Lunsford, A. (1979). Cognitive development and the basic writer. *College English, 41*, 38–46.

McCaulley, M., and Natter, F. L. (1974). *Psychological (Myers-Briggs) type differences in education*. Gainesville, FL: Center for Applications of Psychological Type.

Macrorie, K. (1970). *Telling writing*. Rochelle Park, NJ: Hayden.

Murray, D. M. (1978). Write before writing. *College Composition and Communication, 29*, 375–81.

Myers, I. B. (1980). *Gifts differing*. Palo Alto, CA: Consulting Psychologists Press.

Partridge, R. (1983). Learning styles: A review of selected models. *Journal of Nursing Education, 22*, 243–48.

Perl, S. (1979). The composing processes of unskilled college writers. *Research in the Teaching of English., 13*, 317–36.

Pianko, S. (1979). Reflection: A critical component of the composing process. *College Composition and Communication, 30*, 275–78.

Rohman, G. D. (1965). Prewriting: The stage of discovery in the writing process. *College Composition and Communication, 16*, 106–12.

Shaughnessy, M. P. (1976). Basic writing. Gary Tate (Ed.) In *Teaching Composition: Ten bibliographical essays.* Fort Worth, TX: Texas Christian University Press.

Young, R. (1976). Invention. In *Teaching Composition: Ten bibliographical essays* Fort Worth, TX: Texas Christian University Press.

FRED LEAFGREN has used type for 15 years with communities, faculty, administration, students, and organizations. Currently Assistant Chancellor for Student Life, at the University of Wisconsin (Stevens Point) , Fred received his graduate training at Michigan State University. His current work involves using type to work with an entire campus community as part of a wellness program. Fred has contributed chapters to various books/monographs in higher education; most notable is his chapter entitled, "Educational Programming in College Residence Halls" in the Jossey-Bass New Directions Series, and the 1986 publication *Developing Campus Recreation and Wellness Programs*, which he edited. Fred is an INFP.

CHAPTER 10

Faculty Involvement

FRED LEAFGREN

DIFFERENT PERSONALITY TYPES learn in different ways. Recognizing and reacting to those differences can significantly affect the way we teach and advise students. Other chapters in this book support the idea that taking Jungian psychological type into consideration in advising and instructional programs in higher education can contribute significantly in the areas of self-awareness, career choice, course selection, learning style, writing style, selection of instructor, and peer relationships.

This chapter will discuss strageties for

- introducing the concept of personality type to faculty and staff;

- overcoming resistance to the use of type in education; and

- persuading faculty and staff that personality type is a valid criterion to be considered in developing curriculum, choosing teaching style, and planning teaching strategy.

Strategies for Introducing the Concept of Personality Type

Introducing type theory to faculty has been an enjoyable experience for me. They seem to be interested in and appreciative of gaining insight into their own behaviors and the behaviors of others. In fact, my experience has been that faculty will often ask how or where they can obtain additional information about type theory, application, and research.

My objectives in introducing type are to explain type theory and the relevance of type in the academic community, in one's personal life, and in one's professional life. I am interested in encouraging each individual to grow in self-awareness and self-knowledge, and to recognize his or her unique gifts.

When introducing type theory it is important to emphasize the relevance of type in both the work and personal environments, and to give major attention to the importance of understanding one's own type and style of behavior.

Strategy 1

Find faculty and staff members who are familiar with the concept of using psychological type in educational planning. These people can provide immediate support and increase credibility for the concept among other faculty and staff. They can also serve on planning commit-tees, assist in instructing other faculty and staff, and share with col-leagues personal experiences they have had using the concept in teach-ing and advising.

Strategy 2

Administer the MBTI to administrators, deans, and other influential in-stitutional leaders. I believe that an introduction to the use of psychologi-cal type in educational planning can be achieved best by administering the MBTI to key leaders, interpreting the results, and discussing the relevance of type to working relationships among leaders and adminis-trators, student development, retention, campus environment, counsel-ing, student activities, career planning, learning, and instruction.

It is essential that key leaders receive a thorough introduction to the concept because they are the prime determiners of what happens within the institution. They must accept the validity of the concept and the value of the instrument if they are to influence others to support any proposal for using the type concept within the institution. These key individuals will make decisions regarding the degree of support and funding any proposal receives, so make sure that you spend adequate time in your presentations to them.

Strategy 3

After you have the encouragement or permission of administrators and other key leaders, introduce the concept to faculty and staff through academic departments and committees, and by means of any other faculty development opportunities available to you. It is important that the MBTI be administered to all those who have an interest in using the psychological type concept in their work, and that they have ample opportunity to learn about how the concept can be useful to them.

During the introductory period, emphasize the type concept as a way of improving teaching/learning methods, thereby improving the teacher's and the student's chance of success in the classroom. Also emphasize the importance of understanding type in any communication. Experience indicates that when we approach others from their frames of reference (which may or may not be the same as our own), we communicate more effectively, make a greater impact, and are more effective in persuading them to consider our proposals. (Successful sales people have known and used these techniques for many years.) It is, therefore, important that the individual promoting the use of type be aware of his or her own type and style, and understand how they differ from the types and styles of others.

Approach established groups about the possibility of incorporating the study of psychological type theory into their agendas. For example, a project at Carthage College in which a team of faculty members evaluated the freshman year experience provided an opportunity for the introduction of type theory to that group. They studied the application of the theory and its relevance in their particular college program. Concentrated study which results in a thorough understanding of psychological type is necessary if the theory is to be used effectively in advising and instruction. At another institution, experimental sections were established in which faculty could experiment with using psychological type in their teaching and advising. This gradual introduction, which provided faculty members with a means of testing the value and usefulness of using type theory, got a positive response from many faculty who preferred concrete evidence of its usefulness on their own campus.

Any time faculty members use type concepts in their work, their plans should be clearly detailed and the results evaluated. These results can then be made available for review by others within the institution. I strongly recommend that such plans and evaluations be made jointly by participants so that all of those involved have an opportunity to contribute and feel that they have a significant role in the project. Their motivation and the project's success depend on their attitudes toward, commitment to, and ownership of the concept. Faculty enthusiasm and interest are crucial if such projects are to succeed.

Resistance to Change

People often resist change, and it is not uncommon to find resistance to using psychological type theory to change present patterns in higher education. Just as people differ by type, so do they differ in their response to the concept of using such theory in the academic process. It is important to be patient and allow time.

Strategies for Overcoming Resistance

Following are the two strategies I use when coping with faculty resistance.

Strategy 1

Assess an individual's type and make your approach from his or her frame of reference.

- Introverts need time to think.

- Extraverts want to see some excitement and enthusiasm.

- Sensors need detailed description.

- Intuitives want to contribute their ideas.

- Thinkers need logical reasons.

- Feelers want to understand values and possible reactions.

In planning presentations for Judging types, be as organized as possible, make your plans clear, and have time schedules in place. For Perceivers, avoid deadlines and leave the presentation open-ended as much as possible, encouraging the gathering of more information and data.

Strategy 2

If a faculty member continues to resist the idea of using type concepts, move on to another individual or group. Don't devote such an excessive amount of time to one individual that the whole project becomes blocked or delayed. I have found frequently that individuals will accept the concept later, on their own. I recommend avoiding pressure of intense persuasion to interest faculty in using psychological type in the classroom. Sometimes resisters join in when they see that the majority of their colleagues are interested. There are other ways to help overcome resistance. For instance, when faculty share information from their own experiences about the value of using psychological type, they promote its acceptance by others.

Persuasive Points to Make with Faculty

The following case points out the value of knowing the type composition in a class. One frustrated instructor reported that his class was unresponsive and never asked questions. The instructor made the assumption that the class was not interested in the course material, did not like his teaching style, and was probably learning very little. Much to his surprise, the first examination revealed that the students had learned the material very well. The instructor then asked his students to complete a teacher evaluation and was again surprised to learn that they evaluated him very positively. Finally, the instructor administered the MBTI to the class. What he discovered helped to clarify the dynamics of the group and the reasons for the instructor's frustration. An overwhelming number of the students were Introverts. They were enjoying the class; they were learning; they liked the instructor; they were comfortable listening and reflecting; and they had minimal need to express themselves verbally. The instructor, on the other hand, was a very Extraverted type. He was entertaining in class and created an excellent atmosphere for the group he was teaching. They enjoyed his style, which left them free to listen, quietly and comfortably. The only problem was that the instructor didn't know that. Administering the MBTI at the beginning of the course would have enabled the instructor to anticipate the class dynamics, and kept him from making incorrect assumptions which resulted in his feelings of frustration and disappointment.

This incident illustrates not only the value of knowing the class as a group but also how an understanding of the differences in type can have more positive outcomes for both teacher and student. Teaching others from our own frame of reference is natural. We assume that our preferred teaching and learning style will also be the preference of others. It is important to inform faculty of the significant differences in preferred learning styles among different personality types. In his book, *People Types and Tiger Stripes: A Practical Guide to Learning Styles*, Gordon

Lawrence (1982) discusses the difference in type and preferred learning styles, and in his article "A Synthesis of Learning Style Research Involving the MBTI" (1984), he reports on research and presents, in table form, a synthesis of the findings of studies that directly address learning style questions. The article is extremely helpful to anyone using the type concept in teaching.

You can point out that student evaluations of courses and instructors are affected by type. Why, when students have experienced the same class and the same instructor, is there such a difference in the evaluations? One answer is that students respond according to their type and the relationship of that type to the instructor's type and teaching style. It is likely that a student's performance in class is dependent upon that relationship. In order to maximize the student's appreciation for the course and ability to learn the course material, it is essential for faculty to be aware of how they can make a more positive impact in the classroom and in their advising when they have an understanding of personality type and preferred learning styles. Once again, I strongly encourage using Gordon Lawrence's book, (1982) as a resource in teaching others about type theory and learning styles.

Discussions can also focus on how knowing their own personality types and teaching styles, as well as the types and styles of their colleagues, can help faculty to maintain better relationships within their working units and result in a more positive work environment.

Recruitment, attrition, and retention are words that get the attention of faculty and staff on most college and university campuses today. Improving a student's ability to learn can have a dramatic effect on his or her potential for success, and individuals are more inclined to remain where they are successful. Institutions that can demonstrate a personal approach in assessing and responding to student needs in order to maximize the learning experience will probably find that their recruitment and retention rates are positively affected because successful students are more likely to remain in school, and new students are more likely to be attracted by the personal approach. (A good resource on attrition and type is Judith A. Provost's article "Typewatching in College Attrition"[1985].) There are good reasons for using the type concept in academic advising as well as teaching. Scott Anchors, in his article "Type and Academic Advising" (1985), discusses ways in which using type theory in the advising process can affect problem solving and the selection of a major and career.

Adapting teaching style to a class of a predominately different type can improve students' responses. One instructor, an Introverted Intuitive teaching a class of Extraverted Sensors, was frustrated with student responses. He decided to try altering his teaching style to accommodate his students' learning styles. He began by placing less emphasis on theory and providing more structured activities that permitted students to become involved in an experiential way. He also identified ways in which course content was relevant to out-of-class situations. As a result of these changes, class response improved significantly, and the instructor felt a greater personal reward for his efforts.

Knowledge about the MBTI sharpens faculty skills as good observers of student behaviors and consequently generates a good deal of excitement about using this new tool. Faculty notice differences in behaviors. One faculty member, commenting on a Judging type, said of the student: "The first day she came into class she wanted decisions out so she could make some judgments. She wanted to have her say on how things were to be structured for the class." The same faculty member, observing a group of students being introduced to computers, noticed that the students who were Extraverts moved right in and began operating machines immediately following the introduction.

Knowledge of type enables an instructor to address students in ways that are more likely to stimulate their participation in class. In a writing class, one faculty member explained typology to students and then asked them to analyze the typology of fictional characters from various books they had read. This served to stimulate their thinking about typology and how it relates to and affects the behavior of individuals. This same faculty member also asked his students to predict the MBTI type of each of their instructors. This encouraged students to become aware of their instructors as unique individuals.

Ideally, a student should be personally known and related to by the instructor in each of his or her own classes. Asking students to be five different people in five different classes may increase their frustrations. In some instances these frustrations contribute to a students's decision to drop out of school. However, it may be impractical (especially in large classes) to direct individualized teaching methods based on particular learning styles to specific students. The MBTI offers a humanistic alternative to trying to focus on each individual student. Instead, if the instructor can become sensitive to type when he or she is planning the curriculum, flexibility and variety can be built into the course offerings to accommodate the learning styles of all types.

Example of Classroom Use

In my own psychology class, which has an enrollment of 75 to 90 students, I provide a detailed course syllabus which includes readings, assignments, resources, and a course outline. I try to relate the relevance of the material and its applications. Sensing types and Judging types appreciate this detail and approach because it defines expectations and permits them to structure their own semester activities for the class. At the same time, there is enough flexibility and freedom for the Intuitive types, who prefer opportunities to be creative and like more open-ended assignments, to develop assignments around their interests and needs.

In general, Intuitive types are global learners and Sensing types are linear learners. I try to present material from both frames of reference, varying it throughout the course. The course is designed to present material in such a way that students can apply what they learn to their own lives. Sensing types appreciate opportunities to hear of direct experience or ways in which they can use the material directly.

Extraverts want to participate in class discussion, and I encourage this. However, I do not penalize Introverts for not participating, because I recognize that they more often prefer to process material internally and reflect on what is being presented rather than enter into group discussion. Thinking types frequently prefer, and are very good at, objective tests. This is not always the preference of Intuitives or Perceivers, so course assignments include both objective tests and essay papers to accommodate both types. Exercises in small group interaction are used in class, and these develop greater harmony and class participation. Feeling students are generally very appreciative of feedback, support, and encouragement.

Administration and Interpretation

Even in classes with large enrollments, there are opportunities to work with individual students, and these opportunities are enhanced significantly when instructors know and respond to students' MBTI types. The MBTI can be administered by trained instructors on an individual basis, or, if it is to be used extensively within the institution for teaching and advising, student development and residential living, it can be administered to all students as part of the admission or orientation process.

With the student's permission, the resulting data can then be put on a computer file and made available to faculty or administrators when it is needed. Students' rights to confidentiality must, of course, be maintained. In addition, procedures must be developed to assure that students have adequate information about how the data is to be used so that they can make informed decisions about granting permission for that use. It is also important to make sure that faculty who plan to use typology data in the classroom have adequate instruction and information to assure that the data is used appropriately and optimally to benefit both the instructor and the student.

Using the *Myers-Briggs Type Indicator* in a classroom requires attention to individual styles and assessment of each class by type so that the instructor can provide a variety of experiences and assignments to meet the needs of various personality types. Not only is it necessary to have a general class profile, but also to have individual profiles so that work can be assigned that will result in the maximum benefit to the student.

Summary

To summarize, if we are to be effective in persuading faculty and staff to accept psychological type as a valid factor to be considered in developing curriculum, choosing teaching style, and advising students, we must use every means available to us to acquaint them with the theory. Administering the MBTI and interpreting results for all those who are interested in the concept is important to its eventual acceptance by faculty and staff. There may be resistance to the concept and its use in the academic setting, but the resistance can be diminished by using an appropriate approach, avoiding hard-sell pressure techniques, discussing possible uses of type in an academic setting, and asking faculty members who have used type theory in their work to share their experiences. Colleges and universities want to help students learn as much as they can, and as well as they can. Understanding and reacting to the personal learning styles of students will result in better students, greater personal and professional rewards for faculty and staff, and a more positive institutional environment.

Peggy Dettmer of Kansas State University points out that: "Fitting students to the preference of teachers and the structure of an educational system is dehumanizing; however, fitting the system to individuals and their preferences is humanizing." (1981, p. 52) Her statement has merit. Systems should serve people, not the other way around. Responding to personality types and learning styles is one way in which the educational system can serve the needs of students, faculty, staff, and institution.

References

Anchors, Scott. (1985). Type and academic advising. *MBTI News, 7,* 2, 11–13.

Dettmer, Peggy. (1981). The effects of teacher personality type on classroom values and perceptions of gifted students. *Research in Psychological Type, 3,* 48–54.

Lawrence, Gordon. (1982). *People types and tiger stripes: A practical guide to learning styles.* Gainesville, FL: Center for the Applications of Psychological Type.

Lawrence, Gordon. (1984). A synthesis of learning style research involving the MBTI. *Journal of Psychological Type.*, *8*, 2–13.

Provost, Judith A. (1985). Type watching in college attrition. *Journal of Psychological Type*, *9*, 16–23.

JUDITH A. PROVOST, Ed.D., is a psychotherapist, writer, and trainer who has incorporated MBTI concepts in her work for the past 13 years. She currently is Director of Personal Counseling at Rollins College and is on the faculties of the Center for Applications of Psychological Type and the Association for Psychological Type. Her research interests in higher education have resulted in several journal articles and a dissertation, "Personality type and leisure satisfaction as factors in college attrition." Other books by Judy are *A Casebook: Applications of the Myers-Briggs Type Indicator in Counseling* (CAPT) and *The Freshmen Year—Stress or Success* (PPI). As Chair of the Council for Communication and Education of APT, she sits on the executive board; she also serves as Chair of the Ethics Committee of APT. Her education includes an undergraduate degree from the University of Connecticut, graduate degrees from the University of California at Los Angeles and University of Florida, and extensive training with the Gestalt Institute of Florida. She is an ENFP.

BARBARA H. CARSON is an Associate Professor of English at Rollins College. She recieved her B.A. from Florida State University and her M.A. and Ph.D. from the John Hopkins University, after which she taught at Towson State College in Baltimore and at the University of Massachusetts in Amherst. In recognition of her teaching at Rollins, she was named an Arthur Vining Davis Fellow in 1982. In 1984, she was one of eight finalists in the CASE Professor of the Year selection. A specialist in American literature, Barbara's publications have focused on American transcendentalism and on women writers. She is currently writing a study of the works of Eudora Welty. She is an ENFJ.

CHAPTER 11

Effective Teaching and Type: The Words of Outstanding Professors

JUDITH A. PROVOST and BARBARA H. CARSON
with PETER G. BEIDLER

THE INGREDIENTS OF effective teaching are often as elusive as those of effective learning. This chapter reports on a study designed to explore type preferences and excellence in teaching. Outstanding professors are identified annually by CASE, the Council for the Advancement and Support of Education. A sample of these professors agreed to take the MBTI. Their preferences were then compared with their statements about their teaching philosophies and approaches found in *Distinguished Teachers on Effective Teaching* (Beidler, 1986). In this book Peter Beidler, a CASE finalist himself, has solicited and compiled written responses from CASE finalists.

The CASE professors' statements in Beidler's book were examined to pursue the following questions:

1. Among professors identified for their outstanding teaching records, are there similarities in personality types and in preferred styles of teaching and learning?

2. How have these professors capitalized in their teaching on strengths natural to their personality types?

3. How have they compensated for their lesser preferences, in areas where there is less likely to be natural strength?

Only one of the CASE professors was familiar with type theory at the time Beidler surveyed them. Therefore, this study is not an example of an *application* of the MBTI but rather an *illumination* of type theory and the relationship of MBTI preferences to effective teaching. The implications of these findings suggest specific applications of the MBTI in the teaching process.

Procedure

Peter Beidler was contacted and asked to support the study by introducing the authors to the CASE professors and by providing his draft manuscript of their teaching statements. Beidler also offered to provide additional unpublished responses from the CASE finalists to a query about why they thought they had been selected for this honor. After this introduction through Beidler, the authors sent letters to the CASE professors describing the study, the nature of the MBTI, the relationship of type to learning, the procedure for the study, and a postcard to return, indicating willingness or unwillingness to participate in the study.

Those respondents willing to participate in the study gave permission to use their MBTI results and teaching statements. Subjects were then mailed the MBTI Form G, with instructions. These were scored and the results compared with the professors' statements in Beidler's manuscript and in the additional unpublished responses.

The Sample

CASE instituted the Professor of the Year program in 1981 to honor outstanding teachers of undergraduates, using the following criteria (according to a CASE brochure):

- extraordinary effort as a scholar or teacher

- service to the institution and/or the profession

- a balance of achievement in teaching, scholarship, and service to the institution

- evidence of impact and/or involvement with students

- evidence of achievement by former students

- the quality of nominations by former students

Each year, after the several hundred nominations from colleges and universities across the country have been narrowed to about thirty, a panel chaired by the president of the Carnegie Foundation for the Advancement of Teaching chooses a small group of finalists and the

TABLE 1

Case Finalists Compared to Danforth Associates ($N = 18$)

| | Sensing Types | | Intuitive Types | |
| with Thinking | with Feeling | with Feeling | with Thinking |

ISTJ	ISFJ	INFJ	INTJ
N = 1	N = 0	N = 1	N = 0
% = 5.56	% = 0.00	% = 5.56	% = 0.00
I = .70	I = 0.00	I = .66	I = 0.00*†

ISTP	ISFP	INFP	INTP
N = 0	N = 0	N = 1	N = 1
% = 0.00	% = 0.00	% = 5.56	% = 5.56
I = 0.00	I = 0.00	I = .94	I = .80

ESTP	ESFP	ENFP	ENTP
N = 0	N = 0	N = 4	N = 0
% = 0.00	% = 0.00	% = 22.22	% = 0.00
I = 0.00	I = 0.00	I = 4.49*†	I = .0.00

ESTJ	ESFJ	ENFJ	ENTJ
N = 2	N = 0	N = 1	N = 7
% = 11.11	% = 0.00	% = 5.56	% = 38.89
I = 1.73	I = 0.00	I = .66	I = 2.18

Side labels: Introverts Judging / Perceptive; Extraverts Perceptive / Judging

	N	%	I
E	14	77.78	1.60*
I	4	22.22	.43*†
S	3	16.67	.69
N	15	83.33	1.10
T	11	61.11	.95
F	7	38.89	1.09
J	12	66.67	.91
P	6	33.33	1.25
IJ	2	11.11	.30*
IP	2	11.11	.75
EP	4	22.22	1.87
EJ	10	55.56	1.52
ST	3	16.67	1.02
SF	0	0.00	0.00
NF	7	38.89	1.40
NT	8	44.44	.93
SJ	3	16.67	.82
SP	0	0.00	0.00
NP	6	33.33	1.46
NJ	9	50.00	.94
TJ	10	55.56	1.10
TP	1	5.56	.40
FP	5	27.78	2.16
FJ	2	11.11	.49
IN	3	16.67	.42
EN	12	66.67	1.84*
IS	1	5.56	.47
ES	2	11.11	.90

I = self-selection index; ratio of % of type in group to % in sample. *p ≤ .05 level. ** p ≤ .01 level. *** p ≤ .001 level. † Indicates Fisher's exact probability used instead of chi square. Base population used in calculating selection ratio: University faculty selected as Danforth Associates, base total N = 202. Sample and base are independent.

TABLE 2

Case Finalists Compared to University Professors (N = 18)

Sensing Types		Intuitive Types				N	%	I
with Thinking	with Feeling	with Feeling	with Thinking					

ISTJ N = 1 % = 5.56 I = .43	**ISFJ** N = 0 % = 0.00 I = 0.00	**INFJ** N = 1 % = 5.56 I = .74	**INTJ** N = 0 % = 0.00 I = 0.00	Introverts Judging	
ISTP N = 0 % = 0.00 I = 0.00	**ISFP** N = 0 % = 0.00 I = 0.00	**INFP** N = 1 % = 5.56 I = .69	**INTP** N = 1 % = 5.56 I = 1.03	Perceptive	
ESTP N = 0 % = 0.00 I = 0.00	**ESFP** N = 0 % = 0.00 I = 0.00	**ENFP** N = 4 % = 22.22 I = 2.45	**ENTP** N = 0 % = 0.00 I = .0.00	Extraverts Perceptive	
ESTJ N = 2 % = 11.11 I = 1.71	**ESFJ** N = 0 % = 0.00 I = 0.00	**ENFJ** N = 1 % = 5.56 I = .69	**ENTJ** N = 7 % = 38.89 I = 4.03*	Judging	

	N	%	I
E	14	77.78	1.70**
I	4	22.22	.41**†
S	3	16.67	.46
N	15	83.33	1.30
T	11	61.11	1.14
F	7	38.89	.83
J	12	66.67	1.01
P	6	33.33	.98
IJ	2	11.11	.30*
IP	2	11.11	.66
EP	4	22.22	1.29
EJ	10	55.56	1.94*
ST	3	16.67	.75
Sf	0	0.00	0.00
NF	7	38.89	1.19
NT	8	44.44	1.42
SJ	3	16.67	.56
SP	0	0.00	0.00
NP	6	33.33	1.20
NJ	9	50.00	1.39
TJ	10	55.56	1.39
TP	1	5.56	.41
FP	5	27.78	1.35
FJ	2	11.11	.43
IN	3	16.67	.52
EN	12	66.67	2.08**
IS	1	5.56	.25
ES	2	11.11	.81

I = self-selection index; ratio of % of type in group to % in sample. *p ≤ .05 level. ** p ≤ .01 level. *** p ≤ .001 level. † Indicates Fisher's exact probability used instead of chi square. Base population used in calculating selection ratio: University faculty selected as Danforth Associates, base total N = 2282. Sample and base are independent.

National Professor of the Year. Of the 27 professors chosen as CASE finalists or Professors of the Year from 1981 to 1985, 20 contributed to Beidler's book by responding to questions about the way they taught, what they expected from themselves and their students, and their values about teaching.

Eighteen of these 20 finalists agreed to participate in the study. The sample included 14 men and 4 women, with equal representation from state universities, small private four-year colleges, and private universities granting doctorates. The professors represented a range of academic disciplines:

English - 7
Religion/philosophy - 3
Anthropology/sociology - 2
Economics - 2
Biology - 2
Astronomy - 1
Geography - 1

Although the sample is a small and very select one and generalizations cannot be made concerning specific types and excellence in college teaching, several MBTI patterns are worth noting. Of the 18 professors, 9 are ETJs; 7 of these are ENTJs. The four women in the sample are INFJ, INFP, ENFJ, and ENTJ. There are few Sensing types, consistent with the larger CAPT university sample. There are four times as many ENTJs in the CASE sample than would be predicted based on the percentage of this type in the CAPT University Professors sample of 2,282. Compared to the percentages of each type in a sample of Danforth Associates, there are two times as many ENTJs and four and a half times as many ENFPs than would be expected. These findings are statistically significant, as noted on the type tables (Tables 1 and 2).

Using Natural Strengths for Effective Teaching

How have these master teachers capitalized on strengths natural to their type preferences in their teaching? Their statements in Beidler's book reveal how their teaching styles have been shaped by their types. Most revealing were responses to Beidler's questions:

- "What qualities, skills, or attitudes do you want your students to have after a semester in one of your classes?"

- "How do students learn—by example, by rote, by reading, by discussion?"

- "What do you feel you have done to earn your college's nomination and the CASE committee's selection of you?"—"What is most distinctive about your teaching?" (Note that this last question was not included in Beidler's final manuscript.)

Quotations from professors' responses in Beidler's book are included here for each of the types in the sample.

ENTJ

Basic Style

There were 7 ENTJs in the sample of 18. Several in this group discussed their role as teacher in terms of *power*. None of the other types referred to their roles in a similar way. An English professor said:

> I love the power knowledge gives me. I know how uncomfortable and reverential I feel in the presence of people who have more knowledge than I have, and I like knowing that others feel slightly uncomfortable and reverential in my presence. When I discuss two pieces of freshman writing with my freshmen we generally both know which piece is better, but they think they are just guessing, whereas I *know* that I know which is better. I also have the power of knowing that I can find the words to explain why one theme is better. My freshmen often cannot do that, for they are going by true, but to them unexplainable, instinct when they pick one theme over another. I like knowing more than my freshmen do because knowing puts me in control, gives me the power not to sound like a fool when I try to talk about writing. (p. 44)

A biology professor talked about power this way:

> I am the "Vince Lombardi" of modern biology. I am the "Godfather" of biochemistry. Winning is everything. Contracts must be fulfilled by both parties to that contract . . . or else! As I flog, so do I caress. I know I alienate as I gain respect (unpublished).

He goes on to speak of several awards for his teaching by saying, "It says I am winning more than I am losing. I am still not satisfied. I want to win more" (unpublished).

It is clear that both of these professors convey a great deal of vitality and most likely inspire their students with it. Their language of power gives some clues to the motivations and values behind this vitality.

The other ENTJs commenting on their teaching styles also reveal aspects that type theory would suggest for dominant Extraverted Thinkers (objective decisiveness, tough-mindedness, logical structure). One English professor reported that her colleagues described her as "a compassionate hard-ass":

> Students who want Mickey Mouse courses are unlikely to enroll in mine. On the other hand, I try to be exceptionally clear. I try to allow students ample time to adjust to my expectations, and I try through midterm evaluations to adjust *my* expectations to any specific group of students. (unpublished)

An astronomy professor reflects the tendency of ENTJs to take a strong leadership role. In answering the question about why he was chosen as a CASE professor, he said, "I was among the leaders in the innovation of our general education program which became a very important part of the curriculum here . . ." (unpublished).

Extraverted Teaching

The extraverted energy of the seven ENTJs' teaching approaches is apparent in all of their statements:

> I generally learn best and most permanently by *doing* something. It is useful in some ways to have someone tell me what to do or show me how to do it, but it is still theirs when they are finished. It is mine when I have done it myself. In my classes, then, I almost never lecture. When I do, I never lecture for more than fifteen minutes. I am not much good at lecturing anyhow, so no one is missing much when I refrain from doing so. I suppose I could learn to be better at it by doing more of it, but my heart would never be in it. There are better ways for students to learn what I have to teach. (pp. 51–52)

This same English professor gives an example of involving his students in "doing" during a composition class. Instead of using a published handbook on writing, he had them collectively create their own handbook for the class.

A biology professor comments, "When I stand before my class they know that they are being exposed to the real me. . . . I go 'all out' to make the course powerful and relevant. I expect them to go 'all out' in the learning process" (unpublished).

An English professor puts it this way: "I am able to translate my own love for literature into an energy level which allows me to be 'on' in what has been called a contagious way for the hour(s) of class time" (unpublished).

A professor of geography emphasizes his belief in the value of "doing" to learn:

> Facts, concepts, and relationships are meaningless unless students know the places in which these elements of the natural and cultural environments are located. I have tried to facilitate their knowing about such places by developing what I call the audio-visual-tutorial independent method of learning. . . . I have also conducted field trips by air so that my students can see for themselves. . . . (p. 24)

The astronomy professor further illustrates this extraverted orientation: "So for me, field work . . . in the observatory or on-site among the ancient Mexican ruins—is the best way I can help students to learn by doing" (p. 55). Extraverts prefer to learn by externalizing so they can manipulate ideas through talking and action; this preference is clear in the previous statements.

Thinking Judgment

> "I suppose that one reason for my good teaching ratings, as far as students are concerned, is that they know I spend a lot of time preparing my courses" (unpublished).

> "I regularly distinguish between the 'facts' of literature and the 'interpretations' which must be based on those facts. I am alert to boredom and adapt techniques accordingly" (unpublished).

> "I feel that students learn best from carefully prepared and well-delivered lectures" (p. 55). This same professor continues later, "During the preparation, I type up notes, draw diagrams, synthesize relevant literature, and consider examples from current events. The morning of the lecture I write three to six key thoughts on a five-by-eight card" (p. 69).

These are examples of the ENTJ's emphasis on preparation and structure (J) and on use of facts and objectivity (T) to evaluate theories and interpretations (N). The ENTJs put more stress on grades and a system of grading than the Feeling and Perceiving types did. They used language such as "principles," "systems," and "objectivity," and relied on structured evaluation through carefully scheduled testing.

An English professor discusses his grading system:

> The grading process was more successful than before, in part because those freshmen, in writing the criteria themselves [also Extraverted *doing*], had "bought into" them. These were not principles of good writing that came down from high in some egghead lectures or from some grand principle-maker in the sky. No, these were *their* principles, principles at least half-understood because they had discovered and articulated them themselves (p. 53).

This same professor gave daily quizzes on the assigned reading *before* discussing the reading because he felt this structure involved them more actively (extraversion). Students were allowed to ask as many questions as they wanted to before the daily quiz. As the term progressed, the quiz was given closer and closer to the end of the class period. This strategy reflects expression of both the professor's Extraversion in getting the students to do the work of learning, and Judgment in structuring these daily evaluations and markers of progress.

ESTJ and ISTJ

The two ESTJs also revealed their Extraverted Thinking in their statements but with more of an emphasis on practical applications and public service (Sensing instead of Intuition). They share the ENTJs' preference for learning by doing (E). It is interesting to compare the ESTJs' with the ISTJs' teaching statements here and see how the dominance of introverted Sensing shifts the TJ focus.

ESTJ Style

One of the CASE professors who is also an academic administrator explains CASE's recognition of his teaching:

> . . . because I put so much effort into communicating the importance of the subject, because my syllabi are organized, clear, detailed, because I work like hell in preparing every class, because I have published enough to win the respect of my colleagues, I have managed to convince a lot of students and fellow teachers that what I do is important, is good and will have a lifelong influence. (unpublished)

This same professor also says, "My courses are pretty traditional, large lectures on general humanities subjects with no prerequisites. I am not an innovative teacher" (p. 56).

He indicates that he stimulates participation, although the classes are large, by throwing out "about 10 questions with the intent of provoking" (p. 56). He continues:

> In my classes students seem to get the most out of the material
> when I succeed in getting them to think about their place in
> the scheme of things. I love to take them back, to place them in
> a historical context, to make them feel that it is important to
> understand their place in this grand scheme. (p. 56)

His comments illustrate a desire most ESTJs have to place information in a sequential and historical context and to bring immediacy to material by connecting students' lives to this material. His advice for successful teaching is, "Be scared. Be a worrier. Be afraid of failure. Then translate these feelings into energy, careful preparation, and ambition" (p. 81). These words reflect a prevailing ESTJ style which is painstakingly conscientious, concerned with tradition and maintenance of existing structures, and reliant on sensing data.

An ESTJ anthropology professor states his beliefs about teaching succinctly:

> The most important way students learn is by being involved in
> a research project. If it is in a laboratory science, they learn more
> by being in the lab and working with junior and senior or
> graduate level students as well as faculty. They learn equipment
> techniques and are in a position to listen to discussions about a
> particular field and its problems (p. 55).

An interesting quotation from this same professor may not be so relevant to his teaching as to type expression through his chosen field:

> I have difficulty separating teaching from public service.
> Because I am a forensic anthropologist who identifies decayed
> bodies or skeletons for law enforcement agencies, I make public
> service a part of my work. (p. 22)

ISTJ Style

An ISTJ professor of sociology shares many of the STJ characteristics of the ESTJs, such as reliance on facts and structure, but with two distinct differences. With the Introverted attitude, the emphasis is not placed on externalized energy and doing. The dominant function is introverted Sensing, resulting in a different emphasis from the ESTJs:

> I like to try new arrangements of information. . . . My talent is less a matter of performance . . . than an ability to assemble resources in support of the efforts of others who I respect greatly as colleagues. (unpublished)

The language of the Thinking preference is apparent in this ISTJ quotation:

> Students learn by measuring their ideas against those of others. As a consequence, the effective teacher starts by recognizing that students already know a good deal and simply provides a yard-stick and some things to measure. . . . (pp. 56–57)

ENFP and INFP

The NFPs provide a dramatic contrast to the TJs. This group uses a different language to talk about teaching and emphasizes different motivations and strategies. The ENFPs exemplify a high energy level and focus on doing, as the ETJs do, but the *style* of that energy is dissimilar. An ENFP English professor writes:

> I believe Alice in Wonderland was essentially right when she said, 'How can I know what I think until I see what I say?' We learn about experience of others by reading, but we best learn about ourselves by writing. (p. 58)

The first sentence shows the extraverted way of sorting ideas. His comment about writing is one way ENFPs can access their introverted auxiliary Feeling to understand their own inner world. The statement reflects an appreciation for the importance of ways of learning both in the external and the internal "worlds." He further stresses his extraverted style: "It is hard for me to see how anyone can stand still and be interesting. . . to teach, move" (p. 81).

Student-Centered Focus

To remain stimulated intellectually an ENFP professor says, ". . . keep the focus upon the student as much as possible, rather than on the material taught. As a teacher I try to assist the students on their route to self-knowledge" (p. 66). This quotation and the following one show ENFP characteristics of process rather than outcome orientation, student-centered versus teacher-centered focus, and desire to be a catalyst or facilitator: "I prefer another image, that of the teacher as a wise but lonely wanderer, a kind of singing peddler, who comes upon a group of innocent and ignorant youngsters and convinces them the sparkling rocks he carries in his old buckets can enlighten their lives. . ." (p. 66).

Several of the ENFP teachers reflect a theme of mutuality:

> I do not have a two camp image of education—'We andThey.'
> I see us all as learners. Some of us are simply further along the path than others and only a cooperative effort on the part of all participants will ensure a successful outcome to the process.
> (unpublished)

A naturalist describes a shared experience during field work: "[I] . . . lie there in the grass like any human, and reach out to them. And then, with friendships established, I can help guide their university experience" (unpublished). Elsewhere he claims, "When two minds are caused to meet, then all flows from that bonding" (p. 61). A philosophy professor asserts, "The teacher-student relationship is much like a master-apprentice relationship" (p. 59).

Spontaneity and Performance

According to type theory, the EPs and particularly the ENFPs, often exhibit a flare in their presentations and thrive on spontaneous response to people and the environment, often producing their best work under such conditions. A naturalist illustrates these qualities: "Out in the field, also, my students can see me in unrehearsed action, learning and doing and failing" (p. 23).

An economics professor reveals his ENFP style:

> . . . the most distinctive thing about my teaching is my enthusiasm. . . . I must admit that I have a streak of 'ham' in me and I don't mind some of that showing in the classroom: it helps keep the students awake and they certainly can't learn while asleep. I treat students as adults, have confidence in them, as Gandhi put it, to realize his or her potential. Finally, I am willing to 'lend an ear,' which means a lot of office time is spent with students who are *not* dropping by to get help in economics. (unpublished)

Perhaps the clearest contrast of the ENFP teaching style with the TJ style is the following:

> First of all I work hard—every day—and as a rule I teach with abandon. I despise lesson plans, overhead projectors, and indeed any device that is supposed to aid the teacher in the classroom. I know this is utterly rejected today, but I feel that all a teacher needs is a decent text and a piece of chalk, perhaps only a piece of chalk if he knows enough. I do use a syllabus and frequently pass out bibliographies which makes me in a way, I suppose, as dependent on machines as anyone else.
>
> In class I have to admit I frequently 'perform,' though I don't intend to be eccentric or a "character". . . . I will use any technique that is legal to try to get the students to perform. . . . I frequently feel absurd in the classroom, but never ashamed of what I'm doing. In absurdity there is abandonment and with abandonment quite often a good deal of fun. (unpublished)

This last comment about feeling absurd is in striking contrast to the ENTJ's comment about wanting "the power not to sound like a fool" in the classroom.

INFP

An INFP English professor shares many stylistic similarities with the English and economics professors who are ENFPs. The main difference is much less emphasis on classroom performance; instead, there is persuasiveness expressed through a gentle, almost seductive approach:

> . . . I make it clear that it is their enjoyment that I am after, not their grade . . . My aim is to make them comfortable with the (to them) strange manner of writing that poetry is; and then, when they are used to that, to enable them to perceive the means the poet is using to enact experience. (unpublished)

Again the gentle approach is illustrated:

> If your students are hostile to your subject, that is probably because they were taught it badly in high school, were frightened of it because of its terminology . . . In any case, the thing is to present it as enchantingly and interestingly as possible,

without reference to any of their hostility. Refer to your subject always as if it were irresistible and full of gaiety. Soon your students will find it so. (p. 78)

Notice the NF language and especially the expression of dominant introverted Feeling in the above passage. The INFP, like the ENFPs, sees herself as a facilitator to student learning.

A last quotation from the INFP reveals the introverted orientation to learning, in contrast to that of the Extraverts:

I do not think it is possible to learn without reading. It consolidates what one hears in lectures and many people take in material better through the eyes than through the ears. I think studying is better done when it is focused by practical assignments. I find that students 'get more' out of a poem when they are asked to think about several questions while they read it, in preparation for discussion in section meeting. (p. 58)

ENFJ and INFJ

The two NFJs in the sample are women who teach English. Their language reflects much of the idealism and romanticism of the other NFs' words, with some specific differences. The ENFJ and INFJ use extraverted Feeling in their classroom. They also prefer more structure than the NFPs do.

Extraverting Feeling in the Classroom

The ENFJ has as dominant extraverted Feeling, clearly shown both in word choice and in approach described here:

When I was young I harbored a dream of becoming an Aimee Semple McPherson kind of evangelist. I think what I wanted as much as redeemed souls was the sense that I had redeemed them. . . . I think I have kept the evangelism. I want to make a difference in people's lives. I believe in teaching I do that. I teach, too, because it makes me feel good. (p. 90)

An INFJ's reference to "faith" has a similar ring:

Have faith in the greatness of teaching as a vocation. Have faith in your students. Have faith in yourself. Bishop Tutu said no Christian can be anything but an optimist. He would not mind, I think, if I said that of the teacher. (p. 81)

None of the other CASE professors talked about teaching with this kind of "religious" flavor.

> I would like to think that in my courses some students develop a view of life that can accommodate loss and suffering, an awareness that love almost always calls for self-sacrifice, an ability to be joyfully surprised by a single flower of the horse chestnut tree, a reverence for words . . . (p. 48)

While the ENFJ has a dominant extraverted Feeling function illustrated earlier, the INFJ has as dominant introverted Intuition. The difference of the INFJ in the dominant function, though similar on three preferences, causes a shift in emphasis or tone from Feeling to Intuition. Dominant introverted Intuition is represented by the metaphor of a net:

> I teach in a liberal arts college where one discipline touches another, meshes with it, and becomes, paradoxically, a great net to hold an infinite number of questions, and at the same time to release possibilities, intuitions, sometimes even answers to the problems of the "real world". . . (p. 25)

Many professors struggle to achieve some kind of balance between the demands to publish and to teach well. For the dominant extraverted Feeling professor this conflict is poignantly expressed:

> There is a painful conflict for me, because I enjoy teaching more than research and writing. I am better at it, and I get more praise for what I do in the classroom than for what I do in print. It strikes me as nearly impossible to be the kind of teacher I want to be, have a family life I value, and be the kind of published scholar. . . . (p. 39)

Structure

A major difference in teaching style of NFJs compared to NFPs is one of structure:

> I have a purpose and a theme in mind for each part of a course. I enter almost every class with either a detailed lecture or a very careful outline. Then I try to let my students discover these ideas themselves. As I ask questions, provide the framework, clarify, and fill in the background, they create the analysis, building up evidence, connecting, comparing, synthesizing. . . . This tension between order and creativity, between the given and the discovered is, it seems to me, the source of learning. (unpublished)

INTP

The last type in the sample is an INTP professor of English. His motivations for teaching are described here:

> My earliest and highest aspiration was to be a writer. I turned to college teaching because I guessed that I might have a better chance of earning a living by doing it than by writing. Much later, after much writing and teaching, I found out that I had chosen rightly but for the wrong reason. I realized I could not have pursued the solitariness necessary to being the kind of writer my aspirations would want me to be. I realized that some strong part of me needed the interchange with other people over things we were interested ... (p. 91)

Academic involvement seems to have provided him a way to exercise his introverted dominant Thinking through writing and at the same time provide him with stimulation through "interchange" for his extraverted auxiliary Intuition, so that his life does not become too solitary. He has a long list of publications to his credit, serves on many committees, and describes his teaching as having "good solid, scholarly work behind it" (unpublished).

The INTP's approach to teaching is to "be flexible."

> Do not pay much attention to someone who has only one piece of advice about how to teach. It is both a curse and a blessing of teaching that there is no one way. Teaching continues to delight me because the ground is always shifting under my feet. (pp. 80–81)

Summary of Strengths

These CASE professors demonstrate the various strengths of their types in their own words. Their assumptions about how students learn best are influenced by their types. Their words provide a clear contrast and comparison of type styles. The variation in language—the word choice—is most striking. Language reflects internal processes, value systems, and overall style. Their metaphors also reflect preferences: the religious metaphors of the NFJs; the teacher as father from several ENTJs; images of "bonding" and mutuality from the NFPs; and "yardstick" and the "entrepreneur" packaging ideas from the STJs. Readers may make additional connections between the statements and type theory.

These teachers seem able to capitalize on their natural preferences to develop successful teaching styles and to find an arena in which these preferences could be best expressed and encouraged to develop. An ENFP philosophy professor makes this point elegantly: "I suppose that the best one can do is find one's strengths and nurture them" (p. 34).

The next step is to ask if these master teachers are sufficiently self-aware and well developed (having competence in using their dominant and auxiliary and ability to use their less-preferred functions when needed) to compensate for areas outside their natural strengths and preferences. Do they acknowledge learning styles other than their own, and how do they respond to other learning styles? These questions cannot be completely answered by examining their statements, but their statements may provide clues. It is interesting to note that many in the sample reported preference scores above 39, some at the outer ranges. Although one cannot put too much weight on scores in themselves, a natural question to ask is whether individuals who cast all or most of their "votes" for a certain preference will consistently avoid engaging in the opposite preference.

Awareness and Type Development

The question of how aware these master teachers are of their strengths and limitations has actually been partially answered in many of the previous quotations. For example, the ENTJ who discussed the positive aspects of his challenging and demanding approach and at the same time the potential for intimidation and alienation of some students. The ISTJ professor is clear about his strengths lying in organizing resources and serving the team effort instead of in a brilliant classroom performance. In some of their statements the CASE professors have also demonstrated a flexibility to adapt their approach and expectations to student needs. In this section their comments can be examined for additional indications of good type development.

ENTJ

One of the characteristics of some ENTJ professors is their conception of power within the teaching role. One of these professors demonstrates awareness of the limitations of this role and shows his attempts at compensating:

My job as a teacher is to empower my students, to demystify a
subject for them and so give up my power over them. If I am
doing my job, by the end of the semester my students are independent of me. I strive every semester to give my students
power, even though when I succeed I inevitably disempower
myself. I hate that feeling of powerlessness at the end of the
semester. I love it. (p. 44)

There is a lovely paradox in his statement, illustrating both his
natural inclination and his balanced response, and finally his delight in
being able to go beyond his natural preferences.

An ENTJ reveals the alteration of his teaching style in response to
students' reactions:

. . . I teach technique and seeing and criticism and writing and
self-awareness and how to ask questions and, occasionally, little
side dishes like honesty and virtue and truth and beauty. I used
to try to lecture about such subjects, but I have come to see that
my students will learn what I have to teach not by my telling but
by their doing. . . . Gradually, sometimes painfully, I have come
to understand that only doing will convince my students. (p. 52)

The ENTJ who said he was the "Vince Lombardi of modern biology"
also realizes that he "alienates" as he "gains respect." "I know I cannot
be all things to all people." He also says, "I reach out to them in every
possible mode that I know" (unpublished).

The ENTJ who had been called a "compassionate hard-ass" shows
the following awareness:

In providing such a lively, focused, challenging atmosphere I
am troubled by the chance that students may come to depend
upon me and not engender their own pace and excitement. (Is
my strength my weakness?) (unpublished)

This comment sounds much like the earlier ENTJ comment about
striving to give up "the power" to the students.

An ENTJ English professor's comment contains the classic T-F
polarity of hard honesty versus tact. She shows sensitivity to her
inferior function here:

Evaluate others and yourself as honestly as you can, given the
evidence you have honestly worked to collect. Then be forgiving
of mistakes (including your own) and rest in Chaucer's assurance
that the intention is all. One more word: do it all with tact. (p. 78)

Her flexibility to use functions other than her preferred ones is also demonstrated in this statement, "I try alone or with students to create some spectacle, some mutual project or challenge or event which, in a creative and at times outrageous way, serves to embody our learning and be 'fun' "(p. 72). None of the Ps placed the word *fun* in quotation marks; this may reflect a J attitude.

An economics professor shows his appreciation for both his favored Thinking orientation and the least-preferred Feeling function in his comment, "I want them to appreciate that they cannot solve problems unless they marshall facts, sift through data, and establish a framework for solving them. But I also want students to incorporate compassion and values into the solution of a problem" (p. 46).

There seems to be a "mellowing" with maturity of these ENTJs. One advises, "Show that you are human. . . . As young Ph.D.s we often feel like experts ready to hang out a shingle and practice the art of teaching. . . . But pride goes before a fall" (p. 80). Another counsels, "You should be human, interested in students, and willing to poke fun at number one" (p. 79).

Another example of developed flexibility to use functions other than the preferred ones is this comment:

> To be 'responsible' to society seems to require some 'irresponsible' behavior: neglecting committee assignments, common sense security, dependable colleagues, and the fruits of predictability. (p. 24)

He advocates a deliberate letting go of structures when doing so will bring about a rich learning experience. He goes on to give examples of creative and unusual learning experiences he developed which involved not only his students but also his family. This same professor discusses his relationship to students this way: "I have to force myself to listen to them, to find out what they are thinking, singing, longing for. It is so easy to become out of touch, obsolete, a vestigial remnant of the '40s, '60s, Vietnam, graduate school, yesterday." (pp. 69–70)

Occasionally some language more frequently heard from NFs emerges in ENTJ comments about teaching, indicating sensitivity (development?) of Feeling:

> But unexpected (yet dependable) flashes of intuition or dogged discoveries or familiar ideas enlighten and warm me and make my joy complete. Every day. But I must mention also one special pleasure of the profession: friends we could give everything to

cultivate if we were not on the campus, friends we take for granted day after year and discover anew each time an occasion makes dialogue possible. (p. 89)

An ENTJ's appreciation for diversity can be seen in the following:

Surely we must insist on the value of diversity in the professorate, that there is more than one way to show success or progress in a profession as complex as ours. (p. 41)

This professor also points out:

There is no one most important way that students learn, though it may well be that for each student there is at any one moment one best way. Our job as professors is to discover the one best way for as many of our individual students as we can. For most of our students we shall not fully succeed . . . . Helping a student find the best way to learn is sometimes called love. (p. 61)

ESTJ and ISTJ

The ESTJs in this study are similar to the ENTJs in their development of an appreciation for the Feeling dimension and a willingness to use less-preferred functions as needed and to adjust teaching style to students. The professor-administrator expresses it this way:

I love college life. I love being near a gymnasium and being able to work out with the varsity baseball team. I love being able to order books for the library and then being the first person to read them. I love being with young people who are the same age I was thirty years ago. . . . I love making lights go on in people's heads. (p. 87)

Another ESTJ shows modification of his teaching style to accommodate the students:

I lecture not from notes but only from an outline. I encourage students to ask questions and to a certain extent I allow students to lead me in the subject that we discuss in class. I have found as the years go by that attitudes and interests of the students change, and I try to keep abreast of these changes by following a basic outline, but not necessarily teaching exactly the same thing each quarter. (p. 69)

In this quotation the effort to balance control and structure with flexibility and responsiveness to students' needs is apparent. Later he comments, "I think education should be fun and I try to make my lectures as interesting as possible" (unpublished).

The ISTJ who spoke modestly of his strengths shows his self-awareness in his interactions with others and in his academic pursuits:

> I am not fool-hardy enough to venture too far into someone else's backyard [academic area], less out of a respect for turf than the recognition of his or her superior knowledge. The solution to my ambition and my caution is to enlist the help of others to looking at common problems. I am fortunate to work at a college where others share my concerns and penchant for teamwork. (unpublished)

ENFP and INFP

If the TJs have shown good type development through appreciation of diversity and of interpersonal issues as well as by becoming flexible, how have the NFPs shown development? Do they develop beyond strengths such as classroom performance and facilitation? The same economics professor who identified his primary teaching asset as enthusiasm shows development, especially a blending of Sensing and Thinking functions, with his preferred functions:

> I hope my course will help produce a person who has acquired a knowledge of analytical concepts and who can think straight, communicate ideas, evaluate conditions, and discriminate between the important and the unimportant. We do not want skilled barbarians. We want graduates who have technical skills but who know what to do with these skills. (p. 47)

The ENFP English professor seems sensitive to the Sensing student's way of learning in his approach to poetry:

> I tell my freshmen and sophomores that explicating a poem is much like looking at a car that one is thinking of buying. Though a poem and a car are very different, some crucial questions are the same in evaluating them. (p. 26)

He then involves students in evaluating the usefulness of cars and poems.

The naturalist seems to try to reach all four functions in his teaching approach:

> Most lectures can lose some students, so I put an outline on the board and point to it now and then to show where I am in the text [J]. And I watch the audience to see how they are receiving things [ENF]. I try to involve the audience, to get them to ask questions [E]. I tell a story about some class member who has done an interesting thing [SF]. (p. 77)

Elsewhere he adds, "I'm a popular and interesting classroom teacher, though I have my lapses, and sometimes simple organization eludes me" (unpublished). This professor with a Perception preference is conscious of his natural style and tries to balance this in the ways described above. He describes himself as an effective lecturer but "my best teaching by far is in nature, where I become an orchestrator of events for students" (p. 23).

INTP

The INTP professor acknowledges that many of his personal academic interests may be too esoteric for his students. "... my specialized inquiries become of great interest to me but leave the students behind. Knowing too much is as sure a way to be boring as any" (p. 70). He goes on to muse:

> In the end, it is the variety of human life—in the students, in the literature, in myself—that is my subject. One of the advantages we older teachers have is that we can be much freer than younger ones. We can be more ourselves and have more self that is of interest to students. (p. 70)

This last sentence speaks to type development and individuation as people mature. His comments also suggest expression of his inferior Feeling, an appreciation for the human, subjective values.

ENFJ and INFJ

The INFJ's comment illustrates the ongoing nature of development as teacher and person: "Patience, hard thing! But I think I am learning to be patient, to wait—believing in the student—her, his potential" (unpublished).

Perhaps the appropriate way to end this line of inquiry into the awareness and development of these master teachers is with a quotation from the only one of the sample with a prior knowledge of type and the MBTI. This ENFJ sums up the issues:

> For years, I thought there was only one way of learning. That it happened to be precisely the way I learn best never struck me as odd. I catch on easily by reading and by imitation through writing. While not particularly creative, I am good at analysis, at seeing central ideas, identifying supporting specifics, and synthesizing what I have just learned with old knowledge. Expecting my students to do the same, I constructed writing assignments and examinations requiring these skills. Now I know that there are a number of different kinds of learners—from the linear learner who needs step-by-step practical guidance, to the global learner who seems capable of skipping all intermediate stages and with dazzling (and to us more orderly folk, sometimes messy) creativity arriving at a new idea. This recognition of diversity made me rethink many of my writing assignments. I now try to provide choices enabling students to learn and to express ideas in a variety of ways. So, while I require all my American literature students to write an original critical analysis of some work, I now give them options. The global learners can discover and display their knowledge of Poe by writing a short story imitating him, while the more linear learners might begin by summarizing and evaluating major critical articles on "The Fall of the House of Usher." I also try to recognize different learning styles in exams, combining long essays requiring synthesis or original insights with shorter one-paragraph responses based on more specific knowledge of the works studied. (p. 59)

Summary

One *cannot* generalize from this very select sample that most outstanding teachers will be a certain type, or have a specific preference. This study does show how type affects teaching style, assumptions about the learning process, and attitudes about what aspects of teaching are valued and seen as rewarding. The master teachers' own words are like a vivid field study of type dynamics. Although generalizations cannot be made regarding type and teaching excellence, it is interesting to note the distribution of types in the sample and to speculate as to how type might have factored into the selection process, given the nature of the CASE selection procedure.

More interesting than the distribution of types is the way the master teachers have expressed their types through their work and through the language and choice of words used to describe their work. It is evident that they have capitalized on their strengths/natural preferences. At the same time these master teachers have been able "to speak" to other types and to appreciate diversity in students and colleagues. This study suggests that good type development is a primary factor in the sample subjects' recognition for their contributions to teaching.

Implications

Introducing type theory and its implications for learning and teaching early in the careers of faculty can facilitate their personal and professional growth. They can be supported in developing their natural strengths and at the same time encouraged to experiment with a variety of teaching modes to reach students different from themselves. Through knowledge of their MBTI preferences, they can become aware of their own natural biases about the best way to learn. They can realize that there are many other ways to learn and that frequently individuals are more comfortable and successful learning in one of these other ways. By understanding their own natural preferences, teachers can choose work conditions and projects which support and enhance the development and expression of these preferences. Especially in the earlier years, they can also be more tolerant of their shortcomings when they can relate these to their lesser preferences; type gives them a "map" of how they need to develop over a lifetime.

It follows that knowledge of type can influence curriculum development, teaching strategies and assignments, course structure, and method of student evaluation. One of the CASE professors, upon learning his MBTI results, was quick to point out the usefulness of this information in deciphering previously puzzling student evaluations of his teaching. He had received conflicting reviews over the years about "such things as organization of material, clarity of argument, etc." Now he realizes positive and negative comments about the same teaching approach are probably a result of his ENFP style appealing more to the N students and less to the S students. He says, " It casts a whole new light on reviewing student evaluations" (personal correspondence, August, 1986).

Administrators can also be shown that there are many models of excellence among faculty based on productive expression of professors' natural strengths; the CASE finalists provide such models. Therefore, the institution should be prepared to recognize and reward more than one model of excellence. For example, the institution valuing teaching may decide that the ENFJ professor who thrives on classroom interaction and is loved by students for her dedication to teaching should be supported to the same degree as the INTP who, although available to the students, places a higher priority on research for publication.

Those of us not involved directly in the classroom can help students clarify their own learning styles and the relationship of their styles to their success and failures in certain teachers' courses. The examples given by the professors in the sample increase our understanding of differing motivations, value systems, and approaches among faculty. If we are to be effective in the academic community, we must be able to understand and talk the language(s) of the faculty.

Peter Beidler's own comment about the job of professors deserves restatement; he says it is their job to discover the one best way individual students learn. "Helping a student find the best way to learn is sometimes called love" (p. 61). For those interested in a thorough exploration of these themes and others related to college teaching, a complete reading of Beidler's book, *Distinguished Teachers on Effective Teaching* (Beidler, 1986), is recommended.

A special note of appreciation to the CASE Finalists, 1981 to 85: Robert G. Albertson, University of Puget Sound; Anthony F. Aveni, Colgate University; William M. Bass III, University of Tennessee; Peter G. Beidler, Lehigh University; Barbara Harrell Carson, Rollins College; Kenneth Eble, University of Utah; Sister Maura Eichner, College of Notre Dame of Maryland; Julienne H. Empric, Eckerd College; Sol Gittleman, Tufts University; Robert J. Higgs, East Tennessee State University; Parker Grimes Marden, St. Lawrence University; Kenneth S. Norris, University of California at Santa Cruz; Charles E. Ratliff, Davidson College; Benjamin Richason, Carroll College; Paul Saltman, University of California at San Diego; Daniel G. Sisler, Cornell University; Lawrence P. Ulrich, University of Dayton; Helen Vendler, Harvard University.

Reference

Beidler, P. (1986). *Distinguished teachers on effective teaching.* San Francisco: Jossey-Bass.

GERALD MACDAID is the Manager of Research, Computing, and Scoring Operations at the Center for Applications of Psychological Type and has been with the CAPT research department for five years. He worked closely with Mary McCaulley on the revision of the MBTI *Manual*, running extensive databank analyses and compiling studies. Most recently he has co-authored the CAPT *MBTI Atlas of Type Tables*, a compendium of type table data on careers. Previous to his involvement at CAPT, Jerry worked in student development and counseling as a Residence Hall Director and at the Learning Skills Center at the University of Florida, where he also completed a bachelor's degree in Psychology. Jerry's MBTI preferences are ENFP.

CHAPTER 12

Research Approaches Using the MBTI

GERALD P. MACDAID

"THE BRIGHTEST FLASHES in the world of thought are incomplete until they have been proven to have their counterparts in the world of fact."[1] Landmark works in the field of student development, such as Chickering's *Education and Identity* (1969), are built upon this principle, thus enriching the insight of the student development practitioner with the depth and substance of empirical observation. Good research has been an important foundation for the growth of the student development movement.

In the few short years since the MBTI has been generally available to practitioners, a number of applications within higher education have been explored and researched. Yet MBTI research is still very much in its infant stage. While this research has gotten off to a good start, much more still remains to be done. One problem with the research to date is a lack of systematic and thorough exploration of areas within student development. Therefore, practitioners must determine which applications have been tested and are empirically sound and which are simply theoretical speculation.

Practitioners and educators in higher education are in a position to improve upon the body of research concerning the relationship between type and student development. Research can be done in simple straightforward ways and yield valid results. Small studies with a narrow focus can contribute valuable information to the field. Complex research projects have their place, but often serve to scare away the busy practitioner without strong research skills. Yet it is these same professionals who could generate important research from their daily contact with students.

---

1 Quote by John Tyndall on a plaque in the Space Sciences Research Building, University of Florida campus

The June 10, 1985, printing of the Center for Applications of Psychological Type's MBTI bibliography had 1,029 entries. Using a cross-reference index of this bibliography by Ware and Glover (1985), Table 1 was constructed to show the frequency of topics pertinent to student development professionals.

TABLE 1

Frequency of Relevant Topics in CAPT Bibliography

Topic	Frequency	Topic	Frequency
Students	136	Sex Roles	15
Counseling	91	Marriage	15
Education	85	Cognitive Style	15
Teachers	72	Communication	12
Career Development	68	Self-Esteem	11
Careers	59	Values	10
Learning	56	Problem Solving	10
Creativity	43	Conflict	9
Interpersonal Relationships	38	Intelligence	8
Academic Prediction	38	Development, Psychological	7
Academic Achievement	33	Reading	3
Teaching	31	Teamwork	2
Religion	30	Privacy	2
Development, General	27	Memory	2
Decision Making	21	Intimate Relationships	2
Residence and Work Settings	20	Personal Space	1
Group Dynamics	16	Career Success	1
Drugs	16		

This list shows that large global topic areas have the most research while smaller more specific areas have much less. Many pertinent topics are relatively unstudied. This illustrates the dilemma facing practitioners wanting to develop a program with the MBTI in such unstudied areas—the literature often is not solid enough to support the development of applications. This problem not only occurs in the quantity of studies but in the quality of studies as well. Many studies are just starting to describe the relationships between type and a topic area, providing a simple overview but lacking substance. Other studies are just poorly done, often showing the researchers' lack of understanding about the properties of the MBTI.

This chapter examines how the practitioner can contribute valuable and pertinent MBTI research. First, I will present the notion that every

MBTI user is a researcher. Then, I will examine the tools and strategies that lend themselves easily to the analysis of type data. As I discuss the various research approaches, I will give specific examples and the appropriate data presentation and reporting conventions.

Every MBTI User Is a Researcher

With the dramatic growth in the number of MBTI users, the potential for collecting large amounts of data is staggering. In 1986, Consulting Psychologists Press, the publisher of the MBTI, sold approximately 1,500,000 blank answer sheets. A reasonable estimate is that 97% of those are hand scored by professionals, and there are desk drawers across the country teeming with potential but untapped research data. Data are being collected every day within institutions of higher education. Individual feedback sessions with students, career exploration groups, and mediations of roommate conflicts are examples of opportunities to contribute more data to how personality functions in these various areas. Every MBTI user has valuable data.

These unutilized data are important, because right now there are more MBTI users than active researchers. More and more people are using the MBTI and doing so in more varied and creative ways. Yet the documented research to substantiate and transmit these findings from practical applications lags far behind. Often other practitioners are looking for data about these kinds of applications and cannot find anything in the literature. Many times the "wheel is reinvented" because no record of another practitioner's discovery exists.

For the body of research to grow, it will require contributions from the practitioners. All of us should document our discoveries so others may verify and amplify them. Each user taps into unique samples and contributes something no other person can. Even the simplest observations and findings add to our body of knowledge, especially as these various studies are duplicated. This is particularly important for work with small specialty groups. Often these populations are not large enough to make clear or definite statements about type relationships, but when combined with other small groups, patterns become more apparent, and the body of research grows.

Simple First Steps to Research

Since data are collected by many practitioners on a day-to-day basis, often a valuable database accumulates without much effort. However, the data often remain unanalyzed. Identifying simple, manageable, and appropriate methods can make data analysis less intimidating and more accomplishable for busy nonresearch-oriented practitioners.

The simplest approach is to get the data analyzed by someone else. While this statement is purposely facetious, it is also perfectly serious. There are a number of ways to get outside data analysis services. One way is to use the CAPT scoring services. Using the scoring services is a way of participating in large-scale assessment of the psychometric properties of the MBTI as well as generating estimates of normative populations and occupational groups. This databank was started in 1970 by Isabel Myers and Mary McCaulley expressly for the purpose of facilitating research on the MBTI.

The size of this databank recently exceeded a quarter of a million cases. Its growth has been based on MBTI users who scored cases from five students seen for academic advisement to users who administer the MBTI to their entire freshman class every fall. Each addition is important, because the power of this databank comes from the cases in aggregate. The databank is particularly valuable because it provides an opportunity to perform analyses that would be otherwise impossible on such a scale. Studies of the databank recently completed for the revised MBTI *Manual*, (Myers & McCaulley, 1985) revealed many important facts about the Indicator and produced informative tables showing type distributions across various populations.

An example of such findings are the reliability studies reported in the *Manual* (Myers & McCaulley, 1985). Reliability, the ability of an instrument to produce repeatable and consistent results, is very important to the practitioner. Unfortunately, reliability is very difficult for practitioners to assess for every group that they might work with. The databank provides a large enough sample to produce stable reliability estimates of the Indicator scales for males, females, age groups from 15 to 60 plus, and education levels from dropouts to college graduates.

Practitioners who use the computer scoring services get the added benefit of being able to receive the scored data back in a computer-readable format. This can save the hours and expense of having to enter large data sets into the computer by hand.

A useful starting point in research is reviewing the literature. Some practitioners may not be sure what aspects of their practice may be pertinent to research. Others may be clear about their topic but unaware of what others have examined in their topic area. Having a sense of what has been published and what is known helps get a researcher off to a solid start. The CAPT bibliography is a very useful resource for this task.

Descriptive Studies of Type

One basic kind of research study that one can do is a descriptive study. In a descriptive study the researcher examines a sample, looking at one or more characteristics of interest, to describe the nature of the sample, and the population it was drawn from. In MBTI research the frequency distribution of types in a sample is not only used to describe a sample's characteristics, but can also be used to explore the concept of self-selection. The basic notion behind self-selection is that people of different types select for themselves different opportunities and situations that are satisfying, and these selections will be congruent with their type preferences.

Research in type self-selection asks the question: If type truly makes a difference in what is perceived by people as interesting, enjoyable, or tolerable, then what differences would we find in various samples such as academic, career, and recreation groups? For example Sensing types are expected to be found more often in situations involving use of the senses and practical realities, and Intuitive types in situations where abstraction and hypothesizing are demanded.

Self-selection data are reported using the type table. Isabel Myers designed this format of data presentation as a standard way for representing type distributions of groups. In a type table one can get a visual impression of the frequency distribution of that group, as well as determine more carefully the precise breakdown of the percentages and numbers of the types and type groupings.

The reporting of frequency distribution data is valuable on two levels. First, it provides further insight into the nature of the self-selection process for each of the types. There are limits to how much one can safely predict from theory, and self-selection data allow us to expand upon what is known about the attractions and behaviors of each type. With the data in a type table format the practitioner can compile a compendium of activities, interests, programs, etc. by type. This can facilitate the targeting of programming efforts.

Second, self-selection data provide a test for type theory itself. Since the underlying theory is what every application of the MBTI is founded upon, the theory deserves rigorous testing. The confidence we can place in the MBTI is related to our confidence in the validity of our applications. Practitioners are in the best position to contribute valid studies of their own applications.

An example of type data being displayed in this fashion is Table 2, which shows a sample of 225 college leaders from the *MBTI Atlas of Type*

TABLE 2

Leaders in Student Government Activities
(N = 225)

Sensing		Intuition				N	%
Thinking	Feeling	Feeling	Thinking				
ISTJ	ISFJ	INFJ	INTJ	Introverts Judging	E	172	76.44
					I	53	23.56
N = 11	N = 6	N = 9	N = 2		S	112	49.78
% = 4.89	% = 2.67	% = 4.00	% = .89		N	113	50.22
▪▪▪▪▪	▪▪▪	▪▪▪▪	▪		T	135	60.00
					F	90	40.00
					J	134	59.56
					P	91	40.44
ISTP	ISFP	INFP	INTP	Introverts Perceptive	IJ	28	12.44
					IP	25	11.11
N = 8	N = 3	N = 8	N = 6		EP	66	29.33
% = 3.56	% = 1.33	% = 3.56	% = 2.67		EJ	106	47.11
▪▪▪▪	▪	▪▪▪▪	▪▪▪				
					ST	74	32.89
					SF	38	16.89
					NF	52	23.11
					NT	61	27.11
ESTP	ESFP	ENFP	ENTP	Extraverts Perceptive	SJ	80	35.56
					SP	32	14.22
N = 8	N = 13	N = 27	N = 18		NP	59	26.22
% = 3.56	% = 5.78	% = 12.00	% = 8.00		NJ	54	24.00
▪▪▪▪	▪▪▪▪▪▪	▪▪▪▪▪▪▪ ▪▪▪▪▪▪▪	▪▪▪▪▪				
					TJ	95	42.22
					TP	40	17.78
					FP	51	22.67
					FJ	39	17.33
ESTJ	ESFJ	ENFJ	ENTJ	Extraverts Judging	IN	25	11.11
					EN	88	39.11
N = 47	N = 16	N = 8	N = 35		IS	28	12.44
% = 20.89	% = 7.11	% = 3.56	% = 15.56		E S	84	37.33
▪▪▪▪▪▪ ▪▪▪▪▪▪ ▪▪▪▪▪▪ ▪▪▪	▪▪▪▪▪▪ ▪	▪▪▪▪	▪▪▪▪▪▪ ▪▪▪▪▪▪ ▪▪▪▪				
					ET	108	48.00
					EF	64	28.44
					IF	26	11.56
					IT	27	12.00

Note: ▪ = 1% of sample
Data collected by Alice Hadwin of Florida Community College at Jacksonville during October 1983. Subjects were 44% male and 54% female. No other demographic data were reported. These data are used with permission and have not been published elsewhere to date.

	N	%
S dom	38	16.89
N dom	56	24.89
T dom	96	42.67
F dom	35	15.56

Tables (Macdaid, McCaulley, & Kainz, 1986). The table displays the frequencies and percentages of the 16 types plus 36 common type groupings; in addition, a symbol is used to convey a visual impression of the frequency distribution of the 16 types. In Table 2, we can see that the two most frequent types in this sample are ESTJ and ENTJ. The most frequent preference is for Extraversion, while the ET and EJ groups are the largest of the clusters of four types.

Short descriptive studies are often published in many of the professional journals. Practitioners may contribute to their field by submitting for publication simple descriptive studies with data in this format. Descriptive studies of this kind allow practitioners familiar with type to educate colleagues about type and show examples of how types differ in frequency in various populations or subgroupings. Information about sharing data with CAPT or others can be found in the Appendix.

Hypothesis Testing with Statistical Tools

So far I have described a method for reporting and collecting descriptive data. Now I would like to turn to the issue of hypothesis testing and statistical inference. Usually research has the very specific goal of discovering the answer to a very exact question. This question is the hypothesis. Hypothesis testing uses statistical tests to see if collected data support a belief.

Hypotheses are first stated as null hypotheses. Instead of predicting a difference related to type, a null hypothesis predicts no difference. An alternative hypothesis is proposed which states a difference does exist due to type. Data are analyzed to disprove or "reject" the null hypothesis, thus providing evidence supporting the alternative hypothesis.

In order to reject a null hypothesis, a level of significance or risk level alpha must be set before statistical analyses are done. The level of significance is usually set at .05, .01, or .001, indicating what percentage of the time we will get a particular result by chance alone. If findings are significant at $p<.001$, then there is only one chance in a thousand that the result occurred by chance. You could therefore place a high degree of confidence on such a finding.

Chi-Square and SRTT

One of the most common hypotheses in type research addresses whether certain types are found more frequently in a given sample than would be expected in a base population. The analysis that is most appropriate for determining if a type is more or less prevalent in the sample than expected is a two-by-two contingency table analysis. Here the null hypothesis is: if type does not affect selection into the sample, then the proportion of any type observed in the sample will not differ from the proportion of that same type in a reference population. This analysis tests to see if the observed frequencies are the same or different than the expected frequencies. A chi-square statistic is calculated for the hypothesis test. If the probability of the calculated chi-square value is less than the alpha level we chose, then we can reject the null hypothesis. We can then conclude that type factors are significant in that particular sample.

This approach is built into a computer software program called the Selection Ratio Type Table (SRTT) program, which was written and is distributed by CAPT as an aid for researchers. While this analysis can be calculated by other programs or standard statistical packages, the SRTT program allows for the convenient analysis of type data, and it produces output from 44 separate analyses on a one-page type table format. Furthermore, the SRTT program calculates a selection ratio obtained by dividing the observed frequency by the expected frequency. The selection ratio thus is equal to 1.00 when the observed and expected frequencies are the same, grows increasingly larger as the observed frequency becomes larger than the expected frequency, and grows increasingly smaller as the observed frequency becomes smaller than the expected frequency.

An example of the SRTT analysis comes from a study by Macdaid, McCaulley, and Kainz (1984). The question of what types excel academically was raised as part of a follow-up study of college freshmen. In theory, the Introverted Intuitives would be expected to excel because of their orientation to ideas and theory. College graduates elected to the Phi Beta Kappa honor society were selected as examples of excellence in academic performance. Since the sample of all college graduates already had a high percentage of IN types, simply examining the frequency distribution of the Phi Beta Kappa sample for a majority of IN types would not provide evidence for the hypothesis. So the Phi Beta Kappa sample was compared to the entire graduate sample using the SRTT analysis.

Table 3 shows the results of this SRTT comparison. The right-hand column, under the letter "I," Index, displays the selection ratios for the various combinations of types. Next to the selection ratio is a symbol denoting the level of significance reached. The lack of a symbol means that the selection ratio Index for that type combination failed to reach the lowest level of significance, indicating the sample probably does not

TABLE 3

Phi Beta Kappas by Type
(*N*= 75)

Sensing		Intuition				N	%	I
with Thinking	with Feeling	with Feeling	withThinking					

ISTJ	ISFJ	INFJ	INTJ	Introverts Judging	E	26	34.67	0.66**
N=6	N=3	N=8	N=10		I	49	65.33	1.37**
%=.8.00	%=4.00	%=10.67	%=13.33					
I=1.12	I=0.48	I=2.20*	I=3.43***		S	18	24.00	0.52***
					N	57	76.00	1.42***
					T	36	48.00	1.33*
					F	39	52.00	0.81*
ISTP	ISFP	INFP	INTP	Perceptive	J	40	53.33	1.07
					P	35	46.67	0.93
N = 81	N = 152	N = 294	N = 138					
% = 2.90	% = 5.44	% = 10.52	% = 4.94		IJ	27	36.00	1.49*
I = 1.04	I = 0.51	I = 1.20	I = 2.30*		IP	22	29.33	1.25
					EP	13	17.33	0.65
					EJ	13	17.33	0.67
ESTP	ESFP	ENFP	ENTP	Extraverts Perceptive	ST	10	13.33	0.69
					SF	8	10.67	0.39***
N = 75	N = 139	N = 383	N = 126					
% = 2.68	% = 4.97	% = 13.71	% = 4.51		NF	31	41.33	1.13
I = 0.56	I = 0.53	I = 0.73	I = 0.61		NT	26	34.67	2.07***
					SJ	11	14.67	0.47**
					SP	7	9.33	0.61
ESTJ	ESFJ	ENFJ	ENTJ	Judging	NP	28	37.33	1.07
					NJ	29	38.67	2.07***
N = 176	N = 259	N = 186	N = 113					
% = 6.30	% = 9.27	% = 6.66	% = 4.04		TJ	23	30.67	1.39
I = 0.19	I = 0.15*	I = 1.10	I = 2.09		TP	13	17.33	1.24
					FP	22	29.33	0.81
					FJ	17	22.67	0.81

* p ≤ .05, ** p ≤ .01, *** p ≤ .001.
Source: Jerry Macdaid, University of Florida, 1982.

IN	36	48.00	1.96***
EN	21	28.00	0.97

differ from the base population. The selection ratio reported for the IN group is 1.96 and is significant at the .001 level and the selection ratios for each of the four IN types are also greater than one. This is evidence to reject the null hypothesis that type is not related to academic excellence.

Since the SRTT analysis performs 44 independent contingency table analyses, at least 2 of the 44 tests could be statistically significant purely by chance. Stating the hypothesis before performing the analysis will reduce the danger of claiming chance differences as actual.

Choosing a Proper Reference Sample

The validity of the SRTT depends on the selection of an appropriate reference population. The reference population chosen should be directly related to the hypothesis being tested. For example, suppose we wished to discover if the types of residents in a specialized residence program differed from the types of students in other residence halls. Our null hypothesis would be that the type distribution of our specialized residence program would not differ significantly from the type distribution of our entire residence program. The most valid reference population in this case would be the entire population of residence hall students from which the sample was drawn.

Sometimes this reference population is not available or obtainable. Choosing the next best reference population is a process that requires careful judgment, since the results of the SRTT comparison can be rendered meaningless by an inappropriate comparison. The base or reference population should have as many characteristics in common with the sample as possible. The more differences between the chosen base and the sample, the less the results of the SRTT procedure apply.

In the example above, the next best reference population would be a random sample drawn from the entire resident population. If this comparison population is not available, then finding some other estimate of the entire resident population would be advisable. However, when estimated populations are used researchers must account for all identifiable demographic features so as to avoid an inappropriate comparison. Some reasonable approaches to selecting a reference population are: choosing a resident sample from another college similar in nature to your institution; selecting an aggregate of many colleges' residential students to average out potential biases of differences in colleges; using the next most similar population of students at your college; or using other representative samples of college students in general. Comparing the sample of special residents to a population of high school students, resident advisors, or roommates who have taken the MBTI for conflict resolution only shows how the students in the special residential program differ from these very specific populations. Comparison with any of these groups would not answer the original question of how these students differ in type from the residential students in general.

Correlations

A correlational analysis is another approach to discovering how other variables relate to type. Correlation is a measure of association, permitting examination of the relationship between the individual preference scales of the Indicator and the scores of another variable.

Continuous Scores versus Dichotomous Scores. The MBTI continuous score was created explicitly for the purpose of correlational research. The procedure for creating these scores takes otherwise discontinuous preference scores generated from a measure of dichotomous preferences and mathematically gives them continuous characteristics. The MBTI continuous scores then are simply a recalculation of the preference scores where a score of zero would have a value of 100, the preference scores for E, S, T, and J are subtracted from 100, and the preference scores for I, N, F, and P are added to 100. Thus instead of an E score or an I score, one has an EI score. For example, a preference score of E11 yields a continuous score of 89, while a preference score of I35 yields a continuous score of 135.

This mathematically created continuity points out a basic difference between a type theory and a trait theory. For example an Extravert-Introvert scale on a trait-measuring instrument usually starts out with low scores indicating more introverted traits and high scores indicating more extraverted traits. In the middle is a neutral zone where people are said to possess the traits of both. Proceeding up or down these trait-measuring scales represents small, incremental changes in magnitude and quality. In contrast, type theory holds that there is a definite and clear difference in the characteristics of people on either side of the midpoint, not a small incremental change. This difference is a sudden and dramatic qualitative change analogous to a phase change in chemistry, the point an element crosses as it changes from a gas to a liquid; once it crosses that line it has very different properties.

Continuous scores are artificial transformations which allow the researcher to use the four MBTI scales in correlational comparisons with other scales or numeric variables. For most studies of this nature, the Pearson correlation coefficient (r) will be the statistic of choice. Carlyn (1977) discusses the merits of the Pearson and calls it "a good statistic to use with MBTI continuous scores because differences in the shapes of the two distributions being compared tend to have little effect on the *r* in most cases" (p. 6). She warns that a sample size of at least 30 is recommended by most statisticians. She also notes that the Pearson correlation usually understates the magnitude of the relationship. This correlation coefficient can only be used with continuous MBTI scores, not with the 16 types.

The values of a correlation coefficient range from -1.00 to 1.00. A correlation of 1.00 indicates a perfect positive relationship. In other words, a high score on one variable is associated with a high score on the other variable. A negative correlation shows that a high score on one variable is associated with a low score on the other variable. A correlation of zero shows no relationship; as the numeric value of the correlation moves away from zero in either direction it indicates increasingly related covariance. Correlations do not indicate a causal relationship, but only indicate an association between variables.

When reading correlations of type with other variables, the underlying dichotomy must not be forgotten even when using continuous scores. The sign of the correlation indicates which half of the dichotomy the variable is related to. Positive correlations are related to I, N, F, or P and negative correlations are related to E, S, T, or J. Table 4 shows some examples of correlations with type. The correlations in Table 4 are an example of results from correlational research and demonstrate how different measures of value orientation are associated with type preferences. For example, economic values were related to a preference for Sensing (-.46).

Sometimes correlations are computed with the preference scores instead of continuous scores. In this case eight sets of correlations would be calculated. This is sometimes an advantageous procedure, particularly when the scores on the other measure are expected to increase as a type preference in either direction increases. It can also be helpful if the other measure is believed to relate more to one-half of the type dichotomy than the other. An example is found in data analyzed by Myers in the original MBTI *Manual* (Myers, 1962). For this sample of 249, a correlation of student gregariousness as rated by faculty using continuous scores on the EI scale was .42. When correlations were calculated for each preference score, the results were -.21 for Introversion and .05 for Extraversion. Myers' interpretation of this was:

> Apparently, to the faculty eye, gregariousness is a general characteristic of extravert students, not perceptibly related to the degree of preference for extraversion. Introverts, of any degree, however, are seen as definitely less gregarious. (p. 100)

TABLE 4

Correlation of MBTI Continuous Scores with Values

Source	N	Sex	EI	SN	TF	JP	Relation
Study of Values (Allport, Vernon, & Lindzey, 1960)							
(5) Theoretical	1,351	M	11**	26**	−37**	−05*	-NT-
(5)	236	M	14*	20**	−36**	−03	-NT-
(5)	238	M	09	22**	−35**	−02	-NT-
(9)	65	M,F	09	−16	−42***	−13	—T-
(5)	877	M	10**	28**	−38**	−07*	-NT-
(5) Economic	1,351	M	−11**	−46**	−16**	−12**	-S—
(5)	236	M	01	−52**	−24**	−14*	-ST-
(5)	238	M	−22**	−55**	−07	−06	ES—
(9)	65	M,F	08	−58***	−39**	−54***	-STJ
(5)	877	M	−11**	−41**	−16**	−13**	-S—
(5) Aesthetic	1,351	M	20**	34**	−01	16**	IN—
(5)	236	M	17**	40**	05	22**	-N-P
(5)	238	M	25**	44**	06	25**	IN-P
(9)	65	M,F	−13	50***	10	45***	-N-P
(5)	877	M	20**	30**	−05	12**	IN—
(5) Social	1,351	M	−05	−06*	34**	01	—F-
(5)	236	M	−11	00	38**	02	—F-
(5)	238	M	02	03	30**	−05	—F-
(9)	65	M,F	00	23	33**	26*	—F-
(5)	877	M	−05	−11**	34**	02	—F-
(5) Political	1,351	M	−20**	−21**	−16**	03	ES—
(5)	236	M	−12	−26**	−18**	−03	-S—
(5)	238	M	−26**	−29**	−18**	04	ES—
(9)	65	M,F	−04	−30	−19	−06	——
(5)	877	M	−20**	−17**	−14**	05	E—
(5) Religious	1,351	M	00	08**	29**	−04	—F-
(5)	236	M	−15*	04	32**	−11	—F-
(5)	238	M	08	13*	20**	−16*	—F-
(9)	65	M,F	02	15	38**	−02	—F-
(5)	877	M	01	07*	31**	01	—F-

* $p < .05$, ** $p < .01$, *** $p < .001$.

From *Manual: A guide to the development and use of the Myers-Briggs Type Indicator,* (p. 187) by I.B. Myers and M.H. McCaulley, 1985, Palo Alto, CA: Consulting Psychologists Press. Copyright 1985 by Peter B. Myers. Reprinted by permission.

Differences Among Types

Further examination of relationships of other variables to type can be pursued by comparing the level of performance or scores on measures of these variables across various type categories. Here the goal is to see if there are different mean scores between types or groupings of types. If the theory predicts that types will vary in tasks, developmental measures, academic achievement, etc., then the mean scores for the types should reflect the disparity. To statistically test to see if these differences are not likely to have been caused by chance, the *t* and *F* test statistics are employed.

The *t* statistic is used to test the likelihood that two means are significantly different. For example, you might test for difference in mean achievement levels between Sensing or Intuitive types. A one-way analysis of variance (ANOVA) employing the *F* statistic must be used to examine differences in performance for type groupings of more than two groups. Examples of groupings that would be tested in this way are IN, EN, IS, and ES, or the 16 types.

An example of this analysis is a study by McCaulley and Kainz (1974). The hypothesis being tested was that grade point averages would be higher for the Introverted and Intuitive group. The outer right-hand column in Table 5 shows the test statistic used (either *t* or *F*) and its significance level. For this hypothesis, the *F*-statistic (17.4) indicates a significant difference among the four groups. The IN group has the highest average GPA of any grouping and the *F*-test for the differences in variances is significant at the .001 level. Furthermore, the four IN types' GPAs are ranked 1, 2, 3, and 5.

Case Studies

Another method for practitioners to capture and report data is by case studies. Often in teaching, counseling, or supervision one has the opportunity to gather deeper insights about how type preferences manifest themselves in an individual's functioning. Since many practitioners have one-to-one contact with students, case study data are appropriate to collect. The case study allows documenting and reporting of observations of characteristics, behaviors, and phenomena that are often too complex to capture or observe in large sample studies.

Case studies also provide a chance to verify theoretical premises about type dynamics and uncover more complex patterns of type-related behavior. For example, from theory one could make a prediction about the probable process an ESTP might utilize to make decisions. Using a

TABLE 5

University of Florida Students Cumulative Grade-Point Average
Mean 2.76   S.D. 0.58

Sensing Types with Thinking	Sensing Types with Feeling	Intuitive Types with Feeling	Intuitive Types with Thinking	
ISTJ N = 193 % = 6.91 Mean 2.78 S.D..60 6	**ISFJ** N = 232 % = 8.30 Mean 2.84 S.D..59 4	**INFJ** N = 131 % = 4.69 Mean 2.95 S.D..59 2	**INTJ** N = 116 % = 4.15 Mean 3.00 S.D..55 1	*Introverts Judging*
ISTP N = 81 % = 2.90 Mean 2.64 S.D.57 13	**ISFP** N = 152 % = 5.44 Mean 2.63 S>D>.61 14	**INFP** N = 294 % = 10.52 Mean 2.83 S.D. .58 5	**INTP** N = 138 % = 4.94 Mean 2.88 S.D. .59 3	*Perceptive*
ESTP N = 75 % = 2.68 Mean 2.59 S.D. .55 15	**ESFP** N = 139 % = 4.97 Mean 2.54 S.D. .57 16	**ENFP** N = 383 % = 13.71 Mean 2.76 S.D. .57 9	**ENTP** N = 126 % = 4.51 Mean 2.66 S.D. .60 12	*Extraverts Perceptive*
ESTJ N = 176 % = 6.30 Mean 2.65 S.D. .57 11	**ESFJ** N = 259 % = 9.27 Mean 2.75 S.D. .55 10	**ENFJ** N = 186 % = 6.66 Mean 2.77 S.D. .61 7	**ENTJ** N = 113 % = 4.04 Mean 2.77 S.D. .66 8	*Judging*

	N	Mean	S.D.	F/t
E	1457	2.71	.58	24.8***
I	1337	2.82	.59	
S	1307	2.71	.58	22.8***
N	1487	2.81	.59	
T	1018	2.76	.60	0.2
F	1776	2.77	.58	
J	1406	2.80	.59	11.8***
P	1388	2.72	.58	
IJ	672	2.87	.59	
IP	665	2.77	.59	12.6***
EP	723	2.68	.57	
EJ	734	2.74	.59	
ST	525	2.69	.58	
SF	782	2.72	.58	
NF	994	2.81	.59	7.9***
NT	493	2.82	.61	
SJ	860	2.76	.58	
SP	447	2.60	.57	
NP	941	2.78	.58	17.5***
NJ	546	2.86	.61	
TJ	598	2.79	.60	
TP	420	2.71	.59	
FP	968	2.73	.58	4.2**
FJ	808	2.81	.59	
IN	679	2.89	.58	
EN	808	2.75	.60	
IS	658	2.75	.60	17.4***
ES	649	2.66	.56	

Notes: *$p < .05$ ** $p < .01$ *** $p < .001$ [based on t test for EI, SN, TF and JP, and on F test for one way ANOVA for other groupings.] One way analysis of variance for all 16 types df 15,2778 F 6.22***. Study conducted at CAPT by M. H. McCaulley & R. I. Kainz as a follow-up of University of Florida entering students 1–2 years after admission in 1972.

case study approach, one could examine each step an ESTP might use during a decision-making process. Obviously with this approach one can compile more detailed observations about what transpires. The richness of the observations help give more depth to our theoretical predictions, and subtleties that are discovered by this approach then become new hypotheses to be tested with larger samples. The hypothesized behavior is examined to see if it is common to all of this type and not prevalent in other types.

Good examples of the case study can be found in *A Casebook: Applications of the Myers-Briggs Type Indicator in Counseling* by Judith A. Provost (1984). In this book Provost presents vivid descriptions of how she integrates type theory into the counseling process, giving examples of the behavior of clients and tying it to type theory predictions.

The case study approach can also produce quantitative data. If the researcher can precisely label and define the nature of the behavior being observed, the occurrences of the behavior can be counted and compared using methods already described. For example, in theory we might expect Introverts to feel more uncomfortable getting to know new people. Furthermore, specific behaviors might be good indicators of discomfort. If the researcher counted the number of occurrences from logs of initial interviews or counseling sessions, then an analyzable database is created. These data could be analyzed using the SRTT procedure comparing high and low occurrences, or a correlation of the occurrences and MBTI scores, t or F statistic could then be calculated.

Field Research

Field research is similar to case studies in the sense that quantifiable observations are systematically made during the course of natural interaction with subjects in their environment. More variables can be observed and collected if the researcher is an observer and not participating in the interaction with the subject. A practical suggestion for the practitioner who works alone is to focus on collecting the one or two variables of most interest. This helps avoid making the data collection too intrusive to the subject or overwhelming to the researcher.

Collaboration

Having others to collaborate with is another way to help research get done. Networking with other professionals can be stimulating and rewarding, and can also utilize the mutual usefulness of opposites, for good teams can be built balancing strengths and weaknesses as a research team. Three avenues are available for networking. One avenue is the research interest group in the Association for Psychological Type, composed of professionals who are interested in type research. It is often possible to find someone with whom to collaborate or consult. A second avenue is to search your own institution to find other professionals or graduate students interested in research. Often a mutually beneficial mentoring relationship is very productive, giving the less experienced researcher assistance with data analysis and the more experienced researcher more information about type. A final avenue is considering contracting with someone. In a contract arrangement, an outside person is hired to perform all or part of the data analysis. CAPT's research department may be a resource to consider for this service.

Conclusion

For others who are more experienced researchers there are many other methodological approaches that can be considered. The appropriate choice always rests on the nature of the hypothesis in question, the nature of the data in hand, and of the sampling methods used. Complex multivariate statistics are getting easier to use with the advent of computer statistical packages. An important point to remember is the dichotomous nature of type data. Knowing this fact will help avoid any grievous traps.

This introduction to MBTI research approaches in student development is intended to help demystify research, give the practitioner some simple yet useful tools, and generate more interest in doing research. The field of student development and the use of the MBTI as a tool in that field is young and open to new research. Now is an exciting time to be contributing. It is possible to be a cutting-edge contributor since there are so many new horizons to explore and so few explorers. Take a good look at the work you are doing. What do you have to contribute?

References

Carlyn, M. (1977). *Current research practices involving the Myers-Briggs Type Indicator—design and methodology.* Paper presented at the Second National MBTI Conference, East Lansing, MI.

Chickering, A. W. (1969). *Education and identity.* San Francisco: Jossey-Bass.

Macdaid, G. P., McCaulley, M. H., & Kainz, R. I. (1984). *The University of Florida longitudinal study: Ten-year followup.* (Unpublished paper.)

Macdaid, G. P., McCaulley, M. H., & Kainz, R. I. (1986). *MBTI atlas of type tables.* Gainesville, FL: Center for Applications of Psychological Type.

McCaulley, M. H., & Kainz, R. I. (1974). *The University of Florida longitudinal study: First followup.* Unpublished paper, University of Florida.

McCaulley, M. H., Macdaid, G. P., & Kainz, R. I. (1985). Estimated frequencies of the MBTI types. *Journal of Psychological Type, 9*, 3–9.

Myers, I. B. (1962). *Manual: The Myers-Briggs Type Indicator.* Palo Alto, CA: Consulting Psychologists Press.

Myers, I. B., & McCaulley, M. H. (1985). *Manual: A guide to the development and use of the Myers-Briggs Type Indicator.* Palo Alto, CA: Consulting Psychologists Press.

Provost, J. A. (1984). Casebook: Applications of the MBTI in counseling. Gainesville, FL: Center for Applications of Psychological Type.

Ware, R. & Glover, S. (1985). *Index for the Myers-Briggs Type Indicator bibliography.* (Unpublished paper.)

Appendix

THIS APPENDIX IS a compilation of information from a variety of researchers and practitioners around the country; each contribution is carefully acknowledged. The Editors wish to thank these contributors for their efforts in sharing type data. The Appendix contains type tables of specific subgroups within higher education.

The type tables illustrate the similarities and differences among samples within higher education. Type theory suggests that people will move into environments, roles, and situations that reinforce their types. Some of the tables are from the MBTI *Manual* (1985) and from the CAPT MBTI databank, discussed in Chapter 12. Readers are advised to consult the Manual for specific references and additional information concerning type tables from that source. Readers are also encouraged to send the Editors any type tables that might be useful in a future edition of this book.

TABLE 1

Ranking of Colleges by MBTI Preference

College	Percent
Extraversion-Introversion	
St. Louis University	62% E
University of Wisconsin at Stevens Point	61% E
University of Maine at Orono	59% E
Mercer University	59% E
Nicholls State University	58% E
Auburn University	57% E
Adrian College	57% E
University of North Carolina at Greensboro	55% E
Rollins College	54% E
St. Clair College	54% E
University of Florida	54% E
Hope College	53% E
Franklin and Marshall College	50% E
Parks College	50% I
Berkshire Christian College	53% I
Concordia College	54% I
Sensing-Intuition	
Nicholls State University	72% S
St. Clair College	68% S
Berkshire Christian College	67% S
Adrian College	64% S
Parks College	59% S
Mercer University	59% S
Auburn University	57% S
University of North Carolina at Greensboro	57% S
University of Wisconsin at Stevens Point	56% S
University of Maine at Orono	55% S
Concordia College	54% S
Franklin and Marshall College	50% S
Rollins College	52% N
St. Louis University	52% N
Hope College	53% N
University of Florida	55% N

Source: From *Manual: A Guide to the Development and Use of the Myers-Briggs Type Indicator* (p. 137) by Isabel Briggs Myers and Mary H. McCaulley, 1985, Palo Alto, CA: Consulting Psychologists Press. Copyright 1985 by Peter B. Myers and Katherine D. Myers. Reprinted by permission.

TABLE 1 (continued)

Ranking of Colleges by MBTI Preference

College	Percent
Thinking-Feeling	
Parks College	59% T
Franklin and Marshall College	54% F
Nicholls State University	57% F
University of Wisconsin at Stevens Point	60% F
University of North Carolina at Greensboro	61% F
St. Clair College	62% F
Mercer University	62% F
University of Florida	62% F
St. Louis University	63% F
Rollins College	63% F
University of Maine at Orono	67% F
Auburn University	69% F
Hope College	74% F
Concordia College	77% F
Adrian College	80% F
Berkshire Christian College	86% F
Judgment-Perception	
University of North Carolina at Greensboro	60% J
Nicholls State University	54% J
Mercer University	54% J
Adrian College	53% J
Parks College	53% J
Berkshire Christian College	52% J
Franklin and Marshall College	51% J
Concordia College	51% J
University of Wisconsin at Stevens Point	51% P
St. Louis University	51% P
Rollins College	51% P
University of Florida	52% P
Hope College	53% P
Auburn University	54% P
St. Clair College	55% P
University of Maine at Orono	60% P

Source: From *Manual: A Guide to the Development and Use of the Myers-Briggs Type Indicator* (p. 137) by Isabel Briggs Myers and Mary H. McCaulley, 1985, Palo Alto, CA: Consulting Psychologists Press. Copyright 1985 by Peter B. Myers and Katherine D. Myers. Reprinted by permission.

TABLE 2

High School and College Graduates

		ISTJ		ISFJ		INFJ		INTJ	
		n	%	n	%	n	%	n	%
High School	F	129	9.65	256	19.15	48	3.59	32	2.39
	M	137	22.61	46	7.59	7	1.16	14	2.31
College	F	485	10.24	575	12.14	325	6.86	274	5.79
	M	761	17.12	200	4.50	145	3.26	425	9.56

		ISTP		ISFP		INFP		INTP	
		n	%	n	%	n	%	n	%
High School	F	41	3.07	106	7.93	71	5.31	18	1.35
	M	38	6.27	13	2.15	5	0 .83	17	2.81
College	F	66	1.39	144	3.04	351	7.41	168	3.55
	M	144	3.24	85	1.91	203	4.57	248	5.58

		ESTP		ESFP		ENFP		ENTP	
		n	%	n	%	n	%	n	%
High School	F	35	2.62	108	8.08	81	6.06	19	1.42
	M	33	5.45	12	1.98	9	1.49	17	2.81
College	F	40	0.84	142	3.00	453	9.57	193	4.08
	M	117	2.63	69	1.55	264	5.94	251	5.65

		ESTJ		ESFJ		ENFJ		ENTJ	
		n	%	n	%	n	%	n	%
High School	F	126	9.42	189	14.14	39	2.92	39	2.92
	M	186	30.69	38	6.27	8	1.32	26	4.29
College	F	400	8.45	423	8.93	376	7.94	321	6.78
	M	683	15.36	158	3.55	185	4.16	508	11.43

Note: High school female $N = 1,337$, male $N = 606$. College female $N = 4,736$, male $N = 4,446$.

Source: From *Manual: A Guide to the Development and Use of the Myers-Briggs Type Indicator* (pp. 243-292) by Isabel Briggs Myers and Mary H. McCaulley, 1985, Palo Alto, CA: Consulting Psychologists Press. Copyright 1985 by Peter B. Myers and Katherine D. Myers. Adapted by permission.

TABLE 3

Percentage of Teachers in Each Type at Different Levels of Education

	ISTJ		ISFJ		INFJ		INTJ	
	n	%	n	%	n	%	n	%
Preschool	3	3.00	20	20.00	7	7.00	4	4.00
Elementary	86	10.70	144	17.91	41	5.10	17	2.11
Middle & Jr.	126	11.70	138	12.23	56	4.96	51	4.52
High School	77	11.86	68	10.63	50	7.70	35	5.39
Adult	23	10.09	26	11.40	7	3.07	6	2.63
Jr. College	68	12.12	46	8.20	28	4.99	39	6.95
University	293	12.84	139	6.09	172	7.54	248	10.87

	ISTP		ISFP		INFP		INTP	
	n	%	n	%	n	%	n	%
Preschool	0	0.00	4	4.00	8	8.00	2	2.00
Elementary	14	1.74	38	4.73	37	4.60	12	1.49
Middle & Jr.	26	2.30	36	3.19	67	5.94	27	2.39
High School	10	1.54	16	2.47	41	6.32	19	2.93
Adult	10	4.39	11	4.82	14	6.14	4	1.75
Jr. College	4	0.71	12	2.14	45	8.02	26	4.63
University	38	1.67	39	1.71	185	8.11	123	5.39

	ESTP		ESFP		ENFP		ENTP	
	n	%	n	%	n	%	n	%
Preschool	0	0.00	8	8.00	12	12.00	1	1.00
Elementary	7	0.87	46	5.72	82	10.20	12	1.49
High School	7	1.08	15	2.31	74	11.40	23	3.54
Adult	9	3.95	12	5.26	19	8.33	8	3.51
Jr. College	8	1.43	16	2.85	76	13.55	28	4.99
University	27	1.18	38	1.67	207	9.07	121	5.30

	ESTJ		ESFJ		ENFJ		ENTJ	
	n	%	n	%	n	%	n	%
Preschool	6	6.00	12	12.00	8	8.00	5	5.00
Elementary	68	8.46	100	12.44	58	7.21	42	5.22
Middle & Jr.	103	9.13	130	11.52	88	7.80	49	4.34
High School	73	11.25	55	8.47	57	8.78	28	4.31
Adult	26	11.40	31	13.60	10	4.39	12	5.26
Jr. College	38	6.77	46	8.20	44	7.84	37	6.60
University	148	6.49	101	4.43	183	8.02	220	9.64

Note: Data are taken from Form F and Form G databanks of cases scored between March 1978 and December 1982. Levels are based on coding for occupations given by respondents.

Source: From *Manual: A Guide to the Development and Use of the Myers-Briggs Type Indicator* (p. 134) by Isabel Briggs Myers and Mary H. McCaulley, 1985, Palo Alto, CA: Consulting Psychologists Press. Copyright 1985 by Peter B. Myers and Katherine D. Myers. Reprinted by permission.

TABLE 4

Non-Persisters in Higher Education

	ISTJ		ISFJ		INFJ		INTJ	
	n	%	n	%	n	%	n	%
Salem College	0	0.00	11	9.02	8	6.56	2	1.64
Rollins College	11	6.08	5	2.76	10	5.53	10	5.53

	ISTP		ISFP		INFP		INTP	
	n	%	n	%	n	%	n	%
Salem College	4	3.28	8	6.56	8	6.56	2	1.64
Rollins College	14	7.73	15	8.29	19	10.50	11	6.08

	ESTP		ESFP		ENFP		ENTP	
	n	%	n	%	n	%	n	%
Salem College	4	3.28	14	11.48	22	18.03	9	7.38
Rollins College	10	5.53	9	4.97	28	15.47	7	3.87

	ESTJ		ESFJ		ENFJ		ENTJ	
	n	%	n	%	n	%	n	%
Salem College	2	1.64	13	10.66	14	11.48	1	0.82
Rollins College	16	8.84	9	4.97	14	7.73	3	1.66

Note: Salem College *N* = 122, Rollins College *N* = 181.

Source: Salem College (1980–83). [Students entering college between 1980 and 1983.] Unpublished raw data collected by Roger Spearman, Winston-Salem, NC. Rollins College (1984). [Class of 1984.] Unpublished raw data collected by Judith Provost, Winter Park, FL.

TABLE 5

Persisters at Rollins College

	ISTJ		ISFJ		INFJ		INTJ	
	n	%	*n*	%	*n*	%	*n*	%
Male Persisters	6	6.32	5	5.26	1	1.05	5	5.26
Female Persisters	4	3.85	8	7.69	3	2.89	1	0.96
Original Class	21	5.53	18	4.74	14	3.68	16	4.21

	ISTP		ISFP		INFP		INTP	
	n	%	*n*	%	*n*	%	*n*	%
Male Persisters	4	4.2	5	5.26	8	8.42	6	6.32
Female Persisters	0	0.00	6	5.77	10	9.62	4	3.85
Original Class	18	4.74	26	6.84	37	9.74	21	5.53

	ESTP		ESFP		ENFP		ENTP	
	n	%	*n*	%	*n*	%	*n*	%
Male Persisters	7	7.37	4	4.21	7	7.37	4	4.21
Female Persisters	7	6.73	11	10.58	18	17.31	4	3.85
Original Class	24	6.32	24	6.32	53	13.95	15	3.95

	ESTJ		ESFJ		ENFJ		ENTJ	
	n	%	*n*	%	*n*	%	*n*	%
Male Persisters	14	14.74	3	3.16	4	4.21	2	2.11
Female Persisters	5	4.81	11	10.58	8	7.69	4	3.85
Original Class	35	9.21	23	6.05	26	6.84	9	2.37

Source: Rollins College (1984). Unpublished raw data collected by Judith Provost, Winter Park, FL.

Note: Male persisters $N = 95$, female persisters $N = 104$, original class $N = 380$.

TABLE 6

Resident Housing Assistants

	ISTJ		ISFJ		INFJ		INTJ	
	n	%	n	%	n	%	n	%
CAPT databank	5	2.82	12	6.78	8	4.52	5	2.82
University of Maine system	9	6.52	6	4.35	1	0.73	1	0.73

	ISTP		ISFP		INFP		INTP	
	n	%	n	%	n	%	n	%
CAPT databank	3	1.69	8	4.52	16	9.04	6	3.39
University of Maine system	1	0.73	8	5.80	9	6.52	1	0.73

	ESTP		ESFP		ENFP		ENTP	
	n	%	n	%	n	%	n	%
CAPT databank	5	2.82	4	2.26	31	17.51	7	3.95
University of Maine system	2	1.45	8	5.80	27	19.57	5	3.62

	ESTJ		ESFJ		ENFJ		ENTJ	
	n	%	n	%	n	%	n	%
CAPT databank	14	7.91	16	9.04	18	10.17	19	10.73
University of Maine system	12	8.70	28	20.29	11	7.97	9	6.52

Note: CAPT databank $N = 177$. University of Maine system $N = 138$.

Source: CAPT databank (1985). University of Maine system: Combined unpublished raw data from the University of Maine (1985), collected by Irene von Hoffman, Orono, Maine; and from the University of Southern Maine (1985), collected by Joe Austin, Gorham, Maine.

TABLE 7

Campus Assistance and Information Student Staff, Northern Illinois University

ISTJ		ISFJ		INFJ		INTJ	
n	%	n	%	n	%	n	%
0	0.00	2	5.13	0	0.00	0	0.00

ISTP		ISFP		INFP		INTP	
n	%	n	%	n	%	n	%
0	0.00	0	0.00	1	2.56	0	0.00

ESTP		ESFP		ENFP		ENTP	
n	%	n	%	n	%	n	%
0	0.00	1	2.56	10	25.64	2	5.13

ESTJ		ESFJ		ENFJ		ENTJ	
n	%	n	%	n	%	n	%
5	12.82	11	28.21	7	17.95	0	0.00

Note: $N = 39$. Give tours and information as part of the Campus Assistance and Information Office at Northern Illinois University.

Source: Northern Illinois University (1985). Unpublished raw data collected by Denis Rode, Dekalb, IL.

TABLE 8

Disciplinary Offenders Referred to University Conduct Officer
from Residential Life Staff

ISTJ		ISFJ		INFJ		INTJ	
n	%	*n*	%	*n*	%	*n*	%
7	7.69	3	3.30	2	2.20	4	4.40
ISTP		ISFP		INFP		INTP	
n	%	*n*	%	*n*	%	*n*	%
8	8.79	6	6.59	7	7.69	5	5.49
ESTP		ESFP		ENFP		ENTP	
n	%	*n*	%	*n*	%	*n*	%
13	14.29	4	4.40	5	5.49	12	13.19
ESTJ		ESFJ		ENFJ		ENTJ	
n	%	*n*	%	*n*	%	*n*	%
5	5.49	3	3.30	4	4.40	3	3.30

Note: $N = 91$.

Source: University of Maine (1985–86). Unpublished raw data collected by Scott Anchors, Orono, ME.

TABLE 9

Presidents of Greek Organizations

ISTJ	ISFJ	INFJ	INTJ
n %	n %	n %	n %
2 20.00	1 10.00	0 0.00	0 0.00
ISTP	**ISFP**	**INFP**	**INTP**
n %	n %	n %	n %
0 0.00	0 0.00	0 0.00	1 10.00
ESTP	**ESFP**	**ENFP**	**ENTP**
n %	n %	n %	n %
2 20.00	2 20.00	0 0.00	0 0.00
ESTJ	**ESFJ**	**ENFJ**	**ENTJ**
n %	n %	n %	n %
0 0.00	2 20.00	0 0.00	0 0.00

Note: $N = 10$.

Source: Rollins College (1985). Unpublished raw data collected by Judith Provost, Winter Park, FL.

TABLE 10

University of Nebraska Agricultural Undergraduate Majors Ranked by MBTI Preference

	n	Percent
Extraversion/Introversion		
agricultural education	110	61.82% E
animal science	260	52.31% E
agricultural economics	237	51.05% I
ALL AGRICULTURAL MAJORS	1515	51.60% I
agricultural honors	70	52.86% I
mechanized agriculture	70	52.86% I
pre-vet	60	53.33% I
natural resources	128	53.91% I
agronomy	85	56.47% I
general agriculture	111	58.56% I
[agricultural faculty]	126	64.30% I
agricultural engineering	44	70.45% I
Sensing/Intuition		
mechanized agriculture	70	91.43% S
agronomy	85	85.88% S
agricultural economics	237	82.70% S
agricultural education	110	81.82% S
animal science	260	80.38% S
general agriculture	111	76.58% S
agricultural engineering	44	75.50% S
ALL AGRICULTURAL MAJORS	1515	75.30% S
natural resources	128	69.53% S
pre-vet	60	65.50% S
agricultural honors	70	55.71% S
[agricultural faculty]	126	51.60% N

Source: University of Nebraska at Lincoln (1985). Unpublished raw data collected by Leverne Barrett, Lincoln, NE.

TABLE 10 (continued)

University of Nebraska Agricultural Undergraduate Majors
Ranked by MBTI Preference

	n	Percent
Thinking/Feeling		
mechanized agriculture	70	72.66% T
agricultural economics	237	68.35% T
agricultural education	110	66.36% T
[agricultural faculty]	126	65.10% T
agricultural engineering	44	63.64% T
agronomy	85	63.33% T
animal science	260	63.08% T
agricultural honors	70	62.86% T
ALL AGRICULTURAL MAJORS	1515	62.80% T
general agriculture	111	56.76% T
natural resources	128	53.13% T
pre-vet	60	51.67% T
Judgment/Perception		
[agricultural faculty]	126	80.20% J
agricultural honors	70	62.86% J
agricultural education	110	55.45% J
agronomy	85	55.29% J
ALL AGRICULTURAL MAJORS	1515	53.70% J
animal science	260	53.46% J
pre-vet	60	53.33% J
agricultural economics	237	53.16% J
agricultural engineering	44	50.00% P
general agriculture	111	50.45% P
natural resources	128	57.81% P
mechanized agriculture	70	60.00% P

Source: University of Nebraska at Lincoln (1985). Unpublished raw data collected by Leverne Barrett, Lincoln, NE.

TABLE 11

Post-Secondary Health Occupations Majors
Ranked by MBTI Preference

	n	Percent
Extraversion/Introversion		
radiography	61	66.30% E
dental hygiene	58	65.91% E
dental assisting	63	63.64% E
radiological technician	51	61.45% E
respiratory therapy technician	44	61.11% E
physical therapy assisting	15	55.56% E
respiratory therapy	40	55.56% E
ALL POST-SECONDARY HEALTH OCCUPATION STUDENTS	659	55.52% E
occupational therapy	23	54.76% E
surgical technician	18	54.55% E
medical records	28	52.83% E
medical assisting	96	52.46% E
physical therapy	36	51.43% E
med lab technician	53	46.49% I
med technology	82	53.59% I
radiography technician	4	66.67% I
Sensing/Intuition		
medical records	43	81.13% S
surgical technician	26	78.79% S
physical therapy assisting	21	77.78% S
dental hygiene	67	76.14% S
medical assisting	137	74.86% S
physical therapy	50	71.43% S
radiological technician	58	69.88% S
dental assisting	68	68.69% S
radiography	63	68.48% S
ALL POST-SECONDARY HEALTH OCCUPATION STUDENTS	795	66.98% S
radiography technician	4	66.67% S
respiratory therapy technician	42	58.33% S
med technology	89	58.17% S
med lab technician	64	56.14% S
respiratory therapy	40	55.56% S
occupational therapy	23	54.76% S

Source: Indiana University (1985). Doctoral dissertation data collected by Karen Gables, Indianapolis, IN.

TABLE 11 (continued)

Post-Secondary Health Occupations Majors
Ranked by MBTI Preference

	n	Percent
Thinking/Feeling		
physical therapy assisting	5	18.52% T
dental hygiene	18	20.45% T
radiological technician	47	56.63% F
med lab technician	66	57.89% F
med technology	89	58.17% F
respiratory therapy	43	59.72% F
radiography	55	59.78% F
respiratory therapy technician	44	61.11% F
medical records	33	62.26% F
surgical technician	21	63.64% F
ALL POST-SECONDARY HEALTH OCCUPATION STUDENTS	781	65.80% F
radiography technician	4	66.67% F
medical assisting	127	69.40% F
physical therapy	51	72.86% F
occupational therapy	32	76.19% F
dental assisting	77	77.78% F
Judgment/Perception		
surgical technician	24	72.73% J
dental hygiene	61	69.32% J
med technology	104	67.97% J
radiography technician	4	66.67% J
medical records	35	66.04% J
physical therapy	44	62.86% J
physical therapy assisting	16	59.26% J
ALL POST-SECONDARY HEALTH OCCUPATION STUDENTS	700	58.97% J
medical assisting	106	57.92% J
radiography	53	57.61% J
dental assisting	56	56.57% J
respiratory therapy technician	39	54.17% J
radiological technician	44	53.01% J
med lab technician	58	50.88% J
occupational therapy	21	50.00% P
respiratory therapy	37	51.39% P

Source: Indiana University (1985). Doctoral dissertation data collected by Karen Gables, Indianapolis, IN.

TABLE 12

Saint Louis University Academic Majors
Ranked by MBTI Preference

	n	Percent
Extraversion/Introversion		
nursing	178	72.47% E
allied health professionals	320	69.06% E
undecided majors	258	66.67% E
communication	79	65.82% E
psychology	103	65.05% E
business administration	547	63.25% E
TOTAL FRESHMEN 1986	386	62.18% E
pre-medical students	369	58.81% E
political science	56	58.93% E
accounting	188	58.51% E
arts and science	1195	56.07% E
chemistry	83	53.01% E
biology	264	51.14% E
computer science	63	50.79% E
math	27	66.67% I
Sensing/Intuition		
accounting	188	61.70% S
nursing	178	60.11% S
business administration	547	59.05% S
TOTAL FRESHMEN 1986	386	58.81% S
allied health professionals	320	56.88% S
undecided majors	258	54.65% S
chemistry	83	54.22% S
computer science	63	53.97% S
pre-medical students	369	50.95% S
biology	264	50.76% S
political science	56	50.00% N
math	27	51.85% N
arts and science	1195	52.05% N
communication	79	55.70% N
psychology	103	65.05% N

Source: Saint Louis University (1982–85), TRAILS project. Raw data collected by Dave Kalsbeek, Saint Louis, MO.

TABLE 12 (continued)

Saint Louis University Academic Majors
Ranked by MBTI Preference

	n	Percent
Thinking/Feeling		
computer science	63	58.73% T
political science	56	57.14% T
pre-medical students	369	56.10% T
chemistry	83	55.42% T
biology	264	52.65% F
TOTAL FRESHMEN 1986	386	55.18% F
business administration	547	55.39% F
arts and science	1195	56.65% F
undecided majors	258	58.91% F
accounting	188	59.04% F
math	27	66.67% F
psychology	103	66.99% F
communication	79	68.35% F
nursing	178	75.28% F
allied health professionals	320	75.31% F
Judgment/Perception		
biology	264	60.61% J
chemistry	83	60.24% J
pre-medical students	369	59.62% J
computer science	63	55.56% J
TOTAL FRESHMEN 1986	386	54.15% J
accounting	188	52.13% J
nursing	178	51.69% J
psychology	103	50.49% J
arts and science	1195	50.21% J
political science	56	50.00% P
business administration	547	50.64% P
allied health professionals	320	50.94% P
math	27	51.85% P
undecided majors	258	55.43% P
communication	79	59.49% P

Source: Saint Louis University (1982–85), TRAILS project. Raw data collected by Dave Kalsbeek, Saint Louis, MO.

TABLE 13

Students Attending Graduate School Immediately After Graduation

ISTJ		ISFJ		INFJ		INTJ	
n	%	n	%	n	%	n	%
2	4.44	1	2.22	1	2.22	5	11.11

ISTP		ISFP		INFP		INTP	
n	%	n	%	n	%	n	%
2	4.44	0	0.00	1	2.22	7	15.56

ESTP		ESFP		ENFP		ENTP	
n	%	n	%	n	%	n	%
4	8.89	1	2.22	8	17.78	4	8.89

ESTJ		ESFJ		ENFJ		ENTJ	
n	%	n	%	n	%	n	%
5	11.11	1	2.22	1	2.22	2	4.44

Note: $N = 45$.

Source: Rollins College (1984). Unpublished raw data collected by Melinda McDonald, Winter Park, FL.

TABLE 14

Placement Data, Summer Following Graduation

ISTJ	ISFJ	INFJ	INTJ
n % 9 .05 Admin.—Insurance Admin.—Real estate MBA Medicine Sales—Investments (2) Sports professional Unknown (2)	n % 5 .03 Accounting (2) Grad.—Poli. sci. Teaching—Elemen. Unknown	n % 5 .03 Admin.—Government Grad.—Arts/Graphics Reporter Sales—Bus. products Waiter/Waitress	n % 10 .06 Admin.—Government Computer operation Grad.—English (2) Grad.—Psychology (2) MBA Medicine Mgmt.—Retail Teaching
ISTP	**ISFP**	**INFP**	**INTP**
n % 4 .02 Chiropractor Computer operation Grad.—Engineering Sales—Printing	n % 7 .04 Athletic coach Mgmt.—Retail Sales—Bus. products Sales—Insurance Sports professional Teaching—Elemen. Unknown	n % 19 .11 Admin.—Mgmt. co. (2) Advertising (2) Grad.—Comp. sci. Investor (self-employed) Mgmt.—Banking (2) Sales—Insurance Sales—Investments (2) Sales—Retail Teaching—Special ed. Unknown (6)	n % 11 .06 Admin.—Steel industry Grad.—Urban planning Law school (4) MBA (2) Teaching Unknown (2)

(Continued)

Note: $N = 180$.

Source: Rollins College (1984). Unpublished raw data collected by Melinda McDonald, Winter Park, FL.

TABLE 14 (continued)

Placement Data, Summer Following Graduation

ESTP	ESFP	ENFP	ENTP
n %	*n* %	*n* %	*n* %
10 .06	11 .06	29 .16	11 .06
Financial analyst	Computer prog.	Accounting	Admin.—Manuf. (2)
Grad.—English	Coord.—Chmbr. of Com.	Admin.—Publishing	Forensic science
Law school (2)	Counseling—Admissions	Air Force	Grad.—Mathematics
MBA	Grad.—Deaf ed.	Athletics (2)	MBA (2)
Mgmt.—Manufacturing	Interior design	Computer operation	Teaching
Mgmt.—Retail (2)	Mgmt.—Banking	Grad.—Counseling	Unknown (4)
News assistant	Mgmt.—Office	Grad.—Env. mgmt.	
Sales—Travel industry	Mgmt.—Retail (2)	Grad.—MSW	
	Sales—Bus. products	Grad.—Planning	
	Stockperson	Grad.—Theology	
		Law school (2)	
		MBA	
		Mgmt.—Banking	
		Mgmt.—Food/Bev. (3)	
		Mgmt.—Retail	
		Performer	
		Sales—Food/Bev.	
		Sales—Investments (2)	
		Sales—Tele. systems	
		Teaching (2)	
		Waiter/Waitress	
		Unknown (2)	
ESTJ	**ESFJ**	**ENFJ**	**ENTJ**
n %	*n* %	*n* %	*n* %
18 .10	16 .09	9 .05	6 .03
Computer prog. (2)	Advertising/PR (2)	Computer prog.	Admin.—Government
Grad.—Music	Counseling/Personnel	Grad.—Sociology	Law school
Grad.—Theatre	Flight attendant	Mgmt.—Banking	Medicine
Marketing	Law school	Public relations	Sales—Bus. products
MBA	Mgmt.—Banking (2)	Sales—Investments	Sales—Telephones
Medicine	Mgmt.—Hotel	Sales—Paper	Unknown
Mgmt.—Banking (3)	Mgmt.—Retail (3)	Travel consultant	
Mgmt.—Retail (4)	Sales—Manuf.	Waiter/Waitress	
Nursing	Sales—Travel industry	Unknown	
Sales—Automobiles	Stockperson		
Sales—Real estate	Unknown (2)		
Waiter/Waitress			

Note: *N* = 180.

Source: Rollins College (1984). Unpublished raw data collected by Melinda McDonald, Winter Park, FL.

How to Report Type Data for CAPT Databank or Other Studies

When reporting type data to the CAPT databank, it is essential to give an accurate and complete description of the sample for two reasons. First, when demographic characteristics are reported, one can determine more clearly whether the sample is an appropriate model of the large population. Second, CAPT often makes composites of samples. In order for a composite to be helpful, it is necessary to know what it is composed of. Vague descriptions make it risky or inappropriate to combine samples, so a poorly described sample is often only marginally useful.

For example, receiving a contributed type table of 100 teachers without any other description is a problem. Nothing is reported about gender, age, race, subject taught, or grade level taught. All these variables can interact with type, and could be influencing the frequency distribution of the types. Another common problem is receiving a type table described as 67 practicing female architects, in their practice for over 5 years, between the ages of 30 and 50, and 7 secretaries. Since there is no way of knowing which people in the group were secretaries and which were architects, the data are confounded and virtually unusable.

The following pointers will help to minimize such problems:

1. Report samples as distinct groups; do not mix "apples and oranges." If in doubt, report data on separate sheets (it is easy for CAPT to merge them).

2. Describe the subjects thoroughly.

   A. Be clear about their description. Give their role, occupation, or other defining characteristics in clear, precise terms.

   B. Describe how they were selected. Be specific about sampling methods. Was it a random sample or volunteers? State the percentage of the larger population represented by your sample (if known).

   C. Include the major demographic characteristics: age, gender, race, education level, and geographic location, and any other identifying characteristics.

   D. If you wish to report a sample but maintain confidentiality, use global generic descriptions. For example, the Space Needle Power and Light Company in Seattle could be described as an urban public utility company in the northwestern United States.

3. State who owns the data. List the names of all people who participated in collecting the data and the institution they represented at the time of collecting that data (if any). Please state whether data should be reported as collected anonymously to protect confidentiality.

On the following page is a form to copy and use in reporting type distributions to the CAPT databank.

CAPT MBTI Type Table Project

Data submitted by: Give name(s), title, address, project name (if any) as you wish them to be used in referring to your data. Also give telephone number.

❑ Yes, I wish my name, address, and phone number to be given to people inquiring about my data.

Permission: I hereby give CAPT permission to:
❑ Publish these data in the *Atlas of Type Tables*.
❑ Publish these data in composite samples.
❑ Include in confidential archives only.

_____   _____
Signature   Date

Description of data: _____ Males _____ Females _____ Total
❑ Form F   ❑ G   ❑ AV

Were these cases scored by CAPT's computer scoring service?
❑ yes   ❑ no

When collected? _____   Where collected? _____

CAPT plans to report some tables separately and make composites of others. To make a composite, it is important to include only groups that truly share the same characteristics. Please describe your sample, being as specific as possible. (Example: grade, major, career, specialty, age, religion, ethnic origin, etc.)

If these data have been published, directly or indirectly, please cite reference below.

Do you have other measures for this group? (Example: Strong-Campbell, grades, job satisfaction, etc.) If so, please list them below.

Send completed table to: CAPT-MBTI Type Table Project
2720 N.W. 6th Street
Gainesville, Florida 32609

Enter number of males (M), females (F), and total (T) for each type.

ISTJ	ISFJ	INFJ	INTJ
M	M	M	M
F	F	F	F
T	T	T	T

ISTP	ISFP	INFP	INTP
M	M	M	M
F	F	F	F
T	T	T	T

ESTP	ESFP	ENFP	ENTP
M	M	M	M
F	F	F	F
T	T	T	T

ESTJ	ESFJ	ENFJ	ENTJ
M	M	M	M
F	F	F	F
T	T	T	T

When sending in more than one table, save your time by filling in information on the reverse before making copies of this form.

Thank you for sharing your data.